You can smell the caramel popcorn and taste the clown sundaes...

Once upon a shopping center, the Richland Mall was the place to shop, eat, meet, play, and be seen in suburban Johnstown, Pennsylvania. Decades after its closing, this classic mall returns to life in the pages of this one-of-a-kind book. For the first time, the true story of the Richland Mall, its creators, its employees, and the shoppers who loved it has been told, complete with surprising secrets and inside stories from those who knew it best. You'll never forget this trip through an unforgettable period of retail history, from the Mall's miraculous beginnings to its glory days in the 70s and 80s to the struggle to save it from going out of business. Hundreds of rare photos and images, never before gathered in one place, will whisk you back to the people and moments that made the Richland Mall great, then carry you forward to modern-day reunions of Mall employees where the disco music and nostalgia never stop. Relive the story of a lifetime on a magical journey straight out of your favorite memories and dreams. If you've ever longed to return to the Mall where you always felt at home, or you just crave a simpler, sweeter place where the Super Chick sandwiches, Capri pizza, and Sweet William clown sundaes are always delicious, and the customer is always right, step inside. Richie the Pook invites you to the grand reopening of the Mall that comes to life every time we shout...

richland mall

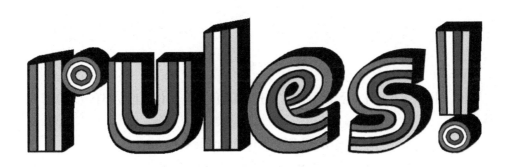

By Robert Jeschonek

pie press publishing

Other Pennsylvania books by
Robert Jeschonek

A Glosser's Christmas Love Story
Christmas at Glosser's
Easter at Glosser's
Halloween at Glosser's
Long Live Glosser's
Death by Polka
Fear of Rain
Penn Traffic Forever
The Glory of Gable's
The Masked Family

DEDICATION

To the people of the Richland Mall, whether they are with us in body
or in our hearts. Without them, there would be no story.
Thanks to them, we will never forget.

To Chris and Debbi,

Enjoy the memories!

Robert Jeschonek

12/19/17

Table of Contents

Courtesy Jim O'Roark

Photo by Chuck Mamula

introduction

No book can truly recapture the magic of the Richland Mall. That is what I've learned while writing this book about the Richland Mall.

Reading about walking through the Mall on a Friday night, smelling the Karmelkorn and Super Chick in the air, hearing the music play from National Record Mart, watching the fish swim in the stream in the middle of it all, is nothing like the real thing. Words on a page can't compare with sundaes in Sweet William, videogames in Time-Out, or movies and popcorn in the Duke and Duchess theaters.

But it sure feels good writing and reading about all that anyway. Because the truth is, a book is still the next best thing to being there. And let's face it, a book is our only option if we want to revisit the Mall these days.

The place itself has been gone since 2003 – and closed for years before that. It has vanished from the face of the Earth.

Which just makes us want to go back there all the more, doesn't it? We want to live the story just one more time, and pass it along to the generations to come so they won't forget why it meant so much to us.

And what a story it is. It's a *big* one, with all those hundreds of stores and thousands upon thousands of shoppers throughout the years. It's a bigger and more important story than you might realize, in fact.

And it has so many parts and pieces, so many details you might not be aware of. Even now, over a decade after its demolition, over 40 years since its grand opening, the Richland Mall is full of surprises. Keep reading and you'll see.

You'll learn the coolest, most unexpected things from the people who were right at the heart of the Richland Mall story, from the original developers to the general manager to the woman who ran the information booth. You'll find out what it was like to dress up as Richie the Pook, to talk to kids at Christmastime as Gus and Melanie, and to party with Ozzy Osbourne at the Encore restaurant.

You'll discover the secrets of Kmart, Sears, Shop 'n Save, National Record Mart, Spencer Gifts, Capri Pizza, Richman Brothers, Hush Puppies, and more, straight from the men and women who managed and worked at those stores and restaurants.

But the best part will be the memories and stories in your own mind, the ones that come back to you while you read. The ones you share or pass along to those around you, so they'll know what the Richland Mall meant to you. That story, the one beyond the page, is what keeps the Mall and its magic alive all these years after its final days...and it is very different for each one of us.

For some, it was a place to make a living. For others, it was a place to shop and dine and have fun. Still others knew it as a place to grow up and experience rites of passage, from meeting friends to going on first dates to learning to drive in the parking lot.

For many of us, though, the Mall was all of these things – workplace, playground, social center, community. It was our Main Street, our Glosser's, our Penn Traffic Department Store, everything we needed under one roof. And it helped to make us who we are, and makes us long for what we've lost.

Speaking as one of those very people who worked and played and grew up at the Richland Mall, I know and feel this story in my bones, in the depths of my heart and soul. I see it now when I close my eyes – my favorite storefronts and arcade games and movies and foods and merchandise, all laid out just as they once were, under those scallop-edged ceilings that looked so much like flowing waves of water or ripples of sound on a scope. I *dream* about it sometimes, and I'll bet you do, too.

Unless the Richland Mall was before your time...in which case, you are even more welcome to dive deep into this book. Because this is the key to another world, one far gone from the one taking shape around you, but every bit as precious.

Reading about the Richland Mall and the way of life it represents – one in which the things we had in common were so much more important than the things that kept us apart – might help you see it really *is* a better way of doing things, and it really *does* work. A place like the Mall can be as important for the way it brings a community together as the way it enables people to buy and sell.

Courtesy Jim Streeter

So here we are now, at the big main doors at the center of the Richland Mall back in the late 1970s. Come with me as I open a door and wave you in, and the sweet smell of Karmelkorn wafts up to greet you...

Strolling past Somerset Trust bank and Watchmaker's Diamonds & Jewelry, you approach a thicket of trees and mountain laurel, shading trout in a trickling stream winding around a central well. You look right, then left along the main axis of the Mall, first toward Sears, then Kmart. Straight ahead, Penn Traffic awaits at the end of a shorter spur.

Happy shoppers flow in all directions, and you want to join them. Which way should you go?

If you're anything like me, you're going to go in *all* of them.

Photos by Chuck Mamula

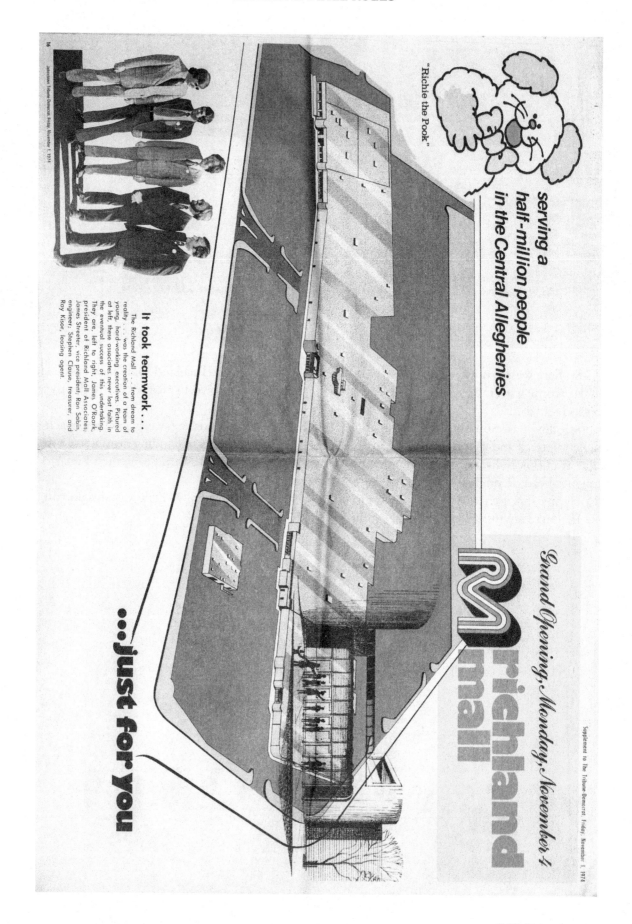

"Richie the Pook"

serving a
half-million people
in the Central Alleghenies

Grand Opening, Monday, November 4

Supplement to The Tribune-Democrat, Friday, November 1, 1974

richland mall

...just for you

It took teamwork....

The Richland Mall . . . from dream to reality . . . was the creation of a team of young, hard-working executives. Pictured at left, these associates never lost faith in the eventual success of this undertaking. They are, left to right, James O'Roark, president of Richland Mall Associates; James Streeter, vice president; Ron Sabin, engineer; Stephen Clause, treasurer, and Ray Kisor, leasing agent.

Johnstown Tribune Democrat Friday November 1, 1974

16

chapter one
richie rides again
april 30, 2016

How long had it been since a Pook had ridden through the site of the old Richland Mall in a bright yellow Volkswagen Thing? Thirty years? Forty?

People stared and pointed from the sidewalks and doorways of what was now the Richland Town Centre. Some of them had no idea what was going on, while others knew Richie the Pook quite well. Some of them went *way* back when it came to Richie.

Now there he was after all that time, riding around as if he were looking for his long-gone Mall, waving at children and grown-ups alike from his original convertible Pookmobile.

When the car finally pulled to a stop, it was in a corner of the Town Centre parking lot where the spirit of the Richland Mall was strongest – home to the latest incarnation of one of the Mall's original tenants.

Photo by Philip Balko

5

Capri Pizza was the perfect place to make a connection to the Mall's good old days...and to have a reunion of employees, shoppers, and fans of that unique place that had once stood on that site.

Dozens of them gathered in that corner of the lot, brought together by newspaper ads, radio interviews, and Facebook posts. They had come on a cloudy, cold Saturday morning in April to be a part of something they loved, something that was making its mark once more after so many years away.

They had come to remember the Richland Mall, and make sure it was never forgotten.

Reunited, and It Feels So Pook

As soon as the Pookmobile parked, people crowded around it, all trying to get close to the Richland Mall's beloved mascot. There were employees from classic Mall stores like Kmart, Sears, and Vitamin World, plus a roll call of some of the Mall's movers and shakers: Shirley DiRosa, owner of Capri Pizza;

Gil Demos, owner of Hush Puppies; Joe Cohen, owner of LaRose; Frank Koscis of Thom McAn; and Joe Fortunato of Richman Brothers. Karen (Bevilaqua) Belle was there, too – the public relations director of the Mall in its earliest days. She and the Pook had done a lot of work together back then, stirring up interest and helping the Mall get off the ground.

But the biggest star of them all was the unassuming, white-haired man in the gray sport coat...the one with the huge smile and occasional tear in his eye. You might not have known it by looking at him, but he was much more than a member of the supporting cast in the story of the Richland Mall. Out of everyone there that day, he had made the biggest impact on that place, those people, and all of us.

His name is Jim O'Roark, and he is the father of Richie the Pook... the creator of Super Chick (the restaurant and the character) and one of the fathers of the Richland Mall itself.

Jim is Richland Mall royalty. Without him, there would have been no Mall and no Pook. Yet there he was, mingling and laughing and reminiscing like all the others, as if his main contribution to the Mall had been working alongside them on the sales floor. But that's the way he's always liked it, keeping the magic of the Mall alive and sharing the joy it brings to people's lives by staying close to them.

And guess what? These days, even without the Mall itself still standing, there's plenty of joy to go around.

You can see it in the photos from the reunion that day. Everybody's smiling, hugging, laughing, and clowning around.

7

Photos by Philip Balko

They're "doing the Pook" – holding both hands up and flapping fingers against palms in Richie's signature move. It looks like one big party in the parking lot, though the Mall they came to celebrate has been gone for over a decade.

Clearly, they treasure their memories and miss the place...but why?

Jurassic Mall
The Richland Mall wasn't that big of a mall, actually. It only had one floor, and therefore no balconies or escalators. It didn't have nearly as many tenants as other malls that came after it, and what tenants it had mostly catered to a middle-class, blue-collar clientele.

It wasn't surrounded by restaurants and big-box stores on outparcel properties, either; there was just the Mall, and Ponderosa Steakhouse, and Sears Automotive.

As an indoor shopping mall, it was part of a dying breed... an early casualty of the ongoing collapse of brick-and-mortar retail merchandising. It was a creature of the 70s and 80s, and a dinosaur by the 90s, doomed to extinction. It was just another step in the evolution of the human marketplace, the shift from classic downtown department stores to suburban malls to big box plazas to online shopping and doorstep delivery. It was just another way to get people to part with their money.

Except that's not nearly all there is to it. Ask any of the people who attended the parking lot reunion or anyone who remembers spending time at the Mall (especially in the years before it lost traction after the nearby Galleria came to be), and they'll tell you the same thing. *This* Mall, *our* Mall, was *special*.

It wasn't special just because it was part of our era, or because it was close and we happened to go there. It wasn't special because there wasn't anything better around back then, or we didn't know any better. It wasn't special because we're small town people with unsophisticated tastes. And no, it doesn't just *seem* special to us now because of the rose-colored glasses of nostalgia.

It was special because of the way it was built, the unique architecture that made it feel inviting and intimate instead of cavernous and cold. It was special because the owners and vendors went out of their way to create a sense of community through special events and spaces for the public. It was special because the people who worked there were a close-knit family who were treated with kindness and respect and did the same for the customers they encountered on a daily basis.

Perhaps most of all, it was special because of the way it came to occupy the center of our lives, and the shoppers, employees, and owners accepted that mutual connection and the responsibility that came with it.

9

Photos by Philip Balko

Right up until the end, everyone involved with the place held up their end of the deal – because they all knew how important they were to each other.

And they all loved each other in their own way, without ever needing to say so.

Photos by Philip Balko

The Key to the Richland Mall

What happens to the love that comes to life around a place when the place disappears from the face of the Earth? It lives on in our memories and hearts and relationships, in the stories we tell and the treasures we cherish.

People brought such treasures to the Town Centre reunion – name-tags and photos and newspaper clippings, menus and business cards and merchandise. Someone brought a Richie the Pook doll, and Jim O'Roark wore a one-of-a-kind silver Richie the Pook ring. Someone else brought the key to the Mall – a symbolic one, surely, but still.

All these objects with their traces of magic, brought together with dozens of Mall employees and supporters on the hallowed ground that had

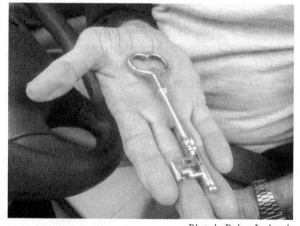

Photo by Robert Jeschonek

once been home to the Mall itself. What if it could have all come together to bring the Richland Mall back to life in its former location? What if, just for one hour, the Mall could have risen from our dreams and given us one last tour of that special place?

It would have been nice, but what followed the reunion was just as nice – and longer lasting – in its own way, because the gathering on that day formed the basis of the book in your hands. The memories shared and photos shot in that parking lot helped immortalize the Richland Mall, to preserve its story for generations to come.

So now we will never forget what the Mall meant to us...how it looked and smelled and sounded and felt....and how it all started with two guys in Michigan with a dream.

I remember when I was in high school, watching them build the Richland Mall. I remember going to the Richland Drive-in, which was on the property where they built it. Then, as a high-schooler taking the bus to school, I watched them build it as we drove by. It was a part of the community for a lot of years.

Terry Miller

I wish the Richland Mall was still here. I remember going there for everything from shoes to clothes to groceries. I remember walking around the inside of the Mall, sometimes just to window shop, and making two or three laps around the place with my husband or friends. But the best part was stopping at Sweet William for a meal or just a snack. That Mall had personality, and that is something malls today are lacking.

Carol Galbreath

My friends and I would walk around the Mall on Friday and Saturday nights, mostly just giggling and looking for boys. I spent a lot of hours and money in Time-Out! I remember almost every day after school, walking to the Mall and picking up ticket stubs outside the Duke and Duchess theaters because a ticket stub would get you a free game!

I also bought *so* many albums in National Record Mart.

I was part of the Bubble Yum bubble blowing contest the Mall had when that gum first came out. I didn't win. I was too nervous and kept blowing small bubbles.

They had some really cool teen stores for girls. I loved their clothes. No Name was my favorite.

My mom always took me to Campus for haircuts. Remember Super Chick? The chicken sandwiches were awesome!

I once played the Easter Bunny when I was around 16. That costume was so hot! I remember going to the restrooms by Hess's and taking the bunny head off because I was sweating, and a little child saw me and screamed. Poor kid.

I loved the smell of Spencer's. I got my Pet Rock there. When I grew up, I became a hairstylist and worked at Regis for a bit. I just loved that Mall. I miss it. But the memories are locked in my heart.

Rebecca Siegrist Marsh

My adolescence was spent in a single hallway, with businesses that became a part of my life: Sweet William, where I worked; Time-Out, where I spent the quarters from my Dad's dresser; Capri Pizza, where I ate; and the Duke and Duchess theaters, where I saw *Animal House* and *Star Wars*.
Ronald P Carnevali Jr.

I remember in the late 80s, growing up and enjoying center court with the "jungle," as I used to call it. I can still picture both the older and newer decorations used for the holidays. I remember riding the carousel not too long after it was put into the updated center court. My mom used

to work at Shoe World as an assistant manager, and I remember when they had meetings before the store would open for the day.

We used to climb the curved walls by Kmart and wait anxiously until McDonald's opened so we could get breakfast. We had many great meals at Sweet William and the Encore. I loved Time-Out, which was across from the old theaters.

I remember the final days after the Mall had closed, when you could peek in through the boarded-up wall along the Kmart hallway to see the empty corridor filled with various memories. I remember how sad it was to see the Mall gradually being demolished in 2003.
Matt Stufft

My mom would take me to the Richland Mall for back-to-school shopping every year. We would visit Sears, Ormond, Kmart, and many others. No visit was complete without a visit to Waldenbooks, the best bookstore ever. We always finished our day with a meal at Sweet William. Such a great Mall, and so many great memories. The Mall would be so crowded on Friday and Saturday nights during the late 70s and early 80s. Families, teenagers, and retirees would just make the rounds, meet friends and neighbors, walk around, shop, and enjoy the atmosphere. What a great time to be alive! What a great Mall!
Michele Krutch-Paonessa

chapter two

the two jims

1970 - 1972

James O'Roark
... president

Jim O'Roark and Jim Streeter had never developed a mall before. In the beginning, they didn't even know that a mall was what they would end up building in Richland Township.

They were just two guys in Grand Rapids, Michigan, working for Lanning Corporation to develop Kmarts across the U.S.

"We did the market analysis and site selection," says O'Roark, who was an executive vice president of Lanning in the late 1960s and early 70s. "Then we flew over the sites in a helicopter with Kmart executives and showed them the view from above and how it all intertwined."

Jim Streeter
.... vice president

Before coming to Lanning, O'Roark and Streeter had worked together for Shell Oil Company, developing service stations. The experience served them well at Lanning, where they teamed up to bring a slew of Kmarts into existence – unknowingly preparing themselves for the biggest project of their lives to that point.

When Lanning started having internal difficulties, the two Jims realized they needed to move on. They decided it was time to leave Lanning and set out on their own to launch a new company called Unimich that would develop commercial properties.

Photos © The Tribune-Democrat

"Our intention was to set up a Kmart somewhere," remembers Streeter. "We traveled all over the East Coast, trying to find a place that didn't have a Kmart...and we ended up in Johnstown."

An Underserved Location

O'Roark, a native of nearby Stoystown, suggested the Johnstown area as a location.

"Johnstown didn't have many major retailers then," says Streeter. "A big reason was that access to Johnstown was limited. Unlike Monroeville, where you had half of Pittsburgh driving by on any given day, Johnstown was stuck between two mountain ranges, with no easy way in or out."

As a result of Johnstown's access problem, retailers who considered setting up shop in the area knew they might have to depend on local residents to drive sales. But thanks to Route 219, which linked Johnstown to Somerset, Ebensburg, and Maryland, the city looked like it might just be connected enough to other clusters of consumers.

The two Jims decided to focus on the Johnstown area and launched a search for the perfect site for their new Kmart. "We looked at all kinds of different sites in the Johnstown area," says Streeter. "We looked at any big parcel we could find. But ultimately, there were only two obvious places where we could do any kind of real-estate development. One was in Richland Township and the other was in Westmont Borough."

Streeter and O'Roark ruled out Westmont, however, because it lacked a large enough site and already had a strip shopping center. That left Richland, which did have a relatively open site and more opportunity to fill a retail void.

O'Roark came up with the location, which was occupied in part by the Richland Drive-In Theater. At the time, it was an out-of-the-way choice for a retail center. "Most retail business was found on Scalp Avenue, Route 56, back then," says O'Roark. "But even on Scalp, there wasn't anything like a shopping mall at that point."

Courtesy Johnstown Area Heritage Association

The team performed exhaustive market studies and liked what they saw. "Richland was an underserved area from a retail standpoint," explains Streeter. "Other than a free-standing Sears and Gee Bee on Scalp Avenue, the township was mostly served by small, independent retailers. The same applied to downtown Johnstown, which was anchored by the Glosser Bros. and Penn Traffic department stores, with small, local independents between them. There was a lack of small tenants with big names."

Courtesy Library of Congress

Courtesy Darrel Holsopple

Richland was looking better all the time to the two Jims, though they knew it was a risky choice for one very obvious reason. Johnstown was the headquarters of Crown American Corporation and Zamias, two regional retail development powerhouses. Was it really a good idea to develop retail property in the backyard of developer giants Frank Pasquerilla and George Zamias? "If we'd had any brains, we'd have gone somewhere other than Johnstown, because two of the largest regional mall developers were based in Johnstown," says Streeter.

At least those developers didn't put up any roadblocks in the early days of the two Jims' project. "I'm sure they didn't think that Johnstown had the demographic to support a mall back then," says Streeter. "As for us, we were well aware that the demographic could be difficult, but we just went ahead and did the project anyway."

To increase the project's viability, the market potential was redefined to include Bedford, Cambria, Indiana, Somerset, and Westmoreland counties.

Backing into the Concept

Satisfied with the location of their project, the two Jims brainstormed what its parameters would be. "Our original intention was to build a Kmart strip center with a few shops and a supermarket," recalls Streeter. "We kind of backed into the concept of a mall.

"Early on, we couldn't get approvals from Kmart, but we just kept working away at it. It was a sizeable piece of land, and we realized that to maximize the property, we should put up something bigger than a mini-mall. The location was better suited to a mall."

The two Jims laid out a site plan for a full-sized shopping mall and proceeded to enlist potential tenants in a unique way. Though small tenants usually held out until large tenants signed with a new mall, Streeter and O'Roark flipped the script. "We got a lot of small tenants to express interest, and then we went to Kmart and Sears and said 'we've got this mall with all these small tenants ready to go, subject to interest from big tenants like you.' That's when interest in the project just exploded."

As anchor stores and small tenants alike jumped on the bandwagon, the two Jims realized this project of theirs might just happen. "We didn't have a lot of money ourselves," remembers Streeter. "We were just trying to pay our own bills at home and make a deal...any kind of deal. And it just morphed into the Richland Mall.

"It was never really planned that way. We didn't come to Johnstown to build a regional mall. We were young and dumb, and we had good luck and help from good people, and the Richland Mall came to life against the odds," says Streeter.

Adding to the Team

As the Richland Mall project moved closer to becoming a reality, the Unimich team expanded to do it justice. Streeter and O'Roark brought in highly skilled specialists, trusted friends who'd worked alongside them at Lanning and Shell.

"Once the deal got to where it was really a deal, we brought in Ron Sabin as an engineering partner," says Streeter. "We also brought in Steve Clause, who had an accounting background, to serve as treasurer.

Ron Sabin
...construction engineer

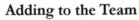

Steve Clause
...treasurer

Photos © The Tribune-Democrat

A few months later, we added Ray Kisor as leasing agent.

"They all became financial partners in Unimich, because O'Roark and I didn't have any money to pay them. We got them to buy into our dream that this was going to be a mall, and we were going to be able to build it, and hopefully we'd make money doing that."

"It was an unbelievable partnership," remembers O'Roark. "I was the president, and Jim Streeter was the vice president. We worked very well together. Then there was Steve Clause, our financial man, who spent probably 90 percent of his time in the office taking care of all the numbers. He was extremely valuable and a treasured friend.

"Ron Sabin was our engineer, and he was outstanding. Ray Kisor was responsible for the bulk of our smaller tenants, and he did a great job. They all did. It was just an incredible team," says O'Roark.

"Well, we were all young men who had great passion for what they did, who came from no particular background in strength from a monetary standpoint. Everything we did, we just worked hard for it. We worked hard, and we struggled, and we made it happen," remembers Ray Kisor.

According to O'Roark, this dream team's commitment to the project had its roots back in Grand Rapids...and one magic moment that stands out in his memory.

"We were all friends, and we had a meeting at my home," remembers O'Roark. "It was a small house, so we went back and sat in the bedroom. Three of us sat on the canopy bed, and the other two sat on the floor.

"I brought up the idea of the location in Johnstown, and everyone agreed that we should focus on that site. For the first time, we all knew we were moving forward, and our future would be in Richland.

"In a way, that was the moment when the Richland Mall was born," says O'Roark, and he smiles.

Ray Kisor
...leasing director

Photo © The Tribune-Democrat

Courtesy Jim Streeter

When they were building the Richland Mall, I lived across the street. I rode my bicycle through the shell of it, up and down the ramps, when the crews retired for the day. Those were the days!

Mark Lodolinski

I was in high school at the time of the Mall's construction and lived near the Mall property. There was a group trying to stop it because of concerns about traffic. They got lots of signatures on their petition, but I don't know what happened with them. I remember some people signing because they thought they were saving the Richland Drive-in.

Fred Shugars

Courtesy Jim Streeter

I worked at Richman Brothers in the Richland Mall. I was in the Mall when they were still building it and worked there until 1984 when Richman's closed.
Elizabeth Gibson

I worked at Teek's Fine Shoes in the Mall from day one. There was still construction going on, and the only place to eat was the Kmart snack bar. To get there, you had to walk to the center of the Mall and go through a door that had been cut in the middle of the walls. The Christmas parties at the Encore were great; so were the ones in later years that took place after hours in the center of the Mall. Christmas Eve was always a hoot. Most of the stores would have small parties in their back rooms, and we all got to visit and share a little cheer.
Cindy Mikula Houghton

I worked at McDonald's in the Mall for two and a half years when I was in high school. It's where I met my husband. We had a lot of good times in the Richland Mall. I remember when it opened, I thought the center court with the water feature was so pretty. Oh, the memories.
Kelly Rollins Drummer

The Richland Mall was such a great place to shop and meet friends. I loved going to Sweet William. They had the best Swiss cheese and crouton salad with a sweet and sour dressing. It makes my mouth water to think of it. The Kmart store was always busy with Blue Light Specials, and on the other end was the Hess's store, which took over when Penn Traffic closed. I also loved the beautiful plants and wishing waters. I just wonder how much money was taken out of there from everyone making their wishes.
Kay Kalinyak

As a child, I remember my father taking us to see our grandmother, who worked at Hannak's. She would buy my sister and me the newest Smurf figures to play with. Hannak's also had almost every Hummel figurine, which many of our family members collected.

I also remember my Aunt Wendy taking my sister, cousin, and me to visit our Uncle Joel at Hess's, where he worked while going to college. I remember the mannequins with suits and fur coats on them. I always thought it was a store where people with a lot of money shopped. I guess it was because we only saw the area where our uncle worked.
Jason Wyandt

Photo by Chuck Mamula

NAME: **James O'Roark**

TITLE: **Founding Partner**
Pook Creator

richland mall MVIP

On a mountain near Jennerstown, the man who created Richie the Pook and helped develop the Richland Mall is still dreaming up new projects. His Memory-O-Stick – a walking stick inscribed with a special memory related to a historic site – gives tourists a new way to experience and learn from local attractions like the Flight 93 Memorial.

And he would still love to build an amusement park based on Richie and the whole Pook family. "We always dreamed of having a Planet Pook park," says Jim O'Roark. "It would be perfect for the cast of characters I created – Richie the Pook, Ribbie the Frog, Round Hound, Lady Fox, Heidi Hedgehog, Piggley G. Pig, Willard Weasel, and Super Chick. I still think it could be very good. I'm positive it would work."

Even so long after the rise and fall of his crowning achievement, the Richland Mall, Jim has a strikingly positive outlook. He still intends to make a difference in the world...as if doing it numerous times already in his life wasn't enough.

He still longs to get back in the game. He still wants to make lightning strike again, the same way he and the Unimich team did back in the 1970s.

Will That Be Regular or Unleaded?

Born and raised in Stoystown, Somerset County, Jim went to college at the University of Pittsburgh. He earned his Master of Business Administration in 1965, then promptly went to work...as a gas station attendant at a Shell station in Cincinnati, Ohio?

It was all part of the plan, according to Jim. He'd set his sights on a job in the corporate headquarters of the Shell Oil Company in Chicago. The best preparation, he decided, was to learn about the company from the bottom up.

Photo by Philip Balko

19

"I pumped gas, installed wiper blades, did tune-ups, you name it," remembers Jim. "I wanted to be able to do everything, and really understand how the company worked."

It paid off when Jim got his next job as senior real estate representative at Shell headquarters in Chicago. In one giant leap, he went from grease monkey to senior analyst in the economic planning department.

Courtesy Jim O'Roark

It was a move that set the stage for his work on the Richland Mall project years later. While at Shell, Jim learned the ropes and met the rest of the group that would later become Unimich: Jim Streeter, Ron Sabin, Steve Clause, and Ray Kisor. Good friends and great teammates from the start, they formed an alliance that eventually gave birth to the Richland Mall.

The Start of a Beautiful Friendship

When Jim jumped ship after five years at Shell for a job as an executive vice president at Lanning Corporation, he brought his four friends with him. They spent a few years developing Kmart locations before Jim left Lanning, and Jim Streeter went with him. Once they'd settled on the Richland Township site for their next project, the other three followed, and Unimich was born.

Together, though they lacked experience in mall development, they made their dream of the Richland Mall a reality. "We were just five crazy young people who really had no fear," recalls Jim, "but we had purpose. We moved forward confidently, as if we'd developed many malls instead of none, and the people we needed to help us got onboard."

Of course, it also helped that Jim was a native son, even if he hadn't lived in the area for years – though that changed soon enough.

Fox on the Run

As the mall project ramped up, steadily demanding more attention, Jim and his teammates needed to spend more time in Richland. For a while, they shared a second-floor apartment in Somerset owned by Jim's in-laws, Charles and Dorothy Brant. "It was rent-free, and we were thankful for the great pillow fights," recalls Jim.

"We lived on a hill above a diner in Somerset, and there were 18-wheelers shifting as they came down the hill, no matter what time of the day or night," remembers Ray Kisor. "We weren't exactly living in grandeur, let me tell you."

Things were a little grander in the team's next residence, a condominium on the golf course at Seven Springs. It never quite felt like home to Jim, though.

Eventually, he decided it was time to make his return to the area more permanent. He bought a farm in Rector, near Ligonier, and moved his wife, Linda, and two children there from Grand Rapids in January 1974.

"It was a beautiful farm with 130 acres with a house and horses," remembers Linda. "It had a horse barn and a multi-purpose barn, a caretaker's house, and another barn and a little milk house and two ponds. It was lovely."

The place had its drawbacks, though. According to a stipulation in the deed, the Rolling Rock Hunt Club had the right to ride through the property at any time.

"They would pull up in the driveway with their trucks full of dogs and their fancy riding outfits and get all set up," says Linda. "Then, someone would blow a bugle, and off they'd go, hunting a fox. I was like, 'this is insane.'"

Jim and Linda put up with the hunts, but the local residents didn't exactly welcome them with open arms. "Some people in Ligonier Valley tried to stop us from buying the property because they found out Jim was a developer. They were worried because there was nothing that said we couldn't develop the land if we wanted to, though we had no such intention. They were afraid he'd divide the property into a bunch of lots and put up houses, so they fought the sale. We won in the end, but there wasn't a lot of goodwill after that," says Linda.

Still, life on the farm suited the kids, especially since they had plenty of family nearby. "We were 20 miles away from my mom and dad, so Jamie and Brook, who were four and eight at the time, were happy as could be," explains Linda. "They had cousins in the area, too, so there was a lot going on. They just loved it."

Like Being in Disneyworld

Life seemed to be almost perfect for a while. The grand opening of the Richland Mall put Jim on the front page of the local newspapers, and the local community turned out in force to support the new venture.

"It was exciting," remembers Linda. "Everybody was talking about it – not only having a mall in town, but having a local guy build it after starting with nothing."

Jim added to his success by launching the Super Chick restaurant at the Kmart end of the Mall. Operated by Jim's brother, Jack, Super Chick had a rustic, down-home décor and featured specialty chicken sandwiches. Other menu items included the Super O'Fish, the Super O'Hambo, Super Chick on a Stick, and a beverage called Afternoon Delight. The restaurant's slogan was "Super Chick Instead."

When Super Chick was a hit, Jim added two

Photo by Jim Streeter

more stores – one in the University Park Shopping Center in Richland and another in the Indiana Mall. He also opened Richie's Corner in the Richland Mall, a store where he sold Richie the Pook memorabilia. It seemed, for a while, like he could do no wrong.

But the good times didn't last. Friction developed over disagreements with the other Unimich partners, and the dream team started to crumble. Jim stepped away from the business to focus on developing Richie the Pook and the Pook family of characters he'd created.

"Jim converted the old milk house on the farm into an office for his company, Ribet Productions," recalls Linda. "I imagine the kids thought it was pretty fun. It was like being in Disneyworld every day, because they were always out there shooting video or film of the characters and doing related stuff. I suppose it was fun for them."

But eventually, career stress and financial pressures took their toll. Family separation occurred, as Linda and the kids moved to Alaska, leaving Jim to consider what the next chapter of his story would be.

The Jonathan Winters and Richard Petty Connection

In the years that followed, the Super Chick restaurants and Richie's Corner closed. Jim sold his interest in the Richland Mall in 1982, cashing out to focus his attention on promoting the Pook Family characters and other business interests.

For a while, he lived in California and shopped a Pook Family screenplay around Hollywood. At one point, his neighbor, comedian Jonathan Winters, was attached to the project, with the possible involvement of Jonathan's friend Robin Williams.

But the movie was never made, and other deals never quite came together. Jim kept working to bring the Pook Family to life on the national level but also found himself involved in other projects that he hoped might help him turn a corner.

For example, he released a 45 single of a song about Even Knievel's jump across the Snake River Canyon, titled "Jumpin' the Gates of Heaven."

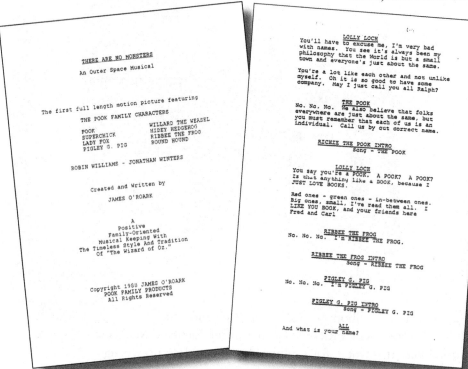

He developed a product with NASCAR driver Richard Petty called "Richard Petty's Chicken on a Stick," which was sold at Food Lion supermarkets.

He also got involved with dwarf car racing, a kind of modified stock car racing featuring scale replicas of vintage race cars. Jim formed the Dwarf World Auto Racing Federation and serving as the national editor of *Dwarf Car Racer Magazine.*

Courtesy Jim O'Roark

Today, at home on the mountain, he still dreams of fresh greatness – taking Memory-O-Stick national or building Planet Pook or bringing back Super Chick to compete with Chik-Fil-A. But to many of us, his most memorable claim to fame will always be the Richland Mall.

"It wouldn't have gotten done without him," says Linda. "He was the driving force and had the vision and wherewithal to do it.

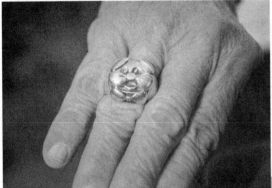

Photo by Philip Balko

"Whatever bad times came after, I still give credit where credit is due. It was a big accomplishment for a young man. He was brilliant."

Photo by Philip Balko

Photo by Philip Balko

Courtesy Jim O'Roark

When I was young, walking around that Mall was such a good time. I remember Kmart, Brooks, Hot Sam, Capri, the movie theaters, and buying half coins at Spencer's. I really miss that Mall.

Tara Robison

I worked at Sweet William and later the Duke and Duchess. There were lots of good memories and friends. From tin roof sundaes to Sunday matinees, it helped pay for school, and Richland Mall was the place to be!

Frank Galasso

I remember when *Star Wars* opened at the Duke and Duchess theaters in 1977. We tried to get tickets for days, but there were never any group seats left. I was seven years old and too scared to sit alone. One night, my mother and brother and I were at the Mall, and we took a chance and stopped by the theater. The manager said there were two open seats in the back row, so my brother and I went in. That's how I finally saw *Star Wars*.

Don Evanisko

Courtesy Jim Streeter

I worked at the Richland Mall for 11 years. I worked at Frank's 'n Stuff near Kmart. One of my favorite Mall stories happened at Christmas during the time of the Cabbage Patch doll craze. The owner of Frank's 'n Stuff went to New York City and bought two dolls for New Day, Inc. to raffle off as a fundraiser. The dolls were such a craze that Security had to go get them each morning and return them every night so there wouldn't be a mob waiting for the dolls to come out of or go into our back room!

Frank's 'n Stuff was the place where lots of people who worked in the Mall ate lunch. We knew all the happenings because we knew so many people who worked there.

There were so many wonderful memories at the Mall. We used to have Christmas parties after hours right in the middle of the Mall. It was awesome and will always live in my heart.

Nancy Morisi

In 1992, I worked as a sales consultant in the Richland Mall at the GTE Phone Mart, which later became Verizon Phone Mart. After the Galleria opened, we moved up there, but it just wasn't the same. I lost my favorite stores, and it wasn't as personal as the Richland Mall.

I had lots of fun at the Richland Mall and enjoyed working there. Sometimes it's sad to see something so good just get up and leave.

Charlotte Amenti

I loved Christmastime at the Richland Mall – the Christmas songs, everyone smiling and having a great time.

Joyce Sell Keller

Courtesy Lynne Dougherty

Going to the Mall in 1979 was a big adventure for my daughter, Erin, at two years of age. My Pap (Clair Malloy, 5/13/08-11/2/80) would go to the Mall every day after lunch and sit on a bench with all his buddies. We always knew where to find him, and my daughter enjoyed visiting him there after we shopped. Pap never had his shoelaces tied, but he'd sit there with his friends all afternoon and people-watch. He only lived a few minutes away, and he was home by 4:00 for supper. It was a beautiful Mall that we utilized often. We were so happy with the indoor shopping away from the elements.

Lynne Dougherty

We had lots of entertainment at the Richland Mall. We had the Vogues there several times. We had line dancers there, and Santa Claus and the Easter Bunny. We did a lot of community-oriented things, like sponsoring an angel tree and having trick-or-treat night, when kids could go through all the different stores. It was just an outstanding place.

Gil Demos

chapter three

laying the groundwork

1972 - 1973

How do you build a mall with no money down? Just ask the two Jims and their partners.

"When we started the project, we didn't have any money to speak of," says Jim Streeter. "None of us invested in the Richland Mall. None of us put any money into the company. All we did in the beginning was agree that we were going to become partners and work full-time on this project and support our families the best we could."

"The five of us might have had a combined net value of ten to fifteen thousand dollars," says Jim O'Roark.

Early on, a businessman in Lowell, Massachusetts co-signed a loan for $10,000 to help jump-start their project...but even in the early 1970s, that money was small potatoes. "We wouldn't have stayed afloat for very long if George Cook at Somerset Trust Company hadn't thrown us a line," says O'Roark.

Courtesy Jim Streeter

"George and Somerset Trust agreed to become a lender for us, to cover some upfront costs we were incurring as the mall development process went along," says Streeter. Somerset Trust loaned Unimich $50,000, then an additional $110,000 to help the Richland Mall project keep going.

"We couldn't have found a better partner. Everything George did was superb," recalls O'Roark.

Still, the money from Somerset Trust wouldn't keep the project rolling forever. The team knew that if they wanted to get the Mall built, they would need to attract some *much* bigger financing.

Winning the Lottery a Couple of Times

As plans for the Mall took shape, and the early funding faded, the team met the next money milestone by capturing millions of dollars in temporary financing from American Fletcher National Bank of Indianapolis. Obtaining the loan was made possible, in part, because of a connection with Unimich from their Lanning Corporation days.

"This lender agreed to do the first part of the construction financing, which is the riskiest part," says O'Roark. "It helped that they knew us from Lanning and our Kmart work."

Next came the biggest piece of the money puzzle: the permanent construction financing. It amounted to a huge chunk of change – $22 million – and came from an unexpected source.

According to O'Roark, the permanent financing for the Richland Mall was provided by the Teachers Insurance and Annuity Association, or TIAA. But none of it would have happened without O'Roark's step-sister Vivian Horner's roommate, Mia, in New York City.

"Mia got a job at TIAA not long before we needed the permanent financing," remembers O'Roark. "She was assigned to be an analyst in the shopping center division, which was an incredible stroke of luck.

"Mia told her co-workers about the Richland Mall project, and she ended up analyzing it as a potential investment. When she was done, TIAA decided to provide $22 million in permanent financing." Later, after Mia helped make the project a reality, Vivian moved to Johnstown and helped Connie Hayes to run the first information booth in the Mall.

"It was just unbelievable, the way the money all fell into place," says O'Roark. "Permanent financing isn't usually something that just happens. It's something that everyone wants, no matter what size shopping center you develop, but it can be hard to obtain.

"Getting it the way we did, and getting the temporary financing and startup loans so easily, was like winning the lottery a couple of times in a row. It was miraculous."

Still, as lucky as it was for the financing to come together the way it did, the Unimich team faced its share of obstacles and hard times.

"Richland Mall was never an easy deal," remember Streeter. "It was not easy to get the zoning. It was not easy to get tenants to commit to Johnstown. But we were too dumb to know we couldn't do it, so we just kept plugging along. And somehow, we got all the pieces put together."

The Mall Stood on Rented Ground

With the financing finally in place, the men from Unimich moved forward with obtaining the next vital piece of the project: the land on which the Mall would be built.

Unfortunately, the owner of the biggest part of the site wasn't interested in selling.

County Amusements, which owned the Richland Drive-In that occupied much of the site, wanted to retain ownership of the property, though Unimich wanted to buy it outright.

This refusal to sell nearly meant the end of the Mall project. Finally, though, County Amusements agreed to *lease* the land instead.

"We negotiated a ground lease with the Troll family, who controlled the land," explains Streeter. "The lease was for 99 years, so we would basically have the use of that property for 99 years." Charles Sheftic, chairman of the board at People's Bank and Trust, was also a partner in the land ownership and integral in the County Amusement decision.

Courtesy Ed Troll

"In any real estate deal, a 99-year lease is as good as owning the land. It's always better to own the land, but if you can't buy it, having a ground lease for close to 100 years is the next best thing. And that allows you to get financing and other lenders to lend money for 30-year mortgages. They know they have fee interests in the land for 100 years, so they're covered," says Streeter.

The Trolls and Sheftic, for their part, were satisfied that the ground lease was a fair deal. "In the first year of the lease, we received twice what we made in a year of running the drive-in theater," remembers Ed Troll, who currently owns and operates the Richland Cinemas on a plot of the same piece of land. "After that, there were periodic increases at different points in time."

As part of the deal, the Trolls would open indoor movie theaters at the Mall – the Duke and Duchess. From the beginning right through to the present day, there has always been a Troll theater on the site.

The Fight to Stop the Mall

With the drive-in land locked down, Unimich moved to acquire or lease the rest of the 35-acre site they'd planned to use for the Mall. They purchased part of the parcel of land from the Berwind-White Coal Company of Windber, conducting negotiations at the clubhouse of the Richland Greens golf course. Next, Unimich proceeded to buy a number of residential properties within the bounds of the designated site, guaranteeing that the full location would be available for construction.

Unimich then sought the approval of the Richland Township Supervisors, aided by local counsel Gilbert Caroff of Richland. After approval was granted by the supervisors, however, a local backlash threatened to derail the project.

Citizens groups claimed Richland Township officials did not consider the interest of township residents when they approved the extension of a commercial zone for the Mall into a multiple-residential dwelling district. The groups filed two lawsuits in Cambria County Court to try to block the Mall's construction.

"I have watched the pattern of growth for 15 years," said John Moorehead, an opposition leader, according to *The Tribune-Democrat*. "At first, the Geistown Shopping Center was the place to shop. Then Bel-Air Plaza, Sears, Gee Bee, Miracle Mart, and Grant City followed. And what did it leave? Empty stores, rundown centers."

Ultimately, though, the citizens gave up the fight and settled out of court with Unimich. "It was a hopeless situation," Wayne Mulligan, who led one of the opposition groups, told *The Tribune-Democrat*. "We could not continue to fight without the money to pay for a court test. We agreed that if we did succeed in stopping one developer, another would come in. We didn't have the money and couldn't get the support of the zoning board."

Another challenge came from William McQuaide, then the executive vice president of W.C. McQuaide Freight Lines, Inc., which was located near the Mall site.

According to *The Tribune-Democrat*, McQuaide opposed the original set of plans because they would affect his business by interfering with development of the Elton Road. Eventually, though, he and Unimich settled their differences, and the Richland Township Supervisors gave the Mall project their blessing.

In return, Unimich agreed to do the following:

- Pay for the installation of a traffic light at Eisenhower Boulevard and Theatre Drive and another at the Donald Lane and Elton Road.
- Install two new 12-foot traffic lanes on Theatre Drive if necessary.
- Make improvements on Route 756 (Elton Road), including the addition of two traffic lanes adjacent to the site frontage along that road.
- Install a traffic island or physical barrier at the Theatre Drive entrance closest to Route 756.
- Install most of the roof drains so they empty on the rear, or easterly side, of the Mall site.
- Provide fire hydrants.

According to *The Tribune-Democrat*, O'Roark said that these improvements to the township would have a combined value of $300,000. When completed, the Mall was expected to bring more than 700 jobs to the area.

Things were looking up for the Richland Mall project. "Everybody became friendly with the knowledge that this was going to become a reality," says O'Roark. "They got used to the idea that a major commercial transfer was going on between downtown Johnstown and the suburbs, just like what was happening in every community in the United States."

The Challenge of Filling a Mall

The financing was in place, the land was acquired, the township supervisors had given their blessing...but would there be enough stores to fill the new Mall?

The occupancy of the Mall was by no means a done deal. Two of the anchors – Kmart and Sears – had committed. Smaller tenants had signed letters of intent, but the letters were non-binding, and there weren't enough interested tenants to fill the Mall as the date of the groundbreaking in May 1973 drew near.

The Mall, when finished, would have 625,000 square feet of floor space. "Filling all that space was difficult," recalls Ray Kisor. "It took quite a bit of time. Johnstown was a hard sell because of the declining population base and diminishing economic base. One of the biggest local employers, Bethlehem Steel, was having serious financial problems."

"The work had just started because we had to lease the rest of the specialty stores," says Streeter. "We had to go from just an expression of intent from those people to getting them to sign firm leases to build their stores. And while we were doing that, we had to get ready to open the Richland Mall. We were 18 months out from the grand opening, which sounds like a long time, but you have to do all the pre-promotion to take it to your marketplace and community.

"Putting up and filling the building were just part of the story."

I loved the Richland Mall. I worked in Spencer's when I was in high school and GNC until I got married and moved away. I still miss it.

Brigid Kapustka Sowinski

It was a pretty awesome Mall in its day. I have so many great memories of it, but I always liked it so much more than the Galleria. Originally, there were many different interesting stores, though the place always lacked a hobby shop.

John Gardner Heckert

I worked in Frank's 'n Stuff when I was in high school, and the woman who is now my mother-in-law worked at the balloon shop right next door. Back then, we didn't know each other, but we worked side by side every day in the 1980s. I'm sure I waited on her many times for lunch or dinner. Who knew, years later, that she would be my mother-in-law?

To this day, I can close my eyes and tell you where every store was located in that Mall. To me, it's still the best Mall that was ever built in Johnstown.

Sherry Harteis

Photo by Chuck Mamula

31

The Richland Mall had personality. I started working at Kmart when the Mall was still new, and I remember the Mall's many promotions over the years. I remember the car giveaway, where you placed your hands on a car, and the last person standing won it. This went on even after the stores closed each day, and people were encouraged to come and support the contestants.

Trick-or-treat night was always a huge success. Mall employees stood outside their stores handing out candy. At one point, I looked out into the Mall and I could see children lined up on both sides. It was a great Mall to work in!

Barb Walukas Ream

Photo by Diane Truscott

When I think of the Richland Mall, I can't help but remember a store called That Pet Place, because I have a pleasant reminder of it in my home every day. One day about 30 years ago, I was in the store with my son, who was around 8 years old at the time. We were just looking around when he saw a box turtle and asked if he could have it. On a spur-of-the moment decision, I said yes. Well, here we are in 2017, and J.D., as we named him, is still alive and going strong. At the time, I never imagined that 30 years later, we would still have J.D. He truly is a part of the family and has been one very spoiled turtle. So when reminiscing about the Richland Mall, I'll remember the various shops, but I'll always have a special place in my heart for That Pet Place.

Diane Truscott

I worked at Sweet William from 1986-87 as a cook, waiter, and ice cream stand attendant. I enjoyed working there, and I really liked the Richland Mall. During my high school years, I liked to constantly drive around outside the Mall.

I do miss it, especially the center of the Mall with all the vegetation and stuff. That's what I miss the most.

Gary Speicher

I was the manager of Somerset Trust in the Richland Mall in the late 70s, after the Johnstown Flood of '77. What I liked best about the Mall was the variety and the small, cohesive friendliness of it.

Richard Stern

We used to go to the Encore when I was in high school, and they made this mistake of having all-you-can-eat chicken. I think it was on a Monday or Tuesday, and my buddies and I ate 120 pieces of chicken in one night. There were eight of us. The owner finally cut us off because when one of us went to stab the chicken, he stabbed the waitress's hand instead.

We loved the Encore. We would go there constantly, and at 200 pounds each, we were big guys. We went in there and just kept eating chicken until they cut us off.

Barry Thomas

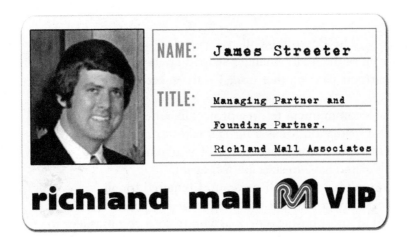

NAME: James Streeter

TITLE: Managing Partner and Founding Partner, Richland Mall Associates

richland mall M VIP

Lots of people are important to the story of the Richland Mall, but only one man had a lead role from the very beginning until the bitter end.

Jim Streeter was part of the first discussions with Jim O'Roark about the project that became the Mall. He was there for the Mall's closing and demolition. And he was there for all the years in between, helping to keep the place on track as managing partner.

No one else can claim the same longevity as Jim in terms of the Mall project. Talking to him is like talking to the history of the Richland Mall in human form.

The Rolling in Cash Myth

Jim remembers the grand opening of the Mall on November 4, 1974. After years of struggle and sacrifice, he and rest of the Unimich crew – Jim O'Roark, Ray Kisor, Steve Clause, and Ron Sabin – cut the ribbon in front of a huge crowd. There's a photo of the five partners huddled together that day, arms around each other's shoulders, basking in the glow of their achievement.

It was a simple, beautiful moment, the culmination of a dream that at times had seemed impossible. It was not, however, the end of the team's struggles.

"You think you made it at the time," remembers Streeter. "You think, 'boy, we actually pulled this off, and we actually got it open, and I bet we're just gonna be rolling in it. Rolling in cash.'

"But that was the furthest thing from the truth. It takes a long time to mature a real estate deal, and we were anything but rolling in cash. But we worked hard and paid our bills and paid our employees."

Courtesy Jim Streeter

33

The Personal Toll

Unfortunately, even as the Mall's finances shaped up in years to come, the Unimich partners paid another price for the success of their venture.

"When you make a commitment to do a project like the Richland Mall, it's a 24/7 situation for as long as it takes to be successful," explains Streeter. "The alternative is, if you're not successful, you go broke and have to start all over again.

"That was the commitment that O'Roark and I required for all our partners. And I'm happy to say that they all gave it 110 percent. That's what is required of most business people who make a commitment to creating something that becomes number one. I'm not saying it's right. I'm just saying that's the way it happened.

"But as part of that, you leave one day, and you come back three years later, and nobody in your family really knows you. Your kids are three or four years older and things change.

"As a result of that, though we were successful getting Richland Mall together and operating, it took a personal toll on us. When the project started, all five original partners were married. By the time it was all said and done, the five of us were all divorced."

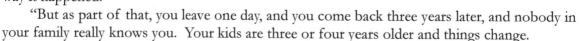

Photo by Linda Dufseth

The Secret of the Mall's Success

In spite of the hardship and personal cost, Streeter looks back at his Richland Mall years as a wonderful part of his life. "It was a wonderful experience with a bunch of young guys who went way beyond their ability and accomplished what was probably a miracle that would never have been done today."

Courtesy Jim Streeter

Even so, Streeter doesn't think of the Richland Mall as a home run in terms of overall success. One perpetual problem was convincing national retailers to move into the Mall, since Johnstown was considered a fringe market. "We never leased 100 percent of the Mall to national tenants because there just weren't enough of them who were willing to come to our market area," says Streeter.

Through the diligence of the Unimich partners, however, this issue became a strong point for the Mall. "Since only 50 or 60 percent of our tenants were major national tenants, we turned to local tenants to fill the balance of our space. With so many local tenants in the mix, we worked really hard at our relationships with those tenants. We worked hard to give local tenants every opportunity to succeed and survive...and they, in turn, added to the unique selection of goods and services available to our shoppers.

Photo by Chuck Mamula

"That is really what made Richland Mall special and successful.
It made it successful for consumers who lived in Johnstown, as well as providing a nurturing environment for local small businesses," explains Streeter.

Ahead of its (End) Time

As managing partner for 25 years, Streeter witnessed much of the Richland Mall's success first-hand. Though based in Grand Rapids, Michigan for much of that time, he was never away from the Mall for very long.

"I returned to Johnstown every week or every other week for 25 years," he remembers. "I was involved with managing the Mall until we sold and closed it."

Streeter watched as tenant defections and loss of business to the Johnstown Galleria sucked the life out of the Richland Mall. "By 1998, it could no longer survive," he says. "I closed the interior of the Mall in March of '98, though Kmart and Michael's, which was in a freestanding building, stayed open for a while longer."

When the Mall was completely closed and torn down to make room for Richland Town Centre in 2003, it was the end of an era – and a tough time for Streeter.

"It was very difficult because I was there the day the Mall was born, the day the concept was born with O'Roark and me," says Streeter. "And I was there at the end.

Photo by James and Frederica Rosenbaum

"The year, year and a half that I was there every week going through the process of holding this piece of real estate that died was like losing a member of my family. It was also terribly difficult because I was responsible for all those people who'd committed their lives to being our employees. And now, it was all disappearing."

In the end, though, the Richland

Photo by Jason Pozar

Mall was ahead of the times in its downfall. "Malls are closing all over the country now because the way people shop today is different than the way they shopped in 1974," explains Streeter.

"In 1974, people would come to the Richland Mall and stay there for two or three hours. They'd have something to eat. They'd shop. They'd make a whole two or three hour trip out of it. Typically, people don't shop that way anymore. If you go to the Mall now, you go in and buy what you need to buy, and you leave. As a shopper, you look for tenants with stores that you can pull up in front of and go in and buy what you want and leave.

"That's led to the disintegration of the way people shop in malls. Malls have disintegrated to the point where they're being repositioned, or if they can't be repositioned, they're being torn down."

Photos by Philip Balko

The Post-Mall Man

After the demise of the Richland Mall, Streeter didn't have a reason to come to Johnstown anymore. Back home in Grand Rapids, he continued to work in the real estate development game, tending other projects that he'd brought to life over the years.

These days, he's mostly retired from the business. His last new deal was ten years ago, in fact – but he still maintains an office and secretary to manage his existing properties and interests.

Without so much business to consume him, Streeter has more free time for his personal interests – like golf – and his family...though the Johnstown connection continues to have an impact. His second wife, whom he married in 1990, was born (but not raised) in Johnstown, and that city is always a special link between them.

Jim Streeter 2017

Jim's Richland Mall days continue to be an important part of his life in other ways, as well. "I still keep in touch with good friends from the Mall," he says. "I see Ray Kisor a couple times a week. I'm the godfather of his daughter, who is now 40 years old with three kids. I also stay in touch with Bob McConnell and lots of other friends who were part of the Richland Mall story.

"It was a wonderful experience, developing and managing that Mall. It's too bad it had to end the way it did, but that's life, you know? Real estate deals don't last forever.

"It's nice to know that we played such a wonderful part in Johnstown, though. I'm amazed at all the people who still love the Mall and stay connected on Facebook, and I'm just delighted that it had such an impact on so many people. That's the true thrill of it for me.

"I don't dwell on the rough spots along the way. I remember only the days when the Richland Mall was the best thing that ever happened to me," says Streeter. "And let me tell you, there were plenty of those."

Courtesy Jim Streeter

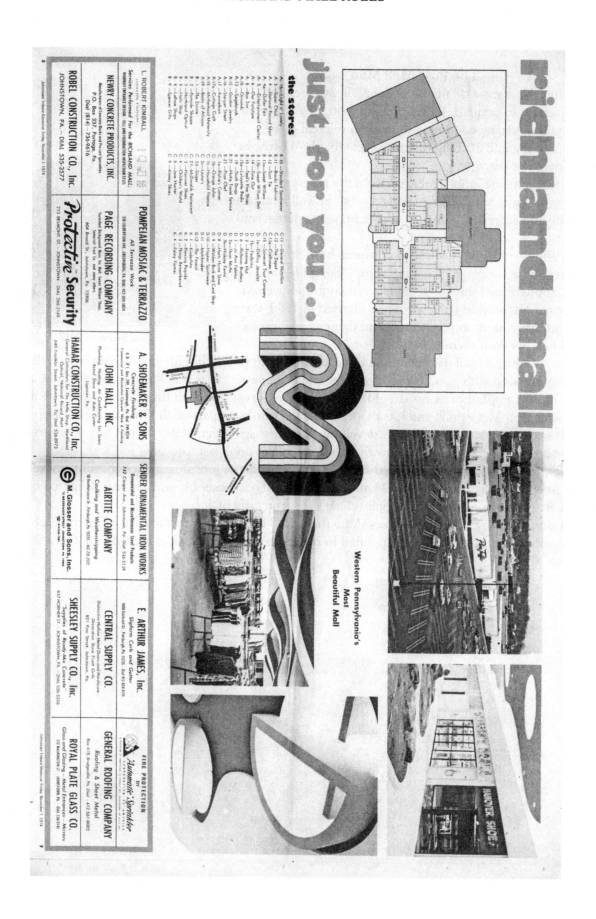

38

The video arcade was Time-Out. I loved the games there. It was my favorite hangout in my early teen years.

I also loved the Easter egg drawing contests they held. We made large cardboard eggs and drew on them. Every year, there was a different theme. The Mall personnel used to judge and hang them from the ceiling all through the Mall. The winners had ribbons that hung from them. It was pretty cool to see a ribbon hang from yours.

Lisa Marie Macri

I loved the one time they were giving away a car to the person who kept their hands on the car the longest. It went on for days.

I also remember working at Kmart, and every Wednesday was macaroni and cheese day at the snack bar. You could get a plate of macaroni and cheese and a roll for $1.99. The line would stretch from the snack bar in the middle of the back of the store to the front door. People loved that snack bar.

Chris Kornprobst

As a student at Pitt-Johnstown, I loved going to Time-Out and Capri. Capri had a great deep-dish pizza.

David H. Plows

I ran the carousel the last year or so the Mall was open, and my daughter worked the lottery booth. I loved that place so much more than the other place, which shall not be named.

Debbie Rosian Penrod

Photo by Chuck Mamula

I remember finally being able to get my ears pierced when I was 12. While I'm not entirely sure of where I got them done, I do know that right afterward, my Mom took me to Sweet William, and I got the best dessert ever: hot apple pie with cinnamon ice cream. Not only is this one awesome memory of spending time with my mom (who happens to be the best ever), but it's also my favorite memory from the Richland Mall!

Hope Weigle

My first date with my husband was at Capri Pizza. A slice of pizza, a side salad, and a soda was a pretty affordable date! Then, we played video games at Time-Out. Galaga was our favorite! Those were the days!

Amanda Fockler

I was assistant manager at GNC. We would grind peanuts for fresh peanut butter and had to stand in front of the store offering samples of that and chewable Vitamin C. We also used to offer samples of Papaya juice. I hated having to stand in front of the store and offer samples.

There were GNC coupons in the Sunday or Wednesday newspaper. With those coupons, you could get a Dannon yogurt or an orange juice for 10 cents each.

Brigid Kapustka Sowinski

We used to have disco dances at the Encore in the 70s, when disco was big. We would all meet at the Encore and dance the night away. It was a happening place. All the merchants would go over there after work and let their hair down, just have a blast. There was always lots of dancing.

Gil Demos

Courtesy Larry Mummert

chapter four
if you build it, they will shop

1973 · 1974

© *The Tribune-Democrat*

It all started with a symbolic shovelful of dirt, turned over by Jim O'Roark and Robert Moore, chairman of the Richland Township Board of Supervisors. Eighteen months later, if everything went according to plan, there would be a Mall on the spot where they stood.

Jim Streeter remembers the momentous occasion well. "The groundbreaking was held on May 3, 1973. It was a big deal, the realization of a dream – but in many ways, it was just the starting line.

Courtesy Jim Streeter

41

Courtesy Jim Streeter

"We were fully financed, and we had our major tenants, Sears and Kmart – but we were nowhere near filling all the retail space we had available. Our marketing efforts were just getting off the ground. And who knew what problems we might face as construction ramped up? We had a very long way to go."

Still, the Unimich team and the rest of the crowd of 100 didn't let worries about the future cloud their enthusiasm. Every speaker had encouraging things to say about the project that was about to move into full swing.

"This is one more in a series of progressive steps toward the development of an even greater Johnstown," said Lou Galliker, president of the Greater Johnstown Chamber of Commerce.

"The more industry and commerce we get, the better for everybody," said Cambria County Commissioner Joseph P. Roberts.

"We feel it is most appropriate that this breaking of ground occurs in Johnstown's All-America City Week," said O'Roark. "We are aware that we must produce a product that will bring pride to the area. The firm will produce what we've said we would produce."

Courtesy Jim Streeter

After the ceremony, O'Roark again spoke at a celebratory dinner at Sunnehanna Country Club in Westmont. "This is not only an important night for us, but it is an important night for the entire community. We believe we should look beyond the first year of our development and down the road to the future."

Look for the Union Label

Once the ground had been officially broken at the Richland Mall site, a fleet of bulldozers, backhoes, trucks, and all manner of earthmoving equipment moved in and went to work.

Courtesy Jason Pozar

Hard-hatted contractors fanned out across the property, most of them local union workers.

Steenwyk Thrall, Inc., based in Grand Rapids, Michigan, was hired to do the architectural design work. Progressive Engineers of Grand Rapids was hired to provide engineering services, and Robert E. Fryling Company, also of Grand Rapids, served as the general contractor managing the project. However, the vast majority of the onsite work was assigned to local laborers.

Already, the Mall was having a positive impact on the local economy. "We made it a point to bring jobs to the area," says O'Roark. "We had total union participation. Everyone was happy because we weren't bringing in workers from Michigan or wherever to do the bulk of the work. The general contractor supplied only supervision."

Local firms involved in the project included Five R Excavating, Inc., Showalter Masonry, Griffith Custer Steel Co. (structural steel), Miller Block Co., Breco Mechanical Contractors (plumbing), Thomas Kinzey Lumber Company, A.J. Confer Co. (plastering, spray fireproofing), L. Robert Kimball (highway entrance design; fill and foundation inspection tests), Sheesley Supply Co., Royal Plate Glass, Wm. M. Chapple, Inc. (heating and air conditioning systems), Church and Murdock Electric, Inc., Wilson Construction Co., M. Glosser and Sons, Newry Concrete Products, General Roofing Company, Hamar Construction Co., A. Shoemaker & Sons, Sender Ornamental Iron Works, Central Supply Co., L.R. Owen Co. (paving), Protective Security, and Southern Alleghenies Disposal Service.

Photos Courtesy Jim Streeter

Bringing in so many local companies to execute the plans of the architects, engineers, and project managers in Grand Rapids was a sound arrangement that encouraged quality workmanship, reduced possibilities for friction and controversy with the community, and earned plenty of local goodwill that would pay off down the line. As with any large construction job, however, the Richland Mall project was not without bumps in the road.

"Deliveries are horrible," said Fryling Project Manager Joseph Ypma while the work was underway. "Shortages of many materials make it very hard to maintain a schedule."

"Every day you're faced with issues," explains Streeter. "You're faced with construction issues, you're faced with business issues, things costing more than you thought. You know the architect is wanting to do things you can't afford and tenants want things you can't help them afford to do. So it was an ongoing process. Every day brought a whole laundry list of issues."

Photos Courtesy Jim Streeter

Curves That Can't Be Beat

Even with the various issues cropping up, everyone stayed focused on bringing to life the unique design of the Mall, as developed by architects Don Steenwyk and Bill Thrall.

One thing was clear to anyone who saw Steenwyk and Thrall's blueprints: this would be a mall like no other. According to O'Roark, this was very much intentional.

"I wanted something that was totally different, that would stand out compared to other malls. That is what we got, and then some."

A great deal of thought went into all the design features, like the serpentine ceilings over the corridors. O'Roark says these ceilings, with their flowing, wavelike appearance, were created "so customers didn't feel like they were going down an alleyway or a dungeon."

The ceilings required a six-step installation process, completed by a small army of professional plasterers.

After constructing a supporting grid system, the plasterers used wire screening to sculpt the scalloped curves. Next, the workmen applied lathing over the screening, followed by a coat of brown plaster coat, a coat of white plaster, and a coat of finish spray. The end result was a fluid, organic look that brought to mind the region's waterways and served as a key component in the Richland Mall's unique and visually rhythmic design.

Walking a Crooked Mall

The curved ceiling was just one aspect of the creative concept applied to the Mall's hallways. By design, the hallways were staggered along an irregular layout intended to enhance the perception of size and variety.

"Most people are used to going down a straight hallway," explains O'Roark. "However, if you look at the design of the Richland Mall, you'll see that our hallways were close but not lined up exactly.

Photos Courtesy Jim Streeter

"They were off just enough to make things different. It enhanced the feeling of going down these different paths that took you to all these different stores.

"From Kmart to center court, for example, was one spur. When you went down the spur from center court to Sears, you had the same kind of hallway with the same curved ceiling, but it was off enough that you were not going down a straight path.

"Maybe the average consumer didn't notice this intentional misalignment, but the design added to the success of the Mall. It influenced foot traffic and perceptions on a subconscious level," says O'Roark.

Another Brick in the Mall

Another unique aspect of the Richland Mall's design was the use of colorful glazed vertical bricks to create eye-catching external surfaces. The main entrance, near center court, was flanked by two cylindrical towers – the left one wrapped in red brick, the right one in yellow. The rooftop skylight over center court was also walled in yellow brick. On the opposite side of the Mall, blue brick covered the exterior of the Duke and Duchess theaters. Other outside walls were encased in white brick, laid horizontally – though Sears had its own grooved, gray masonry wrap around its distinctive façade.

"Those bricks were expensive," recalls O'Roark. "But we wanted to do something totally different, and they were perfect."

Photos Courtesy Jim Streeter

In all, 1,200,000 bricks were used in the construction of the Mall – enough to build a 30-foot-high wall that was one mile, 434 feet long. Years later, after the Mall was remodeled, O'Roark's brother, Jack, used a selection of those bricks to build a U.S. flag in his yard.

Photo by Steven Gavlak

These Fish Weren't Made for Catchin'

The colorful bricks...the staggered hallways... the curved ceilings. All these features added to the Richland Mall's unique character and ambiance. But no element represented the heart of the Mall so well as the wooded parklet in center court, complete with trout-stocked stream.

"It was a recreation of what you'd find in the mountains of Western Pennsylvania," explains Streeter. "It was meant to be like something you'd find in Ligonier or around any trout stream in the area."

The parklet consisted of trees, bushes, and boulders arranged around a central well. A viewing platform overlooked a stream fed by waterfalls and populated with live fish.

Two smaller parklets were also constructed at either end of the main corridor, carrying the nature theme beyond center court and throughout the Mall.

All three wooded features were designed by Richard Leszcynski, a landscape designer with Eichstedt, Grissim, Young & Associates of Farminton Hills, Michigan. The original concept sparked to life when O'Roark took John Grissim, a senior partner of Leszcynski's firm, on a tour of the local countryside during the early planning of the Mall.

Leszcynski took the ideas from Grissim and ran with them. "Basically, we wanted a natural feeling using as close as possible to native materials.

Photos Courtesy Jim Streeter

47

We chose plants that simulated outdoor natural plants in this region. This is a rocky area, and we wanted to include this. The whole court, with its five waterfalls, is laid out just as we wanted it," said Leszcynski.

John Crampton of Holly Hills Nursery in Bloomfield, Michigan supervised the implementation of Leszcynski's design. According to Crampton, the Richland Mall was his first landscaping job *inside* a Mall – and he enjoyed it. "Man relates to plants," he said. "This is a nice concept for a mall."

Though the center court parklet was meant to replicate a Western Pennsylvania outdoor setting, Leszcynski and Crampton filled it with sub-tropical plants from Florida.

John Crampton   Richard Leszcynski

© The Tribune-Democrat

Local plants weren't feasible because they would need a period of cold each year to survive – not the perpetually temperate conditions inside the Mall. Also, though kept indoors, local plants would lose their leaves and be barren for several months each year.

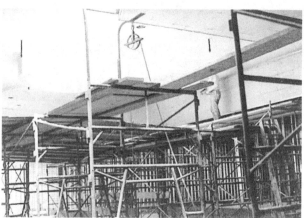

In spite of the non-native vegetation, the wooded center court would prove to be one of the Mall's most popular features. People loved the novelty of having trees and a stocked stream in the middle of the Mall, and they

often paused in their shopping to walk down the short stairs to the viewing platform and watch the trout swim by.

Unfortunately, this very popularity took its toll on the fish.

"We always had a very difficult time keeping the trout alive," remembers Streeter. "There were issues with keeping the water aerated properly. Also, people got in the habit of using it as a wishing well."

Photos Courtesy Jim Streeter

48

"After a while, we took the fish out, and it just became a wishing well," says Bob McConnell, general manager of the Mall.

Still, in the very beginning, center court was a magical, unique place. "It was artfully done," says O'Roark. "It wasn't a matter of throwing in stones and hoping all the water went down a certain way. Every bit of it was carefully designed, and it had a positive impact on the people who spent time there. It was a little piece of serenity in the heart of our bustling Mall."

Photos Courtesy Jim Streeter

Central Court Mapped Out

world premiere
Richland Mall
starring
Sears·K·mart·PennTraffic
with a supporting cast of 35 more stores

Sign Announces Coming Event

Landscapers Use Natural Foliage

Giant Boulders Enhance Interior

© *The Tribune-Democrat*

© *The Tribune-Democrat*

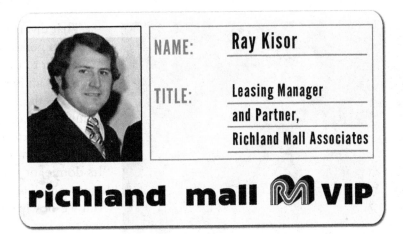

NAME: **Ray Kisor**

TITLE: **Leasing Manager
and Partner,
Richland Mall Associates**

richland mall M VIP

To Ray Kisor, part of the price of success was three new cars. That was how many he wore out while driving 200,000 miles in pursuit of tenants for the Richland Mall.

In the years leading up to the Mall's grand opening in 1974, Ray scoured the country for tenants who would be a good fit for the new Mall. As director of leasing, it was his job to visit and negotiate deals with the inline tenants – the smaller businesses that occupied the Mall hallways between major tenants Sears, Kmart, and Penn

Courtesy Jim Streeter

Traffic (which were landed by Jim O'Roark and Jim Streeter).

It was a challenging job, what with all the travel...and a workload that was nothing short of insane. As the sole leasing agent for the Mall, Ray single-handedly accomplished what most Mall developers assigned to a staff of four or five people.

By the time of the Mall's grand opening, Ray had secured nearly 65 inline tenant leases, accounting for 100 percent of the Mall's available space. It was an achievement, as far as he knew, that had never been tackled by one man before.

Leisure Suit Personality

Ray's hard work quickly paid off. Post-opening enthusiasm for the Richland Mall was contagious throughout the local community – and among the Unimich partners, as well.

"We've been using ourselves as a maximum resource," he said at the time. "The whole thing comes down to a tremendous amount of pride, knowing that five guys could work as well and hard together to produce what I feel will be the most exciting shopping complex that has been created by anybody. Its broad diversity internally is a real asset to the entire community."

Courtesy Jim O'Roark

That diversity extended to Ray's own personal retail project. In addition to the leasing work, he opened an inline business of his own in the Mall – a men's clothing store called Sagebrush, located three storefronts from center court in the Kmart wing. "Its dominant personality was leisure suits," remembers Ray. "But we slowly converted it over to a Levi's store after we determined that was a fashion fad that wasn't going to have legs."

Na Na Na Na, Ray Ray Ray, Goodbye

Not long after the Mall opened for business, Ray stepped back from day-to-day involvement as director of leasing. He didn't need to work so hard at filling space, since the successful Mall practically sold itself to new tenants.

"Our tenant overhead was not that high," explains Ray. "We were able to build the Mall correctly. We were able to do a really good project at a cost that was probably less than that of major malls in and around Pittsburgh, so our tenants achieved better margins. They were doing well, and they were happy."

There was still turnover, but new tenants were eager to jump into the spots vacated by departing tenants. That left Ray, who'd worked a bit of a miracle to fill the place before its reputation had taken shape, with minimal responsibilities to Richland Mall Associates, the partnership that had sprung out of Unimich.

Sagebrush Inc
Sagebrush
Johnstown's newest and most
exciting men's shopping address
Located in the Richland Mall
GOOD LUCK, JETS
Sponsor of "Red Puck"

Courtesy Jim O'Roark

When other hoped-for real estate projects from Unimich didn't materialize to fill the void, Ray knew it was time for him to move on. "I thought we were going to do smart things in the east and we didn't," recalls Ray. "As an organization, Unimich decided not to continue to develop real estate. That's when I personally went into the commercial real estate business in Grand Rapids."

Courtesy Jim O'Roark

By 1976, he was pulling up stakes – leaving the Richland Mall, as well as the home he'd bought in Westmont six months before the grand opening.

"I had a beautiful home that was near Sunnehanna Country Club, situated in the woods on three and a half acres. It was a great place, and I hated to leave it," says Ray.

He also hated to leave Sagebrush, but the time had come. He sold the store to a Pittsburgh retailer when he moved back to Grand Rapids.

From Malls to Moos

In the years that followed, Ray remained a partner in Richland Mall Associates, getting updates as needed from Jim Streeter and Steve Clause and visiting the Mall in person once a year. He also joined a commercial brokerage firm and bought a 400-acre cattle farm.

"We raised some of the finest purebred Angus cattle in the country," says Ray.

"We traveled the country, showing them at major cattle shows. I enjoyed that immensely. I like to think we helped bring a whole new level to the upbringing of the breeding stock of Angus cattle."

Recently, Ray retired from the brokerage, and his involvement with the Richland Mall ended years ago. The last time he visited the site of the Mall was soon after it had been demolished to make way for the Richland Town Centre. "It was depressing as hell," says Ray.

But he still looks back on his Mall experience with great affection. "It's one of the highlights of my life. It's not something you could ever forget, simply because of all the energy and success – the energy that you put into it and the success you enjoyed from it. And the people that you met in the process."

People like Jim Streeter are still a big part of Ray's life. Streeter was best man at Ray's wedding to his second wife, in fact.

All the Unimich partners hold a special place in his heart. "We were all young men who had great passion for what we did, who came from no particular background of strength from a monetary standpoint. Everything we did, we just worked hard for it.

"We were very close to each other, and our different specialties complemented each other. We challenged every odd there was, and we won. That success bound us more closely together as friends.

"Being part of the Richland Mall story was a phenomenal experience. It changed my life. I am certainly very glad that I got to know Johnstown, Pennsylvania and the wonderful people who call it home," says Ray.

Ray Kisor 2017

53

All Courtesy Ray Kisor

Courtesy Jim Streeter

chapter five

filling the space

1974

It's hard enough getting *one* business to commit to do something, let alone *65* of them. Yet that's exactly what Unimich did in the months leading up to the Richland Mall's grand opening. The partners locked down tenants for all 65 open spots on the Mall's roster, ensuring that the first customers would find a shopping wonderland with no empty storefronts when they poured through the doors.

Jim O'Roark brought in Sears and Kmart, and Jim Streeter wrapped up the Penn Traffic deal. Ray Kisor, director of leasing, made all the rest happen, plugging in one piece of the puzzle after another until it was done.

From the Hello Shop to Super Chick to Hickory Farms to Shop 'n Save, the first tenants of the Richland Mall had agreed to join the new venture. National or local, apparel or dining, banking or entertainment, these businesses had all united to make history.

Space Invaders

When construction of the Mall reached the point that storefronts were ready for occupancy, that first team of tenants invaded the space, setting it up for business according to whatever specs their companies required.

Courtesy Jim Streeter

It was an incredibly busy time, as employees and workmen bustled through the Mall, setting up everything from lighting to shelving to checkouts to signage. Hammers banged and power drills whined as each individual shop took on its own distinctive, recognizable form.

Imagine wandering through all that controlled chaos in the last weeks before the grand opening. Just imagine watching as workers installed movie screens in the Duke and Duchess theaters...pizza ovens in Capri...counters and stools in Sweet William...bookshelves in Waldenbooks. Imagine what it must have been like when they hauled in the huge panes of glass for the windows of the many storefronts... or hoisted the giant letter "K" in front of the blue-and-red Kmart sign facing into the Mall... or installed the vaults in Somerset Trust or Watchmaker's Diamonds & Jewelry.

Photos Courtesy Jim Streeter

There must have been dust flying everywhere, and people shouting, and carts and dollies and wheelbarrows zipping in all directions. It was all coming together, like a Broadway show before opening night, with all the tenants and workmen just as excited as the civilians squinting through peepholes in the wooden partitions for a glimpse of the spectacle to come.

Sympathy for the Tenants

Bob McConnell was lucky enough to be there for that historic time, though he had too much on his plate to fully appreciate its significance. As the Mall's general manager, Bob wanted to make sure everything was ready for the all-important and fast-approaching grand opening.

"There were just so many details to pay attention to," remembers Bob. "It was exciting, but there was a lot of pressure, too. I wanted to make sure everything went right in time for the opening, and all the tenants were situated and happy."

Bob McConnell
.... mall manager

© *The Tribune-Democrat*

Tenant maintenance was an important part of the Richland Mall formula from the start. The unique mix of tenants – skewed toward local businesses since attracting national companies to a "fringe market" like Johnstown was difficult – required an emphasis on meeting the special needs of local businesses.

"We always had a strong appreciation of local tenants, and we worked hard to help make them successful," says Jim Streeter. "We did everything we could to give local tenants every opportunity to survive and succeed.

"We gave small local tenants money and opportunities that we would never give to a national tenant because we didn't have to, they didn't need them. We practically became the economic development operation of Johnstown.

"We spent a lot to help small tenants get into business and succeed. For example, when they got behind on rent, we worked with them. In some cases, there were tenants who couldn't pay rent and owed us thousands of dollars, and we worked with them for years to keep them from going under.

"Sometimes, we were wrong about a tenant's viability, and they didn't work out. In those situations, we lost whatever rent they owed. But when they succeeded, we succeeded, too, by getting future rent payments and maintaining a stronger Mall with a richer balance of businesses," says Streeter.

Photos Courtesy Jim Streeter

Special K More Special Than Ever

Though small local tenants got special treatment in the run-up to the grand opening and afterward, the major tenants attracted a great deal of attention, as well. In some ways, in fact, the majors in the Richland Mall made history.

"It was the first time a Sears store and a Kmart had ever been teamed up together in the same shopping center," says Jim Streeter. "They'd been in the same towns before, but they'd never been in the same center. Now there they were, our anchors, one on each end of the Richland Mall."

Discount Store News

THE NEWSPAPER OF THE DISCOUNT-DEPARTMENT STORE INDUSTRY

MAY 6, 1974   Published Biweekly, Every Other Monday, Monthly in December, by Lebhar-Friedman, Inc., publisher of CHAIN STORE AGE   VOLUME 12, NUMBER 10

K mart, Sears to Share 1st Enclosed Mall

JOHNSTOWN, Pa.—For the first time, K mart and Sears will compete head-to-head as co-anchors in the 650,000 sq. ft. enclosed Richland Mall scheduled to open near here this fall.

It will also be the first time any K mart has been located within an enclosed mall.

The 84,000 sq. ft. K mart will be located at the east end of the mall, with the 90,000 sq. ft. Sears at the west end. A 70,000 sq. ft. Penn Traffic store will also anchor the mall. In addition, 90 smaller stores are expected to open their doors when the mall bows in mid-September.

Welcome Aboard

"We are glad to be in the mall with a Sears store," a K mart spokesman said. "We requested a location in the mall and evidently Sears didn't have any objections."

A Sears spokesman said it wouldn't be the chain's first mall location with a discount store. He said Sears already has at least one common location with a White Front store. He added that the K mart should provide increased traffic which would benefit all stores in the mall.

The mall will be located on a 45-acre site five miles southeast of Johnstown, bordered by Routes 219 and 756. The facility will be styled in modern decor and will include a Shop & Save food store and twin movie theaters.

In order to protect its interior merchandising layout, the K mart will have only a single entrance facing the inside of the mall. This will enable the chain to maintain its central checkouts and will save on security expenses.

While the facade of the K mart facing the interior of the mall will be styled to fit in with the mall's decor, the chain spokesman said the remainder of the store will be identical to other K marts.

The K mart will compete head-to-head with Sears on automotive servicing. K mart will have an in-store department and an attached service area. Sears will have a 17,000 sq. ft., 13-bay TBA center in the parking lot.

A K mart spokesman said the chain would join in mall-wide promotions with Penn Traffic and Sears. He said it is K mart's policy to cooperate in promotional events which are designed to boost traffic for every store in the mall.

When the mall opens, Sears will close its nine-year-old store located in downtown Johnstown. The existing K mart closest to the new mall is a 65,000 sq. ft. unit in Greensburg, about 35 miles west of Johnstown.

Courtesy Jim O'Roark

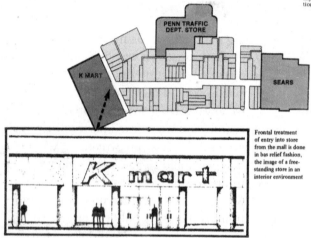

PENN TRAFFIC DEPT. STORE

K MART

SEARS

Frontal treatment of entry into store from the mall is done in bas relief fashion, the image of a free-standing store in an interior environment

"Years later, Sears ended up buying Kmart. But back in 1974, the two retail giants sharing the same mall was big news," says Streeter.

"We're not concerned that Kmart will pull traffic from us," said a Sears executive at the time. ""We'll meet competition no matter what. The focus is on doing whatever makes sense for Sears."

Kmart's very presence in a mall was enough to make headlines back then. The Richland Mall store was Kmart's first time joining a regional mall in the U.S.

"We've taken the blinders off our people on getting into regionals, and at Richland we'll be seeking the answers to a number of questions, such as our effect on center traffic and the effect of center traffic on us," said a Kmart executive.

One of those questions was what impact the new Kmart's unique layout might have on business. Though Kmart stores always had a single entrance to cut security and checkout costs, and that entrance was always outward-facing, the Richland Mall Kmart's entrance faced the interior of the Mall. At the time, it was the first inward-facing store in the Kmart chain.

Photo by Chuck Mamula

Kmart execs were concerned about the experiment. "We hope that a mall entrance will be a successful change of policy. Normally, entry is our trademark, the focal point of the store. It in itself is a big attraction for impulse customers. With Kmart 'buried' in a shopping center, we still need instant identity," said James Kilgore, Kmart's design manager.

Any worries about the layout were soon cast aside, however. "I think the inward-facing entrance increased the traffic into their store dramatically, because shoppers didn't have to go out in the cold and come back in," says Jim O'Roark. "They could just enter from inside the Mall."

To enhance the visibility of the store in spite of the inward-facing position of its entrance, the Richland Mall team arranged to install illuminated signs above the outward-facing entryways closest to Kmart in that part of the Mall.

Another unique aspect of the store's design in the Richland Mall was the location of its auto and garden centers. "The chain has always made every effort in freestanding situations to expose its auto service and garden centers to the secondary road if one exists on the site. Our architects were interested in putting these centers at the back portion of the Mall for better clarity of design," O'Roark told *Chain Store Age* magazine in 1974.

"Kmart educated the architects quickly by pointing out that profit, not design, is the key to a decision on entering a new market. They insisted that the auto and garden centers be exposed to the main access route, rather than having a plain wall. We then incorporated the two centers into the front appearance of the Mall," said O'Roark.

Call it RichlandMallville

All the Mall's tenants, whether majors or minors, raced to put their own distinctive signage, floor plans, and décor in place in time for the grand opening. First impressions mean a lot, and no one wanted to be caught on the big day with sheets over their windows to hide their state of incompleteness.

As each new store put on the finishing touches, the Richland Mall as we would come to know it took shape. When the doors finally opened, shoppers would see it for what it was – "a city unto itself," as *The Tribune-Democrat* put it.

It was an enormous place, a 700,000-square-foot complex with almost every kind of store, restaurant, or facility. There were large communal spaces where people could gather for events of common interest. A piece of the natural world resided in central court, complete with living creatures in a replica of their native habitat. The widest variety of merchandise ever available under one (15-acre) roof in the Johnstown area was for sale from dozens of vendors.

Photo Courtesy Jim Streeter

Arranged along broad corridors like an urban Main Street, these vendors' stores were all worlds apart in terms of design. Their storefronts ranged from a red barn to colonial styling to the rainbow archway of the Time-Out arcade. According to *The Tribune-Democrat*, they employed materials "from gleaming glass and sparkling colored plastic to warm wood paneling and wagon wheel chandeliers."

The Mall had its own maintenance and security forces, its own heating supply, and an air conditioning system with over two miles of ductwork. Sunlight streamed in from skylights over each of the three nature courts, plus recessed circular skylights in the hallways. Outside, the place was surrounded by 30 acres of parking lots.

How could this self-contained city of a mall *not* have a huge impact on the local community?

Great Expectations and Then Some

As anticipation rose for the new Mall, expectations of its immediate and long-term impact – economic, especially – were sky-high. Even before the shopping center had opened, local business people and economic analysts were making predictions about the big splash that was coming.

Jim O'Roark had his own set of prognostications at the time. In addition to the infusion of money from the Mall's construction, he foresaw $20 million in retail sales staying local instead of going to malls in outlying areas. He also predicted a net increase of $10 million in retail sales from adjacent counties.

According to O'Roark, the Richland Mall would bring at least 700 jobs to the area, including many managerial positions. New jobs would create a need for new housing for employees moving to the area. The tax base of the Mall site would be approximately 15 times higher than the base evaluation that existed before the Mall project started.

"The Mall will change the current status of retailing in the Greater Johnstown area," said O'Roark. "The Richland Mall, combined with the beautiful University of Pittsburgh at Johnstown campus, the modern Industrial Park, and the convenient Route 219 and Johnstown Expressway should help Greater Johnstown grow economically in the critical years ahead."

NAME: Ron Sabin

TITLE: Engineer and Partner, Richland Mall Associates

richland mall M VIP

NAME: Steven Clause

TITLE: Treasurer and Partner, Richland Mall Associates

richland mall M VIP

Ron Sabin and Steve Clause might not have been the most high-profile members of the Unimich partnership, but the Richland Mall would not have become a reality in the same way without them.

The Tallest Man in Unimich

As construction engineer, Ron executed a host of tasks related to the building of the Mall. He was often seen in the construction trailer headquarters or striding across the site with a fistful of blueprints and a hardhat on his head.

A native of Martin, Ohio, Ron got his civil engineering degree from the University of Toledo. Like Jim O'Roark and Jim Streeter, Ron worked for Shell Oil and Lanning Corporation before the dawn of Unimich and the conception of the Richland Mall.

In the early days of that project, Ron performed the engineering required for land studies and site examinations. As the project unfolded, he was in charge of all engineering and construction efforts, ensuring that the work of an army of contractors to execute a library of plans while adhering to a plethora of government regulation all came together seamlessly.

"The only way this could have become a reality in two and a half years was to move rapidly and have everybody be part of the team," said Ron.

Courtesy Jim Streeter

"We all had to work together – the developer, architect, and contractor. This working together started even before plans were off the drawing board."

While spearheading the engineering work related to the Mall project, Ron put together the architect and construction team and worked with the builder and architect to formulate plans. He met with the state of Pennsylvania on highway permits and roadway improvement drawings and prepared for sewage and other required permits. He also reviewed subcontracts and supervised the supervisors in the field.

Ron focused on efficient and wide-ranging oversight to keep the Mall project on schedule. "When a drawing was finished, it was bid immediately," he said. "This is the only way this thing could have worked.

"We hashed it all over before it came off the drawing boards, so when it did come off, it was something we could live with. This has worked very effectively."

As a result of his efforts, the Mall was finished as planned, on schedule. Generations of shoppers were treated to a unique realization of architectural style that brought to life Jim O'Roark's vision of childlike, playful colors and shapes melded with local natural beauty.

And the tallest of the Unimich partners moved on to his next project and never looked back.

Courtesy Jim Streeter

Because of Clause

The late, great Stephen Clause was a wonderful guy, according to Ray Kisor. "We were at Shell, Lanning, and the Richland Mall together," remembers Ray. "He was a vital part of Unimich, and he is missed."

As treasurer of Unimich and Richland Mall Associates, Steve worked to manage the financial aspects of the Richland Mall project and associated investments. He joined Unimich in February 1972, helping to get the Mall off the ground by analyzing the market potential of 17 cities under consideration as sites for the project.

After completing his due diligence, Steve and the Unimich partners concluded that Johnstown would be the best location, setting the stage for the new Richland Mall.

"Johnstown was the one that stuck out because of its potential. It had a bigger market area than most and the timing just seemed about right for a major shopping area," said Steve.

After putting together a detailed market study, Steve assembled and distributed statistics and information to the project stakeholders in support of the Johnstown option. His work was key in selling Johnstown – and Richland in particular – as the final choice for the Unimich Mall project.

Next, Steve performed a multitude of duties in support of site preparation and construction. When the Mall was up and running, he focused on his responsibilities as treasurer of the corporation, keeping the paperwork flowing and handling problems day by day from an administrative standpoint.

"We were all owners of the management company, but the day-to-day activity was really communicated through Steve," explains Ray.

"He was responsible for all the accounting of funds, and he paid all the bills. He was, in effect, a chief financial officer (CFO) of the organization, though he didn't officially hold that title," says Ray.

In the early days, he spent a week or so per month in Johnstown, but as Mall operations shifted into a steady routine, he was able to do almost all of his work from the Unimich home office in Grand Rapids, Michigan.

© *The Tribune-Democrat*

Not Forgotten

For years, Steve remained an active member of the Unimich team and Richland Mall Associates, performing a wide range of financial functions. He was instrumental in the remodeling project of 1992 after the coming of the Galleria, and worked with Jim Streeter on plans to secure the Mall's survival.

His untimely death placed a great strain on the Mall partnership. His upbeat personality, strong work ethic, and role as a founding member of the team made his loss difficult to take. Unimich and Richland Mall Associates were never the same.

"Steve was very analytical. He was funny in his own way. His death was shattering," says Ray. "But what he helped us accomplish, and what it meant to so many people, will forever stand as a testimony to his intellect, drive, capabilities, friendship, and connection to the hearts and minds of others."

Steve, like the Mall he helped make a reality, is gone but will never be forgotten.

Photo by Chuck Mamula

I've always had an affinity for Richie the Pook. He's always been a sort of hero of mine. When the Mall had just opened, I was maybe five or six years of age. Mom took me shopping, and we got separated in Kmart. I was so scared. I didn't know whom to ask for help, until I saw Richie the Pook. I went to him, crying, and asked him if he could help me find her. I knew who Richie was and trusted him because I had met him during a promotional visit he made to our neighborhood a week earlier, riding up and down the streets on a golf cart, handing out bumper stickers. My trust in Richie paid off. He went to the service desk, they called for my mom to meet me at the front of the store, and I was saved!

Tonya France

Photo by Linda Dufseth

I still have my Richie the Pook doll. As a matter of fact, I just showed it to my girls when getting holiday decorations down the other night. He is a rough-looking doll after all these years, but I still have him. I loved that Mall.

Patti Yakicic Koeck

I remember as a kid going to the Mall every Friday with my parents just to see Richie the Pook. They were great times. Now I'm 48 years old. I look back and wonder, where did the time go?

Dean Evans

Photos by Philip Balko

I took my girls to the opening of the Mall, and we saw Richie the Pook. My daughter, Lisa Tiger, walked all around this six-foot-tall creature and came back to me and said, "That dog isn't real." I said, "How do you know?" And she said, "He has a zipper up his back!"
Linda Tiger Keeley

I remember the Richland Mall having a contest around Easter. We were to use Richie the Pook in a large cardboard egg design. The eggs were then hung from the ceiling of the Mall for display.
David Seigh

Around 1974, Super Chick restaurant did a commercial. My sons were in the commercial. The last segment featured Super Chick, Richie the Pook, my sons, and some other kids parading around the Mall. WJAC ran the commercial.
Debbie Palmer

Greg & Sharon Kraycirik

Courtesy Jim O'Roark

Courtesy Jim O'Roark

66

chapter six

keep on pookin'

Getting the word out can be almost as important as getting a mall built and filling it with tenants. The Richland Mall team got the word out better than most, thanks to a fur-covered figure with a lolling red tongue, chipmunk cheeks, and a big yellow bow tie.

The brainchild of Jim O'Roark, Richie the Pook became the face and symbol of the Richland Mall. The Pook traveled far and wide, serving as an ambassador of the big new shopping center in Johnstown.

In the months leading up to the Mall's grand opening, Richie (and

Pook director Sally Miles) visited communities throughout the region, handing out over 70,000 bumper stickers with the slogans "Meet Your Neighbor" and "Richland Mall...just for you." Richie also handed out gift certificates to the occupants of cars or houses bedecked with those bumper stickers.

The result? In 1974, it seemed like those stickers were everywhere...and just about everyone knew about Richie and the Richland Mall. Not bad for what was essentially a mascot with a nonsensical name, a character whose design was cobbled together out of the traits of different animals.

Photo by Linda Dufseth

67

The Pook Was A Muppet!

"The Pook was based on an English sheepdog that my family had," explains O'Roark. "We started with the sheepdog, with the same thick white and gray fur, floppy ears, and big red tongue. Even the eyes resemble those of a big, fluffy sheepdog. Then, we added cat whiskers and chipmunk cheeks. We wanted to create a character with the best features of some of the cutest, most lovable animals."

After deciding on the key characteristics of the Pook, O'Roark had a model created...out of cookie dough. He and his wife, Linda, brought the cookie back with them from a trip to California, then used it as the basis of the first on-paper illustrations by Paula Klim, in-Mall graphic artist for all print advertising and an employee of O'Roark's company, Ribet Productions.

After Paula had perfected the Pook's image on paper, O'Roark had it turned into a full-size costume

for use in the field. According to Bernie Pisczek, who worked in advertising and promotions for Ribet, the costume was actually created at the studio of Muppet master Jim Henson, by the same people who'd created the original Muppets.

"The costume was incredibly intricate," remembers Bernie. "It was extremely comfortable and well ventilated. It was very professionally done."

According to O'Roark, the first public appearance of the Pook was a 1974 parade in Somerset for a firemen's convention. The man inside the costume that day was Charlie Breitsman of Ligonier, who became the first person to wear the Pook costume in public.

richie the pook

This is Richie . . . and he's the newest member of the Richland Mall team. Richie will be the highlight of an extensive Mall pre-opening promotional plan and we'd like to involve you!

Photos by Philip Balko

Courtesy Jim O'Roark

In weeks to come, that costume would be worn by a team of designated "Pook People," specially trained to uphold the Pook's image at all times. Usually, these costumed entertainers traveled to their destinations in a bright yellow Volkswagen Thing – a four-door, Jeep-like convertible sold in the U.S. from 1968 to 1983. (Also known as the Volkswagen 181, this four-cylinder model had the same mechanical parts as the Volkswagen Beetle and Microbus.) The yellow Thing – nicknamed the Pookmobile – matched the yellow of Richie's bow tie and fit well with the fanciful tone of the entire Pook campaign.

"Driving around in that Volkswagen Thing, with Richie in the backseat, was something Johnstown had never seen before," says Bernie. "The whole idea was to create top-of-mind awareness and get people shopping, get them used to going to the Mall – and that furry character in the crazy yellow car really got the job done."

Winning Like a Pook

The first of the trained Pook actors was Jim O'Roark's brother, Jack, who was also his partner in the Super Chick restaurant. A graduate of Slippery Rock College, Jack passed up a teaching position to work with Jim at the Richland Mall, making Super Chick a smash hit and setting the standard for all Pook People who came after him.

Jack and the rest of Team Pook made Richie, and the Richland Mall, into household names. The marketing campaign they mounted was tremendously successful in building interest in the Mall to a fever pitch in time for the grand opening.

Courtesy Jim O'Roark

According to Karen (Bevilaqua) Belle, promotions director of the Richland Mall in the months leading up to and just after the opening, using Richie as the face of the Mall turned out to be an extremely effective strategy.

"We took Richie to speaking engagements and all kinds of events in a six-county area," remembers Karen. "That included Cambria, Blair, Somerset, Bedford, Indiana, and Westmoreland counties. We drove him up and down streets in every community in those counties, and he passed out gift certificates and buttons to people who had his bumper sticker. He handed out candy and balloons to children. He just generally made himself and the Mall more well-known."

"People go completely crazy when Richie comes to see them," said Sally Miles at the time. "We get swamped by children and grown-ups. They just love him."

"It was all fun and wholesome and family-oriented," says Karen. "Children particularly related to the Pook. But everyone knew about him. He really helped boost business for the grand opening and the holiday season that followed.

"It was just the most successful promotion that I have ever been involved with," says Karen.

Story of the Info-Pook

Connie Hayes, who eventually ran the information booth in the Mall, was an early member of Team Pook. During the buildup to the Mall's opening in '74, she spent her share of time inside the Richie costume, traveling the region to spread the word about the new shopping center.

"I loved riding around in the back of the Volkswagen Thing, handing out candy to kids," says Connie. "It was a publicity thing, but it was very nice and fun for the community.

"It was very hot in that costume, though. I had to stay hydrated and wear lightweight clothing underneath. When I wasn't in a public setting, I'd open the costume up just enough that a little air could get in and cool me off a bit.

"I had to be careful, though, especially in front of little kids. They really related to Richie. I couldn't just unzip or take the head off in front of them," remembers Connie.

Watching the Pook Drop on New Year's Eve

Encouraged by the local success of the Richie campaign, Jim O'Roark was determined to debut the Pook on a national stage. He came up with a plan to *really* take Richie on the road – all the way to Times Square, New York City, on New Year's Eve.

This was over a year after the Mall's grand opening, at the tail end of 1975. As part of his vision to introduce Richie to a national audience, Jim rented a billboard in Times Square and took a Ribet Productions team to New York for a spectacle he'd concocted.

Courtesy Jim O'Roark

"There were 14 of us on that trip," remembers Bernie. "We went up a week in advance to get everything ready."

Jim arranged to turn the giant Times Square billboard into a tribute to Richie. Huge drawings of the Pook in a patriotic top hat and vest set off a message in massive letters that read, "Help your neighbor...Richie the Pook '76."

In addition to preparing the billboard, Jim and his team worked overtime to install some elaborate props. Using a pulley system, they would hoist a 40-foot balloon that looked like an egg over the New Year's Eve crowd, then "hatch" the egg to reveal an inflatable Richie the Pook figure inside.

It was an ambitious plan, but everything seemed to come together as the week raced by. Jim and his people were confident that they'd covered all the bases...but they missed one.

"It rained like you wouldn't believe on New Year's Eve," recalls Bernie. "It just *poured* nonstop, drenching everyone in Times Square."

"It rained so hard, it put extra weight on the Pook egg balloon," says Jim. "We kept having to pump in more helium to keep it aloft. We probably spent $10,000 on helium, and we had to lug it up three floors to get it to the roof."

In spite of the effort made by Team Pook, the wet weather still won out in the end. "When the time came for Richie to hatch, the props worked fine – but it rained so hard, no one was looking. You had to look right up into the falling rain to see Richie, which of course no one did. It was unfortunate after all the work we'd done, but the weather just killed it," says Bernie.

Courtesy Sal Garcia

From Rouge Plant Blues to Richie the Pook

New Year's Eve in Times Square didn't go as planned, but other Richie projects were more successful in exposing the character to new audiences. For example, the mostly silent Pook was given a singing voice on a record released by Ribet Productions.

And that voice belonged a member of a band called – wait for it – *Stix and Stoned.*

Courtesy Sal Garcia

"The band consisted of me and a guy named Bobby Lewis," says Sal Garcia. "Our song, 'Rouge Plant Blues,' came out in 1972 and was one of the most popular Detroit songs of the time. It was about the guys who work on the Rouge Plant assembly line, and they make decent money, but they still can't afford the cars they make."

Recruited by O'Roark to help market the Mall, Sal wrote the song "Richie the Pook," which featured a chorus of voices singing feel-good lyrics about everyone's favorite Pook.

Between the sung verses, Richie himself lays down some spoken word segments, which is where Sal and his Pook voice appear on the track. "I used the chipmunk technique to record all that," he explains. "What you do is, you read the narrative in your regular voice, but you do it more slowly than usual. Then, when you speed up the recorded track, it sounds like a chipmunk, but it's at regular speed, not garbled. It's a technique I've used many times for commercials."

The Pook and Michael Jackson

Recording Richie's voice was only one part of the story of that record. The chorus of singers, for example, included 10-12 professional backup singers recruited by Sal. He also brought in several children for the recording session, including his bandmate Bobby Lewis and his kids, Wendy and Geo Warner.

Then there were the musicians who played on the record. "I used the best musicians I could find," says Sal. "Some really good people from Detroit. These were people I'd done recordings with back in the day.

"David Van De Pitte, a famous arranger from Motown, played the violin and did lots of other parts as well. That guy had an amazing career, arranging hits by The Jackson 5, Stevie Wonder, The Temptations, and Marvin Gaye...and he was part of the Pook song, too.

"The people who were involved in that Richland Mall project were like the best of the best of Detroit," says Sal.

Those famous connections didn't stop with the recording sessions, though. When Sal was ready to mix "Richie the Pook" and the single's flip-side, "Richie's First Christmas," he ended up in the California studio of The Jackson 5.

"Frank Fischer was a very good friend of mine and Bobby Lewis' from the Stix and Stoned days," recalls Sal. "Joe Jackson hired him to work as a sound engineer for The Jackson 5 in their private studio in Encino, California. When Frank found out I needed a studio to mix down those songs, he set me up with Joe, who gave me a very good deal."

© *The Tribune-Democrat*

During his time mixing the songs in the Jacksons' studio, Sal got to connect with the most famous of Joe's kids – Michael. The future King of Pop was just 15 years old at the time...but even then, he made a strong impression on Sal.

"Michael was the most brilliant musician I had ever met in my life. He knew more about music than most people twice his age...and he was driven. Music was his passion. While his brothers were out playing basketball or running around town, Michael was in the studio creating music."

According to Sal, Michael was so busy in the studio, the Pook songs had to wait until he finally went to bed. Not that Sal minded, as he got to spend time with the musical genius and witness his creative process.

"I got to watch him in action, which was an amazing experience. I talked to him about his work, and even helped with it a little.

"Once, he walked up to me in the studio after he'd recorded something, and he asked what I thought of it. I told him, and he went back and changed it. Then he came back and said, 'You know, I like your ideas.'"

Keep on Pookin'

Sal and Frank did the final mix of the songs at GM Studios in Detroit, then pressed a vinyl single that was sold at the Richie's Corner store in the Richland Mall. It was a hit with young kids at the time and helped cement Richie's popularity as spokes-pook of the Mall.

The song continues to be well thought of by people who grew up in the 70s and remember singing along with the upbeat tune from the 45 single:

Richie, Richie, we all love that little Pook.
Richie, Richie, we all know he ain't no spook.
Richie, Richie, shares his love with all,
We prepare to have some fun when Richie comes to call.

Children and grown-ups all love Richie, yes they do.
Animals, yes animals, they adore that little Pook.
Richie, Richie, shares his love with all,
We prepare to have some fun when Richie comes to call.

Richie's fans could even be heard calling out his slogan from the song: *Keep on Pookin'!* The Pook, in his way, had become a celebrity.

But did anyone other than Jim O'Roark realize just how far his celebrity would take him?

Let the Pookgrass Play

After Jim stepped away from the Richland Mall and dedicated himself to making the Pook a worldwide sensation, Richie got more exposure than ever.

© *The Tribune-Democrat*

Jim and his creation traveled to Philadelphia during the U.S. Bicentennial in 1976, where they rang the Liberty Bell and handed out copies of *Pook Sense*, a patriotic tract along the lines of Thomas Paine's *Common Sense*...if it were written by a Pook. The pamphlet was addressed to "The Inhabitants of America" and covered several topics, including "Thoughts on the Present State of 'There is no end to being Happy'," "Of the Origin and Design of Pooking U.S.A.," and "Help your neighbor, which is inherent to the strength of the country."

The Liberty Bell event was made possible by Jim playing fast and loose when it came to approvals. "We told the Bicentennial Commission that we had approval from the city of Philadelphia, and we told the city of Philadelphia we had approval from the Bicentennial Commission. Then we went ahead and did our own thing. Richie ended up standing with the Liberty Bell for three or four hours, greeting lots of people as they came to visit. To be able to do that was very unique," says Jim.

That Bicentennial moment was only the beginning of Richie's adventures. For a while, a screenplay for a movie featuring the Pook and his friends made the rounds in Hollywood. At one point, stars Jonathan Winters and Barbara Eden were attached to the project, titled *There Are No Monsters*. There was even talk of Jonathan bringing in his friend, Robin Williams, for a role.

Plans for the movie evolved into a proposed TV pilot, but the pilot never got made. Navigating the Hollywood power structure turned out to be even more difficult than building a shopping mall in Johnstown against the odds.

But in years to come, Jim refused to give up on his Pook. Richie appeared on the Jerry Lewis Labor Day Telethon twice in the mid-1970s, working in Las Vegas with Jerry Lewis and Ed McMahon. He also continued to have brushes with celebrities like Joann Worley and Paul Newman.

Richie also formed a bluegrass band – make that a *Pook Grass* band. The Pook Family All-Star Lineup Band featured Super Chick and the other members of the Pook Family created by Jim. The band (consisting of top bluegrass musicians in costumes) even headlined a festival at the Heritage USA Christian theme park in Fort Mill, South Carolina.

The event, called Carolina's Pookgrass & Arts Festival, was held October 6-8, 1989, and was billed as the "Biggest Bluegrass Event in the Carolinas," featuring 16 bluegrass groups and individual artists, including Doc Watson, John Hartford, John McEuen, and Riders in the Sky.

Richie for President

After making a splash in the music world, the Pook jumped into politics. In 2008, Jim launched a political campaign, running the Pook for President.

"The Pook was a candidate of the P.O.O.K. Party, which stood for 'People of Other Kinds,'" recalls Jim. "He ran on the 'help your neighbor' platform, promoting

the idea of helping your country by helping your neighbor."

Richie ran a spirited campaign, mostly by frolicking in patriotic-themed videos shot at Fort Ligonier, the Ligonier Diamond, the Compass Inn at Laughlintown, Quecreek, and the Somerset County Courthouse. The P.O.O.K. Party volunteers handed out plenty of "P.O.O.K. for President" hats and bumper stickers and encouraged folks to join the P.O.O.K. Party.

All courtesy Jim O'Roark

For a donation of $20 (or $15 for children), party members got a membership card, a copy of *Pook Sense*, a sticker, a bumper sticker, and a "P.O.O.K. for President" t-shirt that showed the Pook's head beside the heads of America's great leaders chiseled out of Mount Rushmore.

"The Pook didn't become President," says Jim, "but that didn't stop us from using the campaign to bring up principles and ideals that no one else was talking about in quite the same way.

"'There is no end to being happy.' That was Richie's message, and it holds true today. There really *is* no end to being happy if we help our neighbors."

The Pook Lives!

These days, a "P.O.O.K. for President" bumper sticker still adorns the mailbox outside Jim's home. The Pook Family costumes and memorabilia are in storage in the house, long past the days of the Pookgrass Festival or presidential campaign.

But Jim still dreams of breaking out those characters again...and they might just have some life left in them. After all, Richie showed up at the Richland Mall reunion in April 2016, riding around the Richland Town Centre parking lot in his lemon yellow Pookmobile.

Does this mean there's still hope for the other Pook projects Jim's kept on the back burner for all these years?

Photos by Philip Balko

He hasn't given up on his Pook screenplay, that's for sure. "My dream is to see *There Are No Monsters* produced as a live-action or animated film. A complete motion picture script is done, including 28 original songs and voices from Carnegie Mellon theatrical actors. Maybe we could make a deal with the Pittsburgh Film Institute and have a young tiger there or another young producer who knows everything about technology produce the project. It could be very rewarding for everyone concerned, because the real impact of the film would be to serve as a springboard for merchandising."

Jim also still thinks the Planet Pook theme park could become a reality. He envisions it as a local version of DisneyWorld and says he has the perfect location all picked out. But how likely is it to ever come to life?

As likely, perhaps, as it was for a furry character based on an English sheepdog to hatch from an egg over Times Square on New Year's Eve, have a hit record mixed in Michael Jackson's family's studio, appear on a Labor Day Telethon with Jerry Lewis and Ed McMahon, almost appear in a movie with Jonathan Winters, Barbara Eden, and Robin Williams, or run for president.

Or, let us never forget, to help make the Richland Mall a huge success against all odds.

When the Mall opened up, everyone wanted to see it. The Route 56 bypass was fairly new and was the fastest way to get to Richland. For over a week, the traffic was bumper-to-bumper going up the highway from the Solomon Run on-ramp to the route 56 exit. I took my mother there a week after the Mall opened and couldn't get off 219. The cars were backed up, and the parking lot was full.

My brother dated his wife from 1976 until he got married in 1979. The Mall was the popular place to be, and they went there every weekend.

Mike Meketa

One of the ways we advertised Richland Mall businesses was live local television. WJAC-TV had a show called *Shopper Showcase*, hosted by Steve Richard, the weatherman at the time. He was a great host.

A few of us at a time would go on the show and talk about our products. It was a lot of fun, though I did get nervous sometimes when we were on the air.

Gil Demos

Steve Richard

Courtesy Gil Demos

I worked at Sears for a total of 33 years. I started in 1966 at the University Park store, and I retired in 1999. I worked at the University Park, Richland Mall, and Galleria locations. I started out as a sales clerk in the hats, handbags, and hosiery department, which they don't have anymore.

Betty Kermin

My favorite memory of the Richland Mall is that my grandma took me there on the day it opened. She's long gone, but I remember that day fondly.
Lauren Goff

I loved coming to the Mall entrance by the Duke and Duchess theaters. I always got the best memories a Mall could offer a teen: the excitement of a new movie and the smell of popcorn mixing with the aroma of Capri Pizza. I was then greeted by a feast of digital beeps and flashes coming from the Time-Out "cave." Walking into Time-Out *was* like entering a cave, and once I was in, it was always hard to leave without playing my favorite games, such as Donkey Kong, Cyberball, and Joust.
Scott Jeschonek

Some of my earliest memories involve the Richland Mall in the late '70s. It was a great weekend destination for the family. Mom and Dad would pick up my grandmother and hit the Mall. From the moment we entered the door, I recall being immersed in the whole experience. The Mall had its own sound and smell.

Courtesy Jim Streeter

First, you would be hit by the scent: a combination of tobacco products, Karmelkorn, Hot Sam, and Sweet William. Then the sound: people walking and talking, coupled with the distant sound of the waterfalls in the sunken garden at center court, unless it was Christmas season, in which case the falls would be turned off and replaced with a winter wonderland complete with Santa. I still have all the photos of my childhood visits with the Jolly Old Elf.

Every trip to the Mall brought so many wonderful memories. I remember Dad buying us each a warm pretzel dipped in chocolate from Hot Sam or a clown's head sundae at Sweet William. I also remember the day I met "Spider-man" at center court, and the time I had the chance to sit in the General Lee car from "The Dukes of Hazzard" TV show. There were the toys bought for me at Child World and the strange tables at the Encore restaurant that had real money sealed against the wood for all time to come.

I was long removed from Johnstown the day the Richland Mall closed, but I still shed a tear on the day she was torn down. They don't make malls like that anymore. In fact, they really don't make malls at all anymore.

As a barber, I talk to young people all the time. They have no modern day equivalent of "the Mall experience" and often struggle to understand what I'm talking about. It seems they are too busy with their phones and tablets to have any real connection with people. It is in that stark reality that I realize what the malls of my life were to all of us in a certain age bracket: they were our social experience. They were where we had our first dates. They were where we bought our first bike. They were the places where we would meet up with friends and socialize at the arcade over games of Pac-Man and Q*Bert. I will always miss the Richland Mall, and she will hold a special place in my heart...because she was my "first" Mall.
Jim Norcross

chapter seven
the grandest of openings
1974

The party at Sunnehanna Country Club in Westmont Borough wasn't open to the public. But if you ever go back in time to witness the opening of the Richland Mall, you're going to want to beg, borrow, or steal to get yourself a ticket.

Though the Mall's grand opening was set for November 4, 1974, the pre-opening party at Sunnehanna happened on August 13th of that year. In the weeks before the party,

invitations went out to Mall tenants and VIPs alike, inviting them to celebrate the impending opening at a lavish gala at Sunnehanna.

Photo by Linda Dufseth

According to Gil Demos, owner of C. Gil Shoes and onetime manager of Teeks Fine Shoes and owner of Hush Puppies in the Richland Mall, the soiree was every bit as lavish as expected. "It was the most first-class event I've ever been to in my entire life, and I've been to some pretty nice things," remembers Gil. "Everything related to that Mall was always first class.

"They had an open bar with every kind of alcohol," says Gil. "They had caviar and mountains of shrimp as hors d'oeuvres. Then there were steaks for dinner. You name it. Only the best."

"Those guys did things right," says Joe Fortunato, manager of Richman Brothers in the Mall.

The guests mingled with the Unimich and Ribet Productions teams, getting to know each other and getting the latest news about the grand opening. Everyone seemed to be impressed and excited, on the verge of one of the greatest business opportunities of their lives. There was a distinct sense of optimism in the place, a feeling that history was being made. Now they just had to wait until November 4th to find out how that history would be received.

Photos by Linda Dufseth

Though thanks to Kmart, they wouldn't even have to wait *that* long.

Premature Openings

Kmart just had to be different.

After years of development, negotiation, construction, and promotion, The Richland Mall's grand opening date was set for November 4, 1974 – just in time for the retail industry's biggest time of the year, the holiday shopping season. Plans were made, a band was hired, invitations were sent, ads were purchased, and the media were notified. The Unimich partners and the publicity team of Ribet Productions shifted into overdrive, making sure no detail was overlooked, no matter how small.

After all, this event would be the culmination of everything they'd done. It would set the tone for everything that came after, whatever it might be. Every tenant, boss, and employee would have to work together in perfect synchronization to make the best impression possible on the first waves of shoppers pouring through the doors on November 4th.

©*The Tribune-Democrat*

Richie The Pook Is Looking . . . For This Lady

She was the first shopper ever to set foot into the New Richland Mall and Richie would like her to be his own special guest for the big Grand Opening on November 4

There is a lot in store for this sweet lady and time is running out . . . So Richie is offering a

SPECIAL REWARD of a $25.00 Gift Certificate to the first person who locates her and brings her to the Mall!

Keep watching to see who Richie's special new friend will be...

richland mall ...just for you

See Richie playing Super Scoro between periods at all Johnstown Jets hockey games

© *The Tribune-Democrat*

Imagine their surprise when Kmart decided to open for business on Wednesday, October 9, 1974 instead – nearly a full month before the scheduled grand opening of the Mall.

As you might expect, shoppers and curiosity seekers alike flooded Kmart that day, rushing in for a first look at the big store that was about to become a part of their lives. People scooped up the opening day bargains and flocked to the Blue Light Specials, thrilled to finally be shopping in the place they'd been looking forward to since the groundbreaking in 1973 or perhaps even before that.

The Richland Mall's First Shopper

One woman, Mrs. Angeline Crognale of Railroad Street in Windber, would turn out to be more thrilled than the rest of the eager shoppers at Kmart's grand opening... later, at least.

Mrs. Crognale and Richie

© *The Tribune-Democrat*

Angeline became the first shopper to enter Kmart that day, right after the ribbon-cutting, and therefore the first shopper to set foot in the Richland Mall.

"Someone was pushing me from behind with a shopping cart and I had no choice but to run into the store," said Angeline.

Her historic importance wasn't discovered until later, however. A photo of Angeline entering Kmart ahead of the crowd appeared in a full-page ad in *The Tribune-Democrat,* along with an offer of a reward of a $25 Mall gift certificate for anyone who could identify her.

When Mrs. Paula Virgenock of Windber called in the I.D., Angeline was on the Mall's radar. Her friends, Helen Marcinko and Mary Maruschock, who'd attended the Kmart opening with her, brought her to meet with Mall officials about her prize.

As the first-ever shopper at the Richland Mall, Angeline would attend the full Mall's grand opening as the special guest of Richie the Pook, plus receive a special prize in the bargain.

Penn Traffic Follows the K

Inspired by Kmart's example, Penn Traffic executives staged their own early opening. At 10:00 a.m. on Monday, October 14, 1974, the Penn Traffic Company launched its Mall branch with an opening ceremony attended by various Walt Disney characters. Penn Traffic President G. Fesler Edwards presided over the ceremony, joined by Vice President in Charge of Branch Stores Richard Corbin, store manager John Hanley, and numerous other managers and supervisors.

The first three days of that week were dubbed Preview Days, with a grand opening promotional sale kicking off on Thursday. By the time the *Mall's* grand opening rolled around in November, Penn Traffic – like Kmart – was already thriving, pulling throngs of shoppers through the doors with a string of sales and providing them with the same quality merchandise and customer service that the company's downtown store had been known for since its own opening in 1854.

© *The Tribune-Democrat*

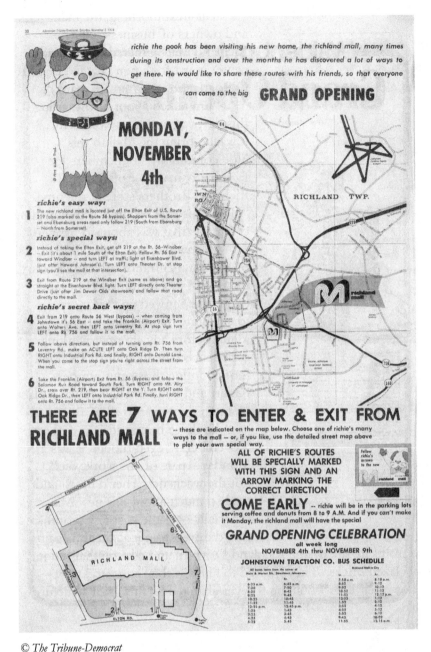

© *The Tribune-Democrat*

The Shape of Openings to Come

Did the early openings of Kmart and Penn Traffic throw off the plans of Unimich and Ribet for a joint grand opening by all the Mall's tenants? Not at all. If Kmart and Penn Traffic wanted to get out in front and highlight their independence, the Mall team couldn't stop them...but they weren't about to change or downgrade their plans in any way.

Looking at the Kmart and Penn Traffic moves as a kind of "soft opening," the Mall team observed the public's response and fine-tuned their own approach. They felt good about the prospects for the Mall-wide event and the sales that would follow – felt better than expected, even.

On October 9th, the parking lots on the Kmart side of the Mall were overflowing. The interior of the store was packed wall-to-wall with customers, and the lines at the checkouts were long.

If that pattern extended to the rest of the Richland Mall, the full-blown Grand Opening on November 4th would be very grand, indeed.

Setting the Stage

The night before the grand opening, an invitation-only event was held in the Mall, open to Mall teammates and tenants and their loved ones.

Jim O'Roark's wife, Linda, was there, of course. "All my family and friends got to come and see the Mall before it opened. I was so proud of what Jim and Unimich had accomplished.

"I thought the Mall was beautiful, and the stores were great. I thought Jim and his team had done a great job in a very short amount of time, and it was wonderful."

SPECIAL SECTION

Introducing the outstanding Richland Mall Tenants...

Company's coming...

so richie the pook

is getting everything

in order at his new home.

Winnie the Pooh,
Leroy the Lion and
Hey-U the Clown
are coming along with some
of richie's other friends...

and richie is personally inviting Everyone
to the GRAND OPENING at the new

richland mall

9:30 a.m., Monday, Nov. 4

...there will be gifts, prizes and some special surprises for all!!!
Join richie in his week-long Grand Opening celebration -- Nov. 4-9
Register to win richie's Volkswagen Thing from Suppes Motors, which will be given away on Saturday, Nov. 9.
Winner need not be present to win. Register free during Grand Opening week.

richie
will be serving
coffee & donuts
between 8 & 9 o'clock

you are
invited
come
early

The new Richland Mall is located
Just Off The Elton
Exit of Route 219

richland mall ...just for you

the stores

K mart
Penn Traffic
Sears
Shop-N-Save *
Super Chick
National Record Mart
Our Furniture
Ormonds
Sagebrush
Gordon Jewelry
Stanyan Street
Karmelkorn
Cottage Craft
Brettis of Altoona
Partside Shoppe
Hello Shop
LaRose Shops
Spencer Gifts
Breaks Fashions
Scot Tie
Sweet William
Sweet William Deli
Time Out
Teak's Fine Shoes
Lafayette Radio
Thrift Drugs
Richie's Corner
Lester's *
Hanover Shoes
Children's World
Jane Hunter
Kinney Shoes
General Nutrition
The Depot
Craftsmen II
Somerset Trust Company
DeRoy Jeweler
Fashions
Framing Hut
Richman Brothers
Jo Ann Fabrics
Thom McAn
Hickory Farms
Hart's Home Store
Waldenbook and Card Shop
The Parasol
Kinderfoto
Piercing Pagoda
Things Remembered
Fanny Farmer
Light n' Lovely *
Dallas Fair *
Entertainment Center *
Ben Tan *
Motherhood Maternity *
The Encore *
Northland Optical *
Standard Sportswear *
Ho-Ko Travel Service *
Pizza Chef *
Orange Julius *
Household Finance *
Singer *
McDonald's Restaurant *
Haynes Sportswear *
Matchmaker *

*Opening soon

The next morning, the managers and owners of businesses in the Richland Mall gathered in the Mall's center court for a pep rally led by Jim O'Roark and the Unimich team.

"Jim talked about how exciting this day was, and how wonderful it was to bring the Mall to this little community," remembers Joe Fortunato, manager of the Mall's Richman Brothers store at the time. "He got us psyched up for the opening ceremony that was about to happen."

Meanwhile, just outside the doors of the main entrance off center court, the crowd was forming. Thousands of people showed up that morning to celebrate the opening of the Mall. Before any shopper had fully experienced the interior of the Mall (not counting those gun-jumpers, Kmart and Penn Traffic), it was a place of intense interest to all of them.

All those thousands showed on November 4th even though it was a Monday – part of the work week, not the weekend. They'd heard and read so much about this new Mall, especially over the past few months; they'd driven past it again and again, watching it rise from the site of the Richland Drive-In and take on that unique, curvilinear shape with the colorful glazed bricks. They wanted to know – they *needed* to know – what all the hubbub was about…how their lives would be forever changed by this great structure and the stores, merchandise, people, and community activities they would surely find inside.

Up, Up, and Away

Buzzing with excitement, the crowd thronged around a stage that was set up outside the main middle doors. They were warmed up by a band brought in from Michigan for the occasion – Stix and Stoned, starring Sal Garcia, the voice of Richie the Pook.

Photo by Linda Dufseth

"I played bass, Bobby Lewis played lead guitar, and Marcus Terry was on drums," remembers Sal. "Plus, we had a group of beautiful dancers from Detroit who performed with us. It was a really dynamic show."

When it came time for the ribbon-cutting ceremony, the Richland High School chorus and marching band filled the air with a series of rousing numbers, further stoking the excitement.

As the music and applause trailed off, all eyes fixed on the stage, which by then was populated by Unimich developers and their wives, Ribet employees, VIPs from the community, the Mall's first shopper Angeline Crognale...and Richie the Pook. The big, furry character who'd helped build interest in the Mall with his whimsical adventures sat front and center, closer to the mic stand than even the Unimich team and their wives.

Richie's creator, Jim O'Roark, stepped up to the mic and made a few remarks to commemorate the day. It was "a big day for all of us," he said, as Richie sat there and nodded in agreement.

After O'Roark was done addressing the crowd, he and the other four Unimich partners cut the ribbon spanning the doors at approximately 10:00 a.m., officially declaring the Mall open for business.

All Courtesy Jim Streeter

Courtesy Jim Streeter

Just as the ribbon was cut, 400 balloons were set loose from the roof of the Mall, floating off into the northeast sky.

As the balloons soared away, the Unimich and Ribet teams ushered the crowd forward. That was all the encouragement the waiting shoppers needed.

Grinning, talking, and laughing, they pushed through the doors, marveling at the neon lights, sparkling storefronts, and natural oasis complete with trout-stocked stream arrayed in front of them.

Courtesy Jim Streeter

Honeymoon of a Mall

By all accounts, the grand opening was an unqualified success. The Unimich partners could not have hoped for a better day.

Photo by Linda Dufseth

"The grand opening was phenomenal," recalls Ray Kisor. "My parents and my wife's parents were able to come in from Ohio, so it was like small town boy does good when they got to see what we'd done.

Courtesy Jim Streeter

"We were fortunate to have most of the stores open or at least committed by the time we opened. The place looked fantastic, and people loved it. There was a lot of excitement all around.

"I had an indescribable feeling of joy and pride, a great sense of accomplishment," says Ray.

The partners' dreams had become reality; now was the time to reap the rewards of their efforts. Fortunately, they didn't have to wait long to see signs of success from this project of a lifetime.

Courtesy Ray Kisor

From the start, money and merchandise changed hands at a breathtaking pace in the newly opened Mall. Sales were brisk and steadily increasing, building momentum from the bump of publicity that came with the grand opening.

There would be challenges ahead, down the line, but it was still too soon to see them. For now, it was enough to bask in the light of early success, restore the energy and resources they'd expended in attaining it, and imagine the heights to come.

Courtesy Ray Kisor

Courtesy Jim Streeter

Courtesy Ray Kisor

Photo by Linda Dufseth

Hi!

My name is Richie the Pook and I want to invite you to join me and the Richland Mall Associates for a private preview of my new home, The Richland Mall.

Sunday, November 3, 1974
6:00 p.m. to 9:30 p.m.

Elton Road at Theater Drive
Johnstown, Pennsylvania
Join us also for the
Grand Opening Ceremonies
Monday, November 4, 1974
9:30 a.m.

Come on out and
we'll Pook together

NAME: **Bob McConnell**

TITLE: **General Manager**

richland mall

If the Richland Mall was like a small city, Bob McConnell was its mayor.

As general manager of the Mall, Bob supervised and coordinated security, maintenance, promotions, advertising, and bookkeeping and accounting. He organized and oversaw anything involving the whole Mall, whether it was community events, holiday decorating, or the Richland Mall Merchants Association. But he did much more than that, too.

"Bob was the glue that held the Richland Mall together," explains Jim Streeter. "He was the guy who was there every day, solving problems and maintaining relationships with tenants.

"He was the Mall's go-to guy, and he was there from the groundbreaking until the day the Mall closed," says Streeter.

"I worked 23 years in the Richland Mall, and I couldn't picture having a better job," says Bob. "It was great, it was fantastic. I really feel blessed."

The Unpaid Apprentice

A native of Pittsburgh and graduate of Carrick High School and Penn State University, Bob served in the U.S. Army for almost two years, beginning in 1968. When he got out of the military, he decided to go back to college and chose the University of Northern Colorado. "I picked the school that had the highest ratio of girls to guys in the United States," says Bob. "I hadn't had a date in a long time after my Army discharge, so I thought, I need to turn this around a little bit."

Bob left the University of Northern Colorado to return to Pittsburgh, where he found a job with the candy manufacturer E.J. Brock & Sons. It wasn't long, however, until another opportunity presented itself.

"My cousin, Jim O'Roark, told me about the Richland Mall project," remembers Bob. "He said they needed someone to manage the shopping center. I said, 'gosh, that sounds exciting, I'd like to get involved in that.' The problem was, I didn't have any experience managing a shopping center."

Fortunately, Jim O'Roark was able to set Bob up with a unique training program – an unpaid internship, basically, with the Rouse Company, which owned and operated a chain of 23 shopping malls. Starting at Exton Square Mall in Philadelphia, Bob learned the mall business inside-out, essentially paying for his training by working without pay at Rouse properties.

"In those days, shopping centers were being developed rather quickly," explains Bob. "The deal was, either train my guy or we'll hire one of yours. Since mall owners didn't want to lose their managers, they were very agreeable to the arrangement. It wasn't going to cost them anything, and the trainee was effectively an extra management person that would be on site to help with daily tasks. They trained me just like they trained any of their managers."

Bob worked at Exton Square Mall for six months leading up to and following its opening, getting a full course of on-the-job training along the way. "One of the best things that happened was two weeks after the mall opened, the manager went to Atlanta and I ran the mall myself for two weeks and then oriented the new manager. It was good experience," said Bob in 1974.

When the Exton Square gig had run its course, Bob moved to his next stop, which was much closer to Johnstown – the Greengate Mall in Greensburg. He worked for six months as assistant manager to Harry Overly, who was recognized at the time as an outstanding all-around mall manager.

By the time Bob was done, he had a year's worth of rigorous training to bring to the Richland Mall. "It worked out great," he remembers. "I worked for nothing for a year, which was the deal, but they paid my expenses. I got expenses and unemployment, and I was single at the time, so it worked out great. I got the training and background I needed from Rouse, and did well enough that they actually offered me a job...but I had given my word to the people in Johnstown. The Richland Mall was where I was headed."

Ramping Up in Richland

Bob moved to Johnstown and went to work at the Richland Mall in January 1974, starting as the Mall's tenant coordinator. He was more than ready to accept the challenge.

"It was exciting! It was the beginning a whole new era, a whole new thing. It was the beginning of the indoor shopping mall development business, and I was right there in the heart of it," says Bob.

With the Mall's opening less than a year away, Bob had no choice but to hit the ground running. "Right away, I started advertising for and interviewing potential employees and putting my staff together," recalls Bob. "I needed to hire a security director, marketing director, maintenance supervisor, and others.

"At the same time, I was working as an assistant to Rob Sabin, who was based in the construction trailer. I did whatever he needed me to do, whether it was looking at drawings, talking to people on the site, or getting materials he needed. Whatever it took to keep the operation on track in every way," says Bob.

In September, Bob phased into the general manager job, turning most of his energies toward getting the Mall and its tenants ready for the grand opening events. "There were so many details involved in getting the Mall ready for the grand opening. We had to make sure the security and maintenance staffs were all trained and scheduled, the floors were cleaned and polished, all the plants were properly installed in the landscaping areas, you name it.

Courtesy Jim Streeter

Courtesy Jim Streeter

And we had to arrange for the stage and performers and balloons for the ribbon-cutting ceremony, too, of course. It was pretty intense," says Bob.

The event went off without a hitch, though. "It couldn't have been better," according to Bob. And the Mall's success from that day forward confirmed his belief in the project's viability.

"I thought Johnstown was really ready for something new like that. I thought the area was ready for a modern shopping facility...and the community proved me right," says Bob.

The Kmart Is Falling

After the excitement of the grand opening in November 1974, Bob settled into a daily routine, working to keep the Mall running smoothly.

"I would spend about half my time in the Mall, checking various aspects of the facility and operations. I would walk around and visit the tenants, hearing their concerns and voicing my own as needed.

"The other half of the time, I spent in the office, completing paperwork and making phone calls and dealing with the myriad of issues that arose every day.

"I also met with the Mall partners when they were in town or needed something. Jim Streeter, for example, came in about once a month. He and I would spend a few days together, touring the Mall and discussing various issues. When we were done, he'd go back home until the next visit," says Bob.

As the Mall partners' onsite representative, Bob had to handle situations as they came up, including potential emergencies that might endanger life or property. One such situation involved a cave-in of Kmart's roof.

"One year, we had so much snow that part of the Kmart roof gave way," remembers Bob. "We had to close a section of the store and hire people to go up on the roof and clear the snow. I hired anyone I could find to go up there with snow throwers to get the snow off that roof.

Courtesy Jim Streeter

"Then, we had to rebuild the section of the store under the collapsed roof. We had to get engineers from L. Robert Kimball in Ebensburg to investigate the site and run tests and give their opinions. Then, we had to bring in construction crews to rebuild the roof and part of the store, making sure it could handle heavy snowfalls in the future.

"It was a real challenge, because it was up to us to fix the problem and pay for the repairs. The Mall partners had built that roof, and it hadn't been strong enough to hold that huge snowfall we got. But at least no one was hurt," says Bob.

Becoming a People Person

Though handling crises was an important part of Bob's job, his everyday work focused on tasks that might have been less urgent but were every bit as important. For example, he consistently put a lot of time into developing and maintaining relationships with tenants.

At first, though, the tone he set in dealing with Mall tenants was very formal. "In the beginning, it was very much a landlord/tenant type of relationship. Because of my training, I approached interactions with the attitude that I was the landlord, and when it came to tenants, I made the rules, and they were supposed to follow them.

John Kohut, part-owner of Records Off the Wall, and Richland Mall Manager Robert McConnell look over some of the movies available to be rented at the store. Records Off the Wall is one of several small businesses that have opened in the mall since the opening of the Galleria.

© *The Tribune-Democrat*

"But over the years, I moved away from that style. I realized that really it's a marriage, and if the tenants don't do well, I don't do well. Conversely, if the tenants do well, then I make more money, we're all happier, and I have a better shopping center. So I changed my approach and my attitude toward the tenants as all of us being in this together rather than me against them. Maybe it's because I got older, or maybe I got smarter, or maybe I just got tired of being a hard-ass," says Bob.

Whatever the cause, the new approach served him well. Bob ended up becoming best friends with many of the Mall's tenants, some of whom he still keeps up with regularly today.

"It took a while for the ice to melt. If you wanted to be friendly, Bob just wouldn't do it," says Gil Demos of Teek's, Hush Puppies, and now C. Gil Shoes. "But eventually, we developed a fantastic lasting friendship. Bob still comes to Johnstown now and then to visit his pals after all these years."

Turnover, Anyone?

In addition to his many other responsibilities, Bob took over the leasing work when Ray Kisor left the Mall after two or three years. "The Mall was on its way to being fully leased, so it was just a matter of filling spaces for tenants who left," explains Bob. "By the time I took over leasing, it wasn't a huge project anymore like in the beginning, when Ray had to start from scratch and fill all the small tenant spaces in the Mall."

According to Bob, tenant turnover wasn't bad in the early years. Four to six tenants would leave the Mall every year for a variety of reasons, leaving him to find replacements. "Some of the tenants we lost would be from companies that were closing everywhere. Other stores would just lose their audience or their popularity, or whatever they were selling would run out, and they couldn't find a new supplier.

"We hated to lose them, whatever their reason for leaving. On the other hand, a certain amount of turnover is natural, and it's not all bad. When tenants leave, you can get fresh tenants to fill their spots with the potential for greater success than the old tenants had. Turnover helps you reinvent your shopping center and keep things fresh for the customers," says Bob.

Wishing for No Wishes

When Bob wasn't working with tenants, managing his staff, or handling emergencies, he had plenty of smaller tasks to keep him busy. One, in particular, was a real nightmare, though it started as Jim O'Roark's dream for a piece of the great outdoors inside the Mall.

The nature grove in center court was a popular feature from day one. Visitors especially loved the stream stocked with live trout – but they didn't understand that fish and coins don't mix.

"People started throwing money in," recalls Bob. "It became a nightmare trying to keep the water clean enough for the fish, with all those dirty coins in there."

After a while, Bob and his team gave up and removed the fish, converting the stream into a full-time wishing well. But even then, there were plenty of headaches to go around.

"It was up to us to collect and disburse that money," explains Bob. "Typically, we'd get about a thousand dollars a year out of the stream, and we'd donate it to a community organization like the Red Cross. Organizations applied for the donation, and we gave it to a different group each year.

"But cleaning and processing that money was tough. It was nasty by the time we got it out of the water. Our people had to spend hours cleaning and counting those coins. We didn't have coin-counting machines, so it was very time-consuming.

"Eventually, Somerset Trust offered to do the counting, as long we got the coins all cleaned and dried. It was still a challenge for the bank, though, because our people would walk in with five gallon buckets of pennies and nickels and dimes and quarters, and the bank staff couldn't run it all at one time. They had to come up with a process to handle all those coins. It was just a pain for everybody involved," says Bob.

TODD BERKEY/THE TRIBUNE-DEMOCRAT

© The Tribune-Democrat

You Name It, They Had It

Looking back all these years later, Bob has good memories of even the not-so-hot times. He remembers the Richland Mall as a dynamic place that had a lot going for it – a place where shoppers could find just about everything under the sun.

"We really strived to make it a one-stop shopping complex," says Bob. "As a result, we had a really strong mix of tenants. If you needed a tuxedo or wedding gown, you'd come to the Richland Mall. If you wanted to buy a pet, you would come to the Richland Mall. If you needed to go to the dentist, you'd come to the Richland Mall.

"I tried over the years to put at least one of everything in that Mall. The main reason you wouldn't shop anywhere else, or even *think* about shopping anywhere else, was because you knew we had what you needed. And that was a big reason the Richland Mall was so successful in its day."

the stores

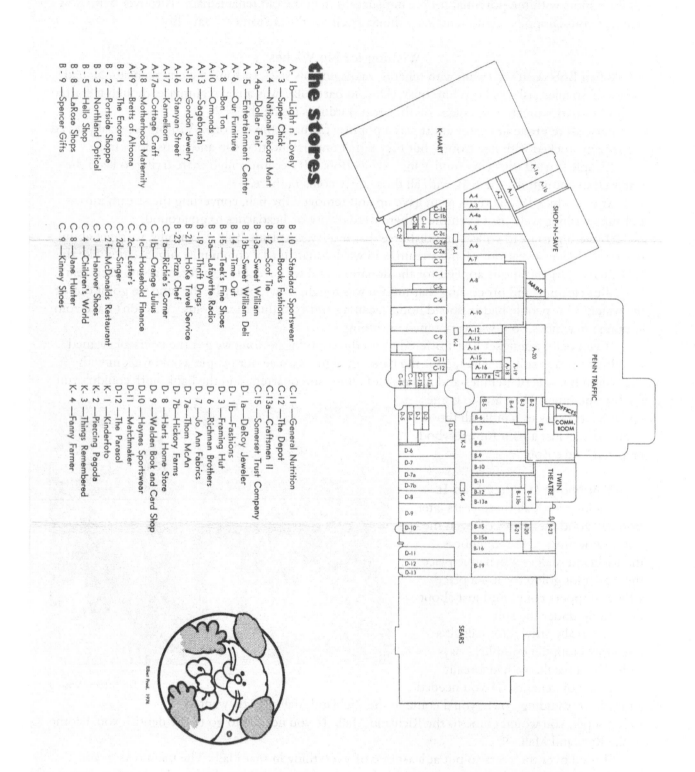

- A- 1b —Light n' Lovely
- A- 3 —Super Chick
- A- 4 —National Record Mart
- A- 4a—Dollar Fair
- A- 5 —Entertainment Center
- A- 6 —Our Furniture
- A- 8 —Bon Ton
- A-10 —Ormonds
- A-13 —Sagebrush
- A-15 —Gordon Jewelry
- A-16 —Stanyan Street
- A-17 —Karmelkorn
- A-17a—Cottage Craft
- A-18 —Motherhood Maternity
- A-19 —Bretts of Altoona
- B- 1 —The Encore
- B- 2 —Portside Shoppe
- B- 3 —Northland Optical
- B- 5 —Hello Shop
- B- 8 —LaRose Shops
- B- 9 —Spencer Gifts

- B-10 —Standard Sportswear
- B-11 —Brooks Fashions
- B-12 —Scot Tie
- B-13a—Sweet William
- B-13b—Sweet William Deli
- B-14 —Time Out
- B-15 —Teek's Fine Shoes
- B-15a—Lafayette Radio
- B-19 —Thrift Drugs
- B-21 —HoKe Travel Service
- B-23 —Pizza Chef
- C- 1a —Richie's Corner
- C- 1b —Orange Julius
- C- 1c —Household Finance
- C- 2c—Lester's
- C- 2d—Singer
- C- 2f—McDonalds Restaurant
- C- 3 —Hanover Shoes
- C- 4 —Children's World
- C- 8 —Jane Hunter
- C- 9 —Kinney Shoes

- C-11 —General Nutrition
- C-12 —The Depot
- C-13a—Craftsmen II
- C-15 —Somerset Trust Company
- D- 1a —DeRoy Jeweler
- D- 1b —Fashions
- D- 3 —Framing Hut
- D- 6 —Richman Brothers
- D- 7 —Jo Ann Fabrics
- D- 7a —Thom McAn
- D- 7b —Hickory Farms
- D- 8 —Harts Home Store
- D- 9 —Walden Book and Card Shop
- D-10 —Haynes Sportswear
- D-11 —Matchmaker
- D-12 —The Parasol
- K- 1 —Kinderfoto
- K- 2 —Piercing Pagoda
- K- 3 —Things Remembered
- K- 4 —Fanny Farmer

Courtesy Jim O'Roark

The Hello Shop was one of my favorite stores to go into with my grandmother. We would visit from New Jersey, and after wandering through Hess's, she and I would head past Karmelkorn to The Hello Shop. I loved it.

My grandmother (Lucy J. Felix) was the seamstress at Penn Traffic, and she married Elit R. Felix, the accountant. My mom and aunt (Katherine Moser and Paula Kellar) and uncle (Elit R. Felix II) were the PT "brats" in the wonderful book, *Penn Traffic Forever*.

I have so many great memories of the Richland Mall. I remember Gus and Melanie at Christmastime. I was terrified and fascinated at the same time…mainly terrified. They were so big, and I was so small. When Gus talked, I would cling to whichever parent happened to be closest! Seeing old pictures of them now still gives me that initial "ack!" feeling.

There was a Christmas elf house with green lighting on the interior near Kmart when I was young. I don't remember much else about it, but I remember loving to go in it. They must have gotten rid of it by the time I was a preteen, because I don't remember my siblings (I was the oldest) going into it.

I remember the holiday train that we could ride in. I remember going in it by myself, and having a blast, waving at my parents and Grandma Lucy and holding my brother Josh (and eventually my sister Rachel) while we chugged around. I don't think my baby brother Andrew ever got a spin in it, unfortunately.

When we visited Grandma when I was a teen, I was allowed two hours to go shopping on my own on Black Friday. Wow! Everyone else would go do their Christmas shopping together, and I was trusted to do my own. I would stop at the Things Remembered kiosk every time, and order ornaments for my siblings. Then, I would go to Claire's for a hair ribbon for myself, then Waldenbooks for old radio shows (Jack Benny, Burns & Allen) on cassettes for my dad. I would swing by The Hello Shop and go into the fancy dress shop (I don't remember the name, but they had prom gowns and wedding dresses), where I would ooh and ah over the pretty fabrics and designs. I would meet everyone at Sweet William or Hess's at the allotted time, and we would regroup and move on.

Grandma loved going to the candy store down by Sears. I want to say it began with a "G," but I can't remember. [Gardners Candies - Editor] The smells were divine, and sometimes she would buy us penny candy. The music store was next to it, and I loved watching the man playing the organ or piano. Then, there was the bank with the second level, and I always wondered if it was a real second level or a false front, because you never saw people up there!

I also remember the Encore…the restaurant with pennies in the tables. We did not eat there often, but when we did, it was a special time with Grandma. I loved the pennies in the tables, as did my younger siblings, and we would count them to see how many there were. The tables were rich!

Sweet William was a treat in the summer months when we would visit over the Fourth of July. We were allowed to choose a chocolate or vanilla ice cream, or possibly a milkshake (budget-friendly treats for a family of 6, you know), and we would enjoy relaxing and spending time with Grandma.

The huge nutcrackers outside Hess's were amazing. We knew it was Christmastime when we saw those on Black Friday. I miss them a lot.

When I was a preteen, and I still had to go shopping with my parents at Christmas, my mom would go off shopping with Grandma, and we would have to go with Daddy. That meant that we would have to carry the bags and go all around Hess's. He would hold up a sweater in the ladies' department and say, "Do you think your mother would like this?" We would say "no," and he would call over a little elderly sales clerk and say "Let's ask the young lady what she thinks." They were the most embarrassing moments ever to a preteen, yet now, we laugh about them and wouldn't trade them for the world. At least, if he planned on shopping in an area for a while, he would plop us down by the mirrors so we could make faces in them and try to amuse whichever youngest sibling happened to be in the stroller. Yes, shopping with Daddy at Hess's was a fun nightmare.

One of the things I loved at the Richland Mall was the Hickory Farms store, especially at Easter or Christmas, because we did not have one in our area in NJ. Hickory Farms had free samples. That was awesome. Daddy would take me (and sometimes my brother Josh) into the store, and we would go around, sampling everything. The honey mustard, the spicy mustard, the varieties of sausages and salamis, and the crackers were so good.

There was also a craft store when I was a child, but I don't remember the name of it. I barely remember it at all, but I distinctly remember going in with Grandma and picking out red and green wooden beads to make a decoration, which I still have to this day. It only comes out at Christmas and hangs on our powder room mirror.

I remember going into Ormond as a teen, and getting some great new clothes to bring home to NJ, especially sweaters. They had the best sweaters during the 80s!

Photo by Chuck Mamula

There was a "path" in Hess's on the floor. I know, it was just the floor pattern, but I loved to follow it when we walked in from the outside entrance. I would run ahead and go (naturally) in the direction my parents did NOT want to go, but I was following the path!

As a teen, I would go into Waldenbooks and check out the books they had available. I have always been a reader, and I would get a classic (*Phantom of the Opera*, *Les Misérables*, etc.) for the long car ride home to New Jersey. I would also get baseball cards; my brother Josh was totally into them, and he and I would get a pack or two each time we visited Grandma and the Mall.

Sarah Milheim

chapter eight

boom times

1977 - 1992

The grand opening was *not* a fluke. The great sales figures tallied by Richland Mall merchants did not sink in the weeks and months that followed that first burst of shopping.

Jim O'Roark, in fact, reported in *The Tribune-Democrat* in January 1975 that business was above expectations in November and December of 1974. According to O'Roark, several tenants had broken national sales records for their chains. All major tenants, including Shop 'n Save supermarket, were delighted with their numbers, and so were the minor tenants, with a few exceptions. Further, O'Roark said the Mall was drawing customers on a regional basis.

Business was so strong, Mall merchants added staff to keep up. Bob McConnell said in November 1974 that employment at the Mall had increased from approximately 700 to 1,000 since the grand opening. A spokesman at the Johnstown office of the Pennsylvania Bureau of Employment said at the time that it had placed approximately 300 people in jobs at the Mall.

All this success was not going unnoticed. O'Roark told *The Tribune-Democrat* that a dozen new tenants had already jumped in to fill unoccupied spaces in the Mall.

Richard Simmons at Richland Mall
Though sales were great right out of the gate, the Richland Mall team knew they couldn't sit back and assume they would stay that way. Right from the start, they worked hard to bring in entertainment and various community activities to promote the Mall and keep shoppers returning often.

97

"From the beginning, our overall goal was to have a family-oriented, one-stop shopping center," remembers Bob McConnell. "As part of that, we wanted to reach the community and incorporate its activities in the Mall. So we brought in anything, any type of a show – car shows, fashion shows, antique and collectible

Courtesy Jim Streeter

shows, cook-offs, petting zoos, you name it. Anything the community was interested in, we would bring it to the Mall.

"Year after year, there was always something going on in the Mall. We hardly had any time when there was no promotion or activity there, because we knew it was always important to keep that going," says Bob.

Shows at the Mall sometimes included celebrities, such as Hallie Bryant of the Harlem Globetrotters. Bryant performed his crowd-pleasing one-man show at the Mall four years in a row.

Photo by Eric Shields

Fitness guru Richard Simmons also appeared at the Mall. "We flew Richard Simmons in from California, and he put on exercise classes in the community room," recalls Bob.

Other shows featured animals, like a wrestling bear. "The bear would wrestle people in the Mall, in a ring," says Bob. "Everybody lost, but people still tried to take the bear down."

Then there was the millionaire chimpanzee, Kokomo

Photo by Doug Brydon

Jr., who performed for kids at the Mall in August 1976. Kokomo, who had his own TV show and newspaper column, worked with Johnny Caron, Merv Griffin, Bob Hope, Ed Sullivan, and other stars before bringing his madcap act to the Mall.

A three-ring circus complete with elephants also made an appearance in honor of the Mall's second anniversary. Murray Hill's Mini-Mall Circus ran from November 1-6 and included aerialist Princess Naja and a trio of young elephants called the Mitie Mites.

Photo by Doug Brydon

"The petting zoo was popular, too. We had it every year for years, and people loved it. We also set up a fishing pond in the Mall every year. It was a huge swimming pool loaded with fish, and people would come in and catch fish right there inside the Mall," says Bob.

When it came to animal-free events, the state lottery drawing on March 31, 1976 got a lot of attention. State lottery officials came to the Mall to draw winners for over a million dollars in prizes, assisted by Johnstown Mayor Herb Pfuhl and a bevy of "local beauty queens."

One of the most memorable events at the Mall, however, revolved around the Guinness Book of World Records. According to Bob, people broke three world records in one weekend during that event, making it into the latest edition of the Guinness Book.

"That weekend, we broke the record for the world's longest submarine sandwich, which folks put together in the hallway in front of Kmart. That sub was a quarter mile long.

"At the same time, a guy from Johnstown and a guy from Wisconsin jumped rope for a day and a half without stopping. They broke the world's record for jumping rope together.

"For the third world record, a guy jumped rope while running around the perimeter of the Mall for an ungodly number of hours. He broke the Guinness record for jumping rope and running at the same time," says Bob.

That's Shopping Centertainment

According to Bob, most of the special events staged at the Richland Mall were dreamed up by promoters who catered to the shopping center trade. "They would go from mall to mall," explains Bob. "They would call us up and say they were coming to Pennsylvania, and they would ask if we wanted them to set up at our Mall.

"The same ones would usually come every year, because our Mall was very busy and successful, and they made good money. For us, it was a way to entertain and build community interest in our business.

"I used to talk with the tenants about that. I'd say, 'Hey, we're bringing in all these people, and this particular time they might not go to your store, but they'll see it, and when they need something, then they'll come and shop there.'

Photos by Eric Shields

"It was all about building that habit, that repetition, building that routine that this is where you go, this is where you shop, this is where you come to be entertained. Eventually, our merchants got their sales," says Bob.

These days, the mall entertainment circuit has gone by the wayside. "I don't see malls doing that anymore. Times have changed, and they're not promoting like that these days," says Bob.

City Flooded Again; Areas Devastated 2 Dead, 5 Missing

... Walnut Grove damage

Looters Roam Streets — *Full Report Inside*

Courtesy Dick Corbin

Flood of Success

Buoyed by the flow of community events and a constant stream of sales and advertising, the Richland Mall merchants continued to post big numbers in the years after the grand opening. Then, midway through 1977, the Mall got its biggest boost yet...in the most terrible way possible.

On July 20th of that year, a freak deluge flooded the city of Johnstown for the third time in its history. The raging floodwaters effectively wiped out all downtown retail business, some permanently. The great downtown department stores, Glosser Bros. and Penn Traffic, were heavily damaged and closed – Glosser's for months, Penn Traffic forever.

Courtesy Fred Glosser

Local residents who'd relied on downtown retail suddenly found themselves with no place nearby where they could get the things they needed – so they turned to Richland.

"The flood really helped the Richland Mall, because downtown for the longest period of time didn't have any retail shopping," recalls Bob. "Local people, whether they wanted to come to the Mall or not, almost had to, so we added a lot of new customers because of the flood.

"From a business standpoint, the Richland Mall benefited from the tragedy of '77. It wasn't something that we would have wished on anybody, but we did benefit from it."

Full Steam Ahead

During the late 70s, the upward trend of business at the Mall showed no sign of slowing or reversing. Whatever momentum had been gained from the '77 flood continued to build.

JOHNSTOWNERS HAVE WHAT IT TAKES TO BOUNCE BACK

And Sears takes pride in being part of Johnstown. We look forward to being involved in the continuing growth and development of such a progressive community.

Sears

©The Tribune-Democrat

By April 1978, the Mall was well above the average in business production – the number of dollars in business produced per square foot of space. Not counting seasonal help, the Mall employed approximately 1,500 people, divided almost equally between full-time and part-time staff.

Ninety different tenants occupied the Mall, which had a maximum capacity of 95. Only eight tenants had left in the three and a half years that the Mall had been open.

Things were going so great, the Mall team was even considering expanding on 10.2 acres purchased from Richland Township by Fetterolf Development Corp., which had become a limited partner when the Mall was refinanced in 1975.

Photos by Chuck Mamula

101

"The space (inside the Mall) is getting so valuable that if you are not doing the amount of business you should, you will be asked if you would like to get out of your lease," Bob said at the time.

All signs pointed to continued success and growth. According to Bob, Sears and Kmart were doing "exceptionally well, among the best in their regions," and Penn Traffic was also doing well. Shoe World was about to open a 4,000-square-foot store, and Tiffany Bakery was setting up shop in the Mall, as well. National Record Mart had big plans, too, for an expansion that would make it the biggest store in the whole chain. Dr. Arnold Hecht's Family Vision Center and DeRoy's Jewelers were leading the charge, ranked as the number one and two tenants in terms of sales per square foot.

The good news just kept coming, quarter after quarter. So how much money had the Mall partners raked in from their creation by April 1978?

"The partners still haven't received a pay day, not a dime," Bob told *The Tribune-Democrat* at the time. "The income is paying off construction costs, operating expenses, and the investors."

In spite of the lack of income, the partners still had their ownership stakes in the Mall to console them. They were not exactly destitute.

And whatever the future held, they were very happy with the result of all their hard work.

"We're extremely pleased," said Bob in '78. "It got off to a good start and it's gotten constantly better. I think proof of that is in the leasing. We've done what we said we would do – provide a one-stop shopping center."

Expansion of '81

By 1981, the numbers were still solid, though some tenants did exit the Mall. By May of '81, in fact, eight stores had closed within a six-month period. An economic downturn in the region was causing belt-tightening among consumers, as once-mighty Bethlehem Steel continued to reduce its workforce.

Photos by Chuck Mamula

102

"With economic conditions as they are, there is only a certain amount of dollars for products," said Joe Cohen, owner of the La Rose women's apparel store.

Still, Bob McConnell announced that first-quarter sales were ahead of the same period the year before. Though an increase in sales did not necessarily indicate an increase in profits, things seemed generally positive for most Mall merchants.

Joe Cohen, for example, said that both stores he owned or had a hand in – La Rose and Franks 'n' Stuff – were doing very well. He pointed to good management, personal service, and a specialized product line as reasons for his ongoing success.

Sportswear shop Self Expression was doing well, too. "Every year has been better than the last," said Michael Piemonte, who operated the store with his wife. According to Michael, business was up 21 percent from 1979 to 1980.

Teeks Fine Shoes was also showing growth, according to Gil Demos, who was a district supervisor for the company in those days. Business at Teeks had increased in each of the seven years that the store had been in the Mall, Gil said.

Still, there were concerns among management and the Mall merchants. Gil and Bob both noticed an oversaturation of tenants dealing with certain popular products, like blue jeans.

Some merchants had a problem with the Mall hours, too. Tenants had to stay open during the same hours every week – 10 a.m. to 9:30 p.m. daily, and 12 to 5 p.m. on Sundays – but some stores didn't do enough business during certain hours to justify the expense of covering the full schedule.

And business wasn't good enough for one store, in particular, to keep its parent company happy.

Photo from Penn Traffic 1977 Annual Report

Hess's Cleans Up

The Penn Traffic Department Store – one of the Mall's three major tenants – had been part of the Richland Mall from the start. Overall numbers in Penn Traffic's department store division were weak enough, though, that the company decided to sell the whole division to Crown American Corporation in January 1982 for $7.3 million in properties.

John Kriak, secretary and treasurer of the Penn Traffic Company at the time, handled the deal. "Essentially, I swapped Penn Traffic stores for Crown real estate. Crown gave us seven parcels, including a shopping center on Scalp Avenue in Richland that housed a Riverside market.

"In return, I transferred to Crown all the assets of the department stores, except the Penn Traffic Building in downtown Johnstown. The assets I transferred included all the remaining inventory for the department stores, as well," explains John.

The Penn Traffic and PT branch stores (and PT Sports in Westmont) were now in the hands of Hess's Department Stores, a subsidiary of Crown. Just like that, Penn Traffic was out of the department store business, which had been its *only* business for so many years.

The Penn Traffic mall-based stores in Richland and State College were kept open and converted to Hess's stores. The PT combination stores in Westmont, Indiana, and DuBois, plus PT Sports in Westmont, were all closed.

Photo by Chuck Mamula

And plenty of jobs were lost in the process. Though Hess's interviewed Penn Traffic employees, they didn't hire many of them for the new Hess's stores.

The change sent shock waves through the Richland Mall. A major tenant had been lost, a new one had taken its place, and the Mall would never be the same. For eight years, Penn Traffic had been a known, dependable quantity, a store whose very name was steeped in local history and tradition. Now Hess's was moving in, and who knew what that would bring?

Those Go Go 80s

Though the Hess's takeover upset the status quo, Bob McConnell and the Mall team continued to expect good things and smooth sailing ahead. For a while, at least, those good things came to pass.

Even as the steel industry cratered and the local economy struggled, sales at the Richland Mall continued to rise every year – until 1985. According to Bob, sales were down by three-tenths of a percentage point that year.

But they bounced back the following year, with 1986 sales exceeding those in 1985 by nine percent.

By early 1987, annual sales at the Richland Mall totaled $85 million, supporting an average of 1,500 full-time and part-time store employees and 30 workers on the payroll of the Mall organization itself.

Things were so good that by 1988, the expansion project that had been in the wind for a decade started to look like it might become a reality.

Super-Sizing the Mall

In December 1988, Jim Streeter confirmed to *The Tribune-Democrat* that a 156,900-square-foot addition would be constructed on the Eisenhower Boulevard side of the Mall. The new addition would include 85,000 square feet of space for a fourth major tenant, plus room for other businesses and expansion of the existing majors – Sears, Kmart, and Hess's.

According to Jim, the project had been slowed by delays in the approval processes. It seemed to be picking up steam, though, as the Richland Township supervisors had just passed an amendment to the township's sewage plan to accommodate the addition.

Rumor had it that the new fourth major tenant would be J.C. Penney, which would be a real coup for the Mall. Jim wouldn't confirm that, though, until a final agreement was signed.

It was a heck of a plan, considering the general economic climate of the region at the time. It showed that Jim and his team were still betting on the success of their Richland project, willing to make visionary moves to ensure its future.

They had made history at the same location 14 years before. It seemed like a sure thing to expect them to make history there again.

But this time, the stakes were higher than they'd ever been, though Jim played it down for the newspaper. "We believe we'll take care of our business as we have for the past 14 years," he said.

Meanwhile, a new interchange was being built just up the road, along Route 219 near the Johnstown Industrial Park. Rumor had it that another developer was getting ready to make his own brand of history on a piece of property adjacent to that interchange.

Photo by Chuck Mamula

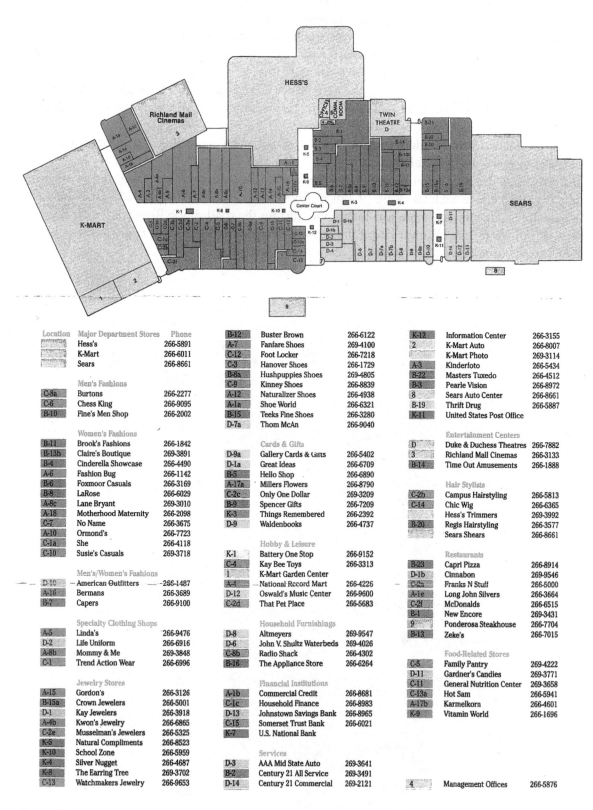

Location	Major Department Stores	Phone
	Hess's	266-5891
	K-Mart	266-6011
	Sears	266-8661

	Men's Fashions	
C-8a	Burtons	266-2277
C-6	Chess King	266-9095
B-10	Fine's Men Shop	266-2002

	Women's Fashions	
B-11	Brook's Fashions	266-1842
B-13b	Claire's Boutique	269-3891
B-4	Cinderella Showcase	266-4490
A-6	Fashion Bug	266-1142
B-6	Foxmoor Casuals	266-3169
B-8	LaRose	266-6029
A-8c	Lane Bryant	269-3010
A-18	Motherhood Maternity	266-2098
C-7	No Name	266-3675
A-10	Ormond's	266-7723
C-1a	She	266-4118
C-10	Susie's Casuals	269-3718

	Men's/Women's Fashions	
D-10	American Outfitters	266-1487
A-16	Bermans	266-3689
B-7	Capers	266-9100

	Specialty Clothing Shops	
A-5	Linda's	266-9476
D-2	Life Uniform	266-6916
A-8b	Mommy & Me	269-3848
C-1	Trend Action Wear	266-6996

	Jewelry Stores	
A-15	Gordon's	266-3126
B-15a	Crown Jewelers	266-5001
D-1	Kay Jewelers	266-3918
A-4b	Kwon's Jewelry	266-6865
C-2e	Musselman's Jewelers	266-5325
K-5	Natural Compliments	266-8523
K-10	School Zone	266-5959
K-4	Silver Nugget	266-4687
K-8	The Earring Tree	269-3702
C-13	Watchmakers Jewelry	266-9653

B-12	Buster Brown	266-6122
A-7	Fanfare Shoes	269-4100
C-12	Foot Locker	266-7218
C-3	Hanover Shoes	266-1729
B-8a	Hushpuppies Shoes	269-4805
C-9	Kinney Shoes	266-8839
A-12	Naturalizer Shoes	266-4938
A-1a	Shoe World	266-6321
B-15	Teeks Fine Shoes	266-3280
D-7a	Thom McAn	266-9040

	Cards & Gifts	
D-9a	Gallery Cards & Gifts	266-5402
D-1a	Great Ideas	266-6709
B-5	Hello Shop	266-6890
A-17a	Millers Flowers	266-8790
C-2c	Only One Dollar	269-3209
B-9	Spencer Gifts	266-7209
K-3	Things Remembered	266-2392
D-9	Waldenbooks	266-4737

	Hobby & Leisure	
K-1	Battery One Stop	266-9152
C-4	Kay Bee Toys	266-3313
1	K-Mart Garden Center	
A-4	National Record Mart	266-4226
D-12	Oswald's Music Center	266-9600
C-2d	That Pet Place	266-5683

	Household Furnishings	
D-8	Altmeyers	269-9547
D-6	John V. Shultz Waterbeds	269-4026
C-8b	Radio Shack	266-4302
B-16	The Appliance Store	266-6264

	Financial Institutions	
A-1b	Commercial Credit	266-8681
C-1c	Household Finance	266-8983
D-13	Johnstown Savings Bank	266-8965
C-15	Somerset Trust Bank	266-6021
K-7	U.S. National Bank	

	Services	
D-3	AAA Mid State Auto	269-3641
B-2	Century 21 All Service	269-3491
D-14	Century 21 Commercial	269-2121

K-12	Information Center	266-3155
2	K-Mart Auto	266-8007
	K-Mart Photo	269-3114
A-3	Kinderfoto	266-5434
B-22	Masters Tuxedo	266-4512
B-3	Pearle Vision	266-8972
8	Sears Auto Center	266-8661
B-19	Thrift Drug	266-5887
K-11	United States Post Office	

	Entertainment Centers	
D	Duke & Duchess Theatres	266-7882
3	Richland Mall Cinemas	266-3133
B-14	Time Out Amusements	266-1888

	Hair Stylists	
C-2b	Campus Hairstyling	266-5813
C-14	Chic Wig	266-6365
	Hess's Trimmers	269-3992
B-20	Regis Hairstyling	266-3577
	Sears Shears	266-8661

	Restaurants	
B-23	Capri Pizza	266-8914
D-1b	Cinnabon	269-9546
C-2a	Franks N Stuff	266-5000
A-1e	Long John Silvers	266-3664
C-2f	McDonalds	266-6515
B-1	New Encore	269-3431
9	Ponderosa Steakhouse	266-7704
B-13	Zeke's	266-7015

	Food-Related Stores	
C-5	Family Pantry	269-4222
D-11	Gardner's Candies	269-3771
C-11	General Nutrition Center	269-3658
C-13a	Hot Sam	266-5941
A-17b	Karmelkorn	266-4601
K-9	Vitamin World	266-1696

4	Management Offices	266-5876

Courtesy Bob McConnell

Tour
SEARS

In the early days of the Richland Mall, Sears was probably the biggest-name retailer, a giant among tenants. Sears had already been a big part of the Johnstown shopping scene for years, occupying a

Photo by Chuck Mamula

downtown location and a building along Scalp Avenue in the University Park Plaza in Richland; now, it was the linchpin of a new Mall, bringing its trademark Craftsman tools, DieHard batteries, and Kenmore appliances to a new generation of shoppers.

Bernie Roesch

Photo by Philip Balko

In the Bus, Not Under It

Bernie Roesch was there from the start, making the move to the Mall location. An employee at the University Park store since October 23rd, 1972, he helped haul merchandise up the hill to the brand new space.

"It took about a month and half to two months to move merchandise up from the store," recalls Bernie. "Basically, everyone who worked there had a hand it in moving. Meanwhile, we saw the workmen installing fixtures, setting up shelving, and getting in new merchandise, getting the place ready to open."

When the store was finally complete, Sears employees were invited to attend an open house that included the interior of the Mall. "I was awe-struck at the size of Sears and the Mall. Everything was nice and clean and neat. It was quite exciting," says Bernie.

Fellow employee Bob Nedroski was also impressed.

Photo by Chuck Mamula

Bob Nedroski
Photo by Philip Balko

"It was a beautiful store. Everyone was enchanted by having such a beautiful place to work. And when you went out into the Mall with all the different stores, it was like you were in a different world. Not to mention, we had Sweet William and Capri right outside the store, and other restaurants further into the Mall. It was great!"

Bob had worked at the University Park store since 1966, managing the jewelry, luggage, and office equipment departments. When Sears opened in the Richland Mall in 1974, he became manager of the carpet department.

"I remember the grand opening," says Bob. "Everyone was so excited. They transported us employees from the Sears parking lot in the University Park Plaza up to the Richland Mall."

"For about the first week, all the employees parked at University Park," says Bernie. "Sears bused us up to the Mall so there'd be plenty of parking for the crowds they expected."

Leaving extra parking spaces was a smart play, as the crowds of shoppers were indeed huge. "Sears was the number one retailer at the time, and our store was brand new. It would've been a shock if we *hadn't* packed in the shoppers," says Bernie. "We were all busy and putting in lots of hours. There were nights where we had three or four people working in sporting goods and the toy department alone."

"The Richland Mall store was booming," says Bob. "And we all loved working there."

Photo by Chuck Mamula

108

Mall in the Family

Sears' employees had been a close-knit group at University Park, and they continued the tradition at the Richland Mall.

Bernie, a "lifer" who spent his entire 43-year career at Sears – most of it in the appliance department – remembers spending plenty of quality time with his co-workers at the Mall. "It was a big happy family. You got to know everyone well. You not only got to know the person, but their family members.

"No one ever called off. Everyone showed up and helped each other out. I really enjoyed going to work, especially at the Richland Mall store.

"A gang of us ate lunch at Capri and had coffee at Sweet William almost every day. We went out for beer and pizza a lot, too."

Becky Kakamor

"Everyone got along well at Sears," says Becky Kakamor, who worked for Sears for 24 years, starting after the Johnstown Flood of '77. "We had regular customers who would come in all the time, and even people who worked in other stores knew you worked at Sears, and we all got along."

"Sears was a great place to work with a great bunch of people," says Marge Jeschonek, a longtime employee who started at Sears in 1975. "Everybody treated everybody well, and we had a lot of fun. I made a lot of lasting friends there." (One of those friends was Bernie. Marge and her friends introduced him to his future wife, Mary Ann, in fact.)

Marge Jeschonek

Bernie got to know plenty of people who worked at other stores in the Mall, too. "I think that friendly family atmosphere extended out into the Mall. I made a lot of friends in the Mall, and we had some great times. I remember going to Christmas parties there and mingling with people from other stores and having a blast.

"One year in the early 80s, they closed off a quarter of the Mall for our Christmas party and set up tables for the employees. There were bands playing in the middle of the Mall for dancing, and we got to visit with all our friends who worked in the various stores," says Bernie.

Culture Crash

As the years passed, life at Sears in the Richland Mall continued to go smoothly, with no end in sight – at least until 1992, and the coming of the Johnstown Galleria. When Sears' lease came up for renewal that year, the company announced it was moving its local store from the Richland Mall to the Galleria.

The move itself happened in October 1992. According to Bernie, Sears' staff regretted leaving their Richland Mall home but held out hope that the new location would be a success.

"It was a bigger store, classified as an A store, which is the biggest," remembers Bernie. "This was compared to the Richland Mall store, which was a B-sized store.

"When we first opened in the Galleria, there was a big ceremony out in the Mall by the escalator, and we all went out there. It was exciting like any time a new stores opens."

But amid the excitement, there was an undertone of worry and gloom. It was the beginning of the Richland Mall's death knell, and many people knew it.

Photos by Philip Balko

It was also the end of a way of life, as Galleria culture turned out to be quite different for Sears employees than the culture of the Richland Mall.

"Most of us liked the Richland Mall better," says Bernie. "It was older and smaller, but friendlier."

"I liked working at the Richland Mall more than the Galleria," says Jeannine Yannutz, who started working for Sears in 1971. "Co-workers were more like a family at the Richland Mall."

Jeannine Yannutz

Maryann Estbanik, a 25-years Sears employee, agrees. "It was definitely more of a family than the Galleria. Everybody pitched in and helped everybody else."

Maryann Estbanik

"The management of Sears at the Galleria was different," says Becky Kakamor. "It wasn't conducive to the kind of friendly bonding we were used to at the Richland Mall. It didn't help that they hired a lot of young people at the Galleria Sears, and those workers would be there for just a little bit, so there was a lot of turnover. That constant change doesn't give you much of a chance to form lasting friendships."

The Sears Retirees Speak

These days, the Richland Mall is long gone, and Sears is still in business at the Galleria...but times are changing. "Business at the Galleria store declined after about ten years," says Bernie. "I go up there, and the whole Mall is pretty slow. There's just so much competition from online retailers, and a lot of malls are hurting."

The spirit of the Richland Mall lives on, though, in monthly meetings of a crew of Sears retirees.

They meet at Hoss's Steak and Sea House (across from the former location of the Richland Mall) at noon on the third Thursday of every month.

They've been meeting for more than 30 years, getting together to reminisce and talk about the latest developments in their lives and the latest news about Sears. On average, a dozen or so people show up to have lunch with their friends like they used to do at Sweet William, Capri, or the Encore.

Photos by Philip Balko

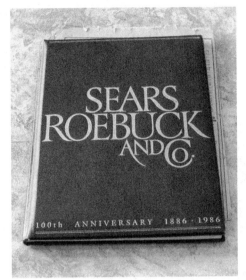

"It's just trying to keep that Sears family together from way back, some from the 60s," says Bob. "We laugh about the old days, remember absent friends, and help each other through life's struggles."

They still talk about Sears at the Richland Mall, too, and how much they miss it.

"The Richland Mall was a great place," remembers Harry Lehman, who worked at Sears from 1948(!) until 1985. "At that time, Sears was a really great place to work. They had good benefits, and the people were really nice."

"The Richland Mall was really nice, and I enjoyed it a lot," says Becky. "That was the first place I worked. I was married and had kids, and I liked it there. Everyone was close and knew everyone else. If something bad happened to someone, folks would rally around them and take up collections to help them."

"I got to know a lot of people at the Richland Mall," says Maryann. "We would go over to Sweet William and Capri and the Encore and have fun. That's what I liked about that Mall."

"It was a great Mall," says Marge. "And Sears was great, too. They really cared about their employees. After the '77 Flood, for example, they provided deep discounts on washers, dryers, and other merchandise to help employees replace what they'd lost."

Glenn Falk

"I enjoyed the Richland Mall," says Glenn Falk, who worked in display advertising at Sears for 32 years. "I hear a lot of people miss that Mall to this day, the size and hominess of it. I do have a lot of good memories of the place."

Photos by Philip Balko

Photo by Chuck Mamula

Photo by Philip Balko

Photo by Chuck Mamula

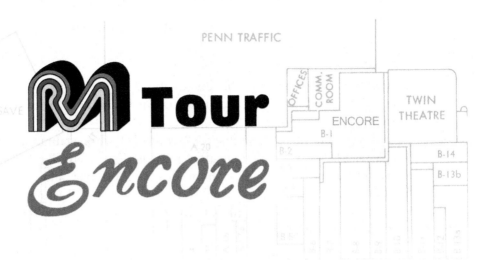

Tour
Encore

Encore owner Larry Mummert will never forget the night Ozzy Osbourne partied at his restaurant. It was after a show at the War Memorial Arena, and hard-partying Ozzy wanted to have a little fun out of the limelight. While the fans swarmed downtown nightspots, Ozzy and his entourage slipped away to the Encore.

"We closed for the night and had a private party just for Ozzy, his wife Sharon, and their crew of 50 or so musicians and roadies," remembers Larry. "We had to bring in a piano player, a D.J., and strippers from New York. We served a fantastic meal of filet mignon, only the best of everything.

"I'll never forget Ozzy dancing with my wife. She went to clear some dishes from a table, and he grabbed her and danced with her.

"Then there were the guys playing poker at two tables in the back, who only cared about their card game. Meanwhile, a girl was dancing on another table wearing nothing but her fingernail polish. It was a wild night.

"When it was all over, I gave Ozzy's manager a bill for $3,000, and he didn't think anything of it. He just said if they were in L.A., it would have been four times as much," says Larry.

The Men from Grant's and Stuver's

Ozzy had a blast, but the Encore was better known for family dining and special event catering than wild rock star parties. Oh, and the Tiffany lamps and Lucite-coated tables with all the coins embedded in them.

"Chuck Campanella, the original owner, brought those to the Encore in the early days. The lamps became a symbol of the restaurant, incorporated into the logo and signage. The tables were made by a relative of Chuck's in Chicago," says Larry.

Photos courtesy Larry Mummert   113

Chuck started the Encore at the time of the Mall opening in 1974. When the restaurant ran into financial trouble a year later, local restaurateur Bob Stuver recruited Larry to join him in buying a share of the business.

Larry had found success running the Bradford Room restaurant at the W.T. Grant Department Store in Richland. He'd landed there after growing up in Gettysburg, Pennsylvania and working for Grant's in York, Lancaster, Chambersburg, Reading, Andover, and downtown Johnstown.

His numbers at Grant's in Richland were phenomenal. "I had the largest dollar profit in the company, bringing in $50,000 in profit in five years. To put the numbers into perspective, I went 118 weeks without a sales loss.

"Grant's had a rating system with a one to five scale. Five meant you should get fired, and one indicated you were outstanding. I received a one three times," says Larry.

As a partner in the Encore, Larry got to put his Grant's experience to good use. He agreed to put on the general manager's hat, while Chuck ran the kitchen.

To get off to a fresh start, the expanded management team remodeled the restaurant and changed the menu to appeal to a different demographic. "We changed the décor, giving it more of an English Tudor look. We added some lights because the place had been so dark, and we got rid of the paintings on the wall. We also changed the menu and added lower-priced options. Since it was located in the Mall, our target audience was Mall shoppers. We didn't want them to think it was too high class to eat there," explains Larry.

Gone and Back Again

Things were looking up for the Encore and its partners. The new menu and décor attracted more customers for dine-in table service. The catering service was going great guns, too.

The three partners seemed to have the right balance of knowledge and expertise to keep growing the business…except, suddenly, there were only two of them. Larry was ousted to make room for Bob's son. He still owned his share of the business, but he was out of his job as general manager.

Soon after, Chuck decided he wanted out completely. He talked to Larry about selling their shares to Bob, making Bob the sole owner – but when financial improprieties came to light, the plan changed. Bob was out, and Larry returned from exile to run the eatery on his own.

Twinkle, Twinkle, Disco Ball

Larry built the business up and made a true success of it over the next 22 years. The Encore became the iconic Richland Mall fine dining restaurant, complete with weekly buffets, a soup, salad, and dessert bar, and disco nights.

"We put in a disco called the Red Lady Disco with two dance floors and brought in bands from New York. We did pretty well with that, but when the disco craze faded, we switched to country music and changed the name to the Silver Dollar Saloon.

"Eventually, we phased out entertainment altogether. The real money was on the food side. We had a lot of volume there.

"Our themed buffets really brought in the customers. Friday nights featured the seafood buffet, with shrimp, fish, and carved ham. Our buffet on Saturday nights featured carved ham and roast beef, and Sundays featured ham and turkey. We also had a complete soup, salad, and dessert bar that people loved."

On weekends and special occasions, the 300-seat, 9600-square foot restaurant was often filled to capacity. Fortunately, space was available to handle the overflow on the busiest of days.

"On Mother's Day and other holidays, we added seating by opening up the Mall community room and setting up tables there. We decorated everything and ran ourselves ragged serving loads of hungry customers."

There were New Year's Eve parties, too, that drew a crowd…and required certain "fun-control" measures. "Tickets were $25 per person. I set up a self-serve bar with kegs of beer, plus a table with chips and pretzels and another table with noisemakers. One year, a drunken brawl broke out, but we never had a problem again. From then on, I hired professional security to check IDs at the door and eject any troublemakers without a refund."

Courtesy Larry Mummert

Red M&Ms Only, Please

According to Larry, the Encore was hugely popular in its heyday. He sustained that success by plowing his profits into upgrades.

"I kept putting all the money back into the business, and it worked," says Larry. "We remodeled many times. By the later years, it was a radically different restaurant than in the beginning.

"We made sure we had all the best equipment. For example, we installed a computer system so our employees could ring up orders better. Each order was time-stamped, so we knew exactly when it was placed.

"We also installed sensors in the hallway from the Mall entrance, so the hostess would know when new customers were coming and needed to be seated."

Larry also invested in the catering business, buying delivery vans and having them painted black with the Encore logo in gold lettering on the side. The logo served as advertising when the vans were on the road or in the parking lot at the Mall.

The advertising paid off, as the catering side continued to boom. According to Larry, the Encore did about 26,000 caterings annually in each of the restaurant's final five years.

Courtesy Larry Mummert

"We did a lot of catering for weddings, funeral receptions, class reunions – big stuff like that. Sometimes, we did three or four weddings in one day.

"We also did all the catering for the crews at rock concerts at the War Memorial. Those concerts were a lot of work! It was challenging sometimes, having to scramble to find unique items that were called for in musicians' contracts. If the special items weren't in the dressing rooms, the performers wouldn't go on stage, and we were the bad guys," remembers Larry.

The Encore also did some catering for the *Slapshot* and *All the Right Moves* movie sets. Larry saw Tom Cruise and Chris Penn during the filming of *All the Right Moves* but didn't get to spend any quality time with them.

No Encore for the Encore

Between the dining and catering, the Encore's business showed no sign of decline – but the same could not be said for the Richland Mall. The coming of the Galleria in '92 put the Mall in a tailspin, leading to an outcome that would have been unthinkable just a few years earlier.

On March 31, 1998, the midsection of the Mall closed for good, leaving the anchor stores, cinemas, and outlying businesses as the only survivors. In spite of the Encore's continued success and support from the community, Larry now had two choices: move the restaurant to a new location or close it.

He chose the latter. "I looked at relocating, but it was going to cost about $300,000, and I wasn't going to spend that much. Not to mention, I'd looked at different locations, and nothing seemed right to me."

Before shutting down for good, however, Larry made a decision that showed his true character. "A friend of mind said I was getting a raw deal and should skim some of it for myself because nobody was going to take care of me. It happens all the time when places go out of business. I went home and slept on it, and I decided that everyone would get paid in full.

"I liquidated and auctioned everything and paid off everyone. I had all the vendors put me on COD and send me their last bill, and after the auction, I paid everybody. My bread man said he'd seen many places go out of business, and this was the first time he'd gotten paid.

"I paid everyone I owed money to. No one lost a penny. I started my life over without owing anyone," says Larry.

These days, he's fully retired and recovering from quadruple bypass surgery. He still stays in touch with employees, friends, and customers from the old days, though. He's still proud of his choice to pay every last debt and clear his karma instead of taking a less forthright path.

And he still remembers closing day at the Encore as if it were only yesterday. "I basically half priced anyone who walked in the door. I cleaned up all the inventory.

"There was a decent crowd. There wasn't much left in the Mall anymore, since all the stores were closed. But we still had a normal-sized crowd for lunch, which was the last meal we served that day, or ever," remembers Larry.

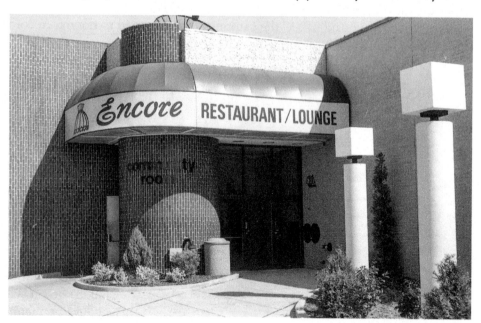

Photo by Chuck Mamula

RM Tour

DUKE + DUCHESS

Since 1949, there has always been a movie theater or drive-in run by County Amusement Co. on the site once occupied by the Richland Mall. Other businesses – the Mall included – have come and gone, but the movies have stayed in one form or another since '49.

And the Troll family has always been a part of them.

The Trolls Arrive

In 1949, Edward William Troll Jr. formed the County Amusement Co. with partners Joe Collins and Charles Sheftic. Sheftic owned two theatres in Boswell – The Sheftic and The Mary Lee – and was interested in Troll's plan to open a new drive-in theater.

To make that plan a reality, County Amusement bought a farm on the future Mall site in Richland Township. The Laub, Collins, and Troll construction company built the new facility, which opened as the Richland Drive-In in June 1949.

All these years later, Troll's grandson – Edward William Troll IV – still operates a movie theater, Richland Cinemas, on the same site. Some things never change in Richland Township.

Others things do change, and grandson Ed and his family have had a front-row seat for the fireworks since 1949.

"My grandfather was a partner in the company that built the drive-in," says Ed. "It turned out to be a good, steady business...and then Unimich entered the picture in '72. They wanted to buy the property and build a Mall on it.

"The thing was, we weren't interested in selling."

County Amusement never did sell the land to Unimich, but they eventually agreed to a land-lease arrangement. As part of the deal, Unimich paid them to shut down the drive-in a year before site-clearing and construction began.

Everyone was happy with the deal, especially County Amusement.

Courtesy Ed Troll

"In that one year leading up to the Mall opening, we received twice what we made in a typical year of running the drive-in," says Ed.

And the Trolls made sure the movie screenings wouldn't be gone for long. When the Richland Mall opened in late '74, it included brand-new indoor twin theaters owned and operated by County Amusement.

The theaters were called the Duke and Duchess.

Photo by Chuck Mamula

Not Named After a Nobleman and Woman After All

If you've ever wondered how the Mall's twin theaters got their names, here's the secret: they had nothing to do with aristocratic titles.

The larger theater was named after Ed's son Ryan, who was born in 1972. "His nickname was 'Duke,' so that's what we called the big theater. Naturally, we called the smaller theater 'Duchess,'" says Ed.

Ed worked with the Mall architects from Michigan to design the theaters. Though his family had been in the drive-in business, he'd spent enough time around indoor theaters to know what he wanted. After all, County Amusement owned the State Theater and Act I and Act II downtown, as well as the Westwood Plaza Theater in Westmont Borough.

The Duke had 450 seats, and the Duchess had 198. Brand-new, state-of-the-art projection equipment was installed in both theaters, including Simplex projectors and Christie Lamphouses. "Simplex made the best projectors, hands down," remembers Ed.

A modern ticket counter and concession stand rounded out the interior, and an illuminated poster display case was set up along the sidewalk outside. The exterior looked fresh and distinctive in its own right, clad in glazed blue brick laid in the same vertical style as the other brick features around the Mall's façade.

118

When the theaters were complete, Mall customers had the perfect new venue to see movie hits in the age of blockbusters – everything from *Jaws* and *Close Encounters of the Third Kind* to *Star Wars*. The mark of true success? Long lines of ticket buyers winding through the Mall.

Photo by Chuck Mamula

"*Jaws* was the first to have those kind of extended lines," says Ed. "They stretched all the way down our hallway and around the corner at Sweet William."

Mall General Manager Bob McConnell remembers that epic line well. "The line for *Jaws* was all the way down through the Mall for day after day after day. There were so many people waiting to get in to that movie, the line went all the way to Sears."

Gil Demos, who was managing Teeks Fine Shoes at the time, wasn't a fan of those long lines for *Jaws*. "They blocked my entrances and kept out potential customers. I lost a lot of business because of that movie."

Portrait of the Usher as a Young Man

Paul Mastovich witnessed plenty of long lines, too – first as a moviegoer and then as an employee at the Duke and Duchess. He started as an usher and cashier, in training to become a projectionist.

"I saw a lot of movies there when I was a kid," remembers Paul. "That was the place to go for movies. I saw *Jaws* and *Star Wars* there at different times. My parents used to drop us off and disappear. They would just give us a few dollars and say here you go, go get some pizza afterward, and we'll pick you up later."

As an employee, Paul got to watch movies for free, which was great...unless a movie overstayed its welcome. "*Dirty Dancing* played there for 14 weeks, and I got a little tired of it. Against my will, I got to learn every line and all the music from that movie. Another one, *Rain Man*, was there so long, we had to act like Dustin Hoffman's character, eating popcorn with toothpicks, to get Jim (Troll) to get rid of it."

According to Paul, the moviegoing experience was very different in the 70s and 80s, before the age of cell phones...but it came with its own set of problems. "People didn't bring babies to the theaters or text during the movie, but kids threw candy a lot more back then. I can't tell you how many times people came out covered in chocolate because kids were throwing it all over the place. Essentially, we were babysitters, and we had to deal with screaming, misbehaving kids.

"Then there were the lovebirds. We would catch people fooling around, doing a little more than just kissing, when the lights went down. There was quite a bit of that going on in the back of the room. We also found beer in the theaters all the time."

People behaved badly in other ways, too. "People would get upset and demand their money back if they saw a bad movie. But we told them it was like McDonald's, where if you eat the whole meal, you can't get your money back," says Paul.

Then there were the constant bomb threats. "It used to happen to us all the time. It doesn't happen that often anymore, maybe because of cell phones, which are traceable, but we used to get bomb threats called in all the time.

"At least every two weeks, we would get a threat called in. When we got one, the staff would gather and draw straws to see who would have to go tell the customers to leave, because they would throw Jujubes at you. Then, we would have to go out into the parking lot, and the cops would show up, and anyone who wanted to go back in to watch the movie could go back in. They'd probably miss a scene or two, though, because the projector would keep running for a bit after the projectionist stopped it," explains Paul.

Another constant problem was the breaking of films during showings. "That's why we had a speaker right outside each theater, so we would know if a film broke. When it did, someone had to run upstairs, splice it, and restart it. It would only take ten minutes or so if you were quick. It was one of the things Ed and Jim Troll were teaching me to do.

"It happened more than people realized. Showing a film four times a day, it wore pretty thin. They'd keep a film for three months and repaired it almost every day. People would get upset and start throwing things, but some people would also come out and buy more concessions, so sometimes I joked that maybe Jim was breaking the films on purpose," says Paul.

(According to Ed, film breakage got to be less of a problem in the late 70s, as the quality and strength of film stock improved. During the same period, Ed installed automation units that shut down the equipment in the projection booth in the event of a break or malfunction, further minimizing damage and delays.)

"What was worse was if one of the lights blew out in the projector, because the lamp and the projector got so incredibly hot, they could explode and ruin the machine and hurt or kill you. That's how dangerous it was, and why you had to be trained. If one those lights went out, you would not be showing the rest of the movie. You would have to wait until it cooled down, and then you had to use these big oven mitts to replace the bulb. It was more dangerous than people thought," says Paul.

In spite of the problems, there were plenty of good times for employees at the Duke and Duchess.

"Jim Troll was a pretty cool boss," says Paul. "As long as we got our work done, he didn't care what we did afterward.

"If we were slow, he would make up this game called office Olympics. He would make up some silly game in the lobby, and whoever won got to go home early.

"The Duchess had a great sound system. If it was a really dead night, Jim would put on some Pink Floyd, and we'd jam out to it on the sound system.

"A bunch of Steeler players showed up at the theaters once. They came into the Duke and Duchess, and we knew who they were right away. Once people figured it out, by the end of movie, there was a mob waiting in the lobby. I was usher that night, so I went in and told the Steelers I could get them out the back door, and they were like, 'No, we love our fans and we'll go sign autographs for people.'"

Paul left after four years and went to work at Time-Out, but the good times at the Duke and Duchess left their mark. "Jim was a great boss. I honestly think it was the best job I ever had."

Supersize My Multiplex

The Duke and Duchess were a smash hit, becoming the highest grossing indoor theaters in town. The wing where they were located, which included the Time-Out arcade and Capri Pizza, became a popular destination for kids and teens looking to have fun and socialize.

The theaters were so successful, County Amusement jumped at the chance to move and expand them in 1990. Space opened up nearby when the Shop 'n Save supermarket closed, providing an opportunity to create a bigger operation with more seats and updated décor.

Photo by Chuck Mamula

County Amusement drew up plans, signed a new 20-year lease, and put the project in motion. The new Richland Mall Cinemas would have eight screens instead of two. The projection equipment from the Duke and Duchess would be reused, and new gear would make up the difference. Almost everything would be new and improved.

But would the new, expanded seating fill up often enough to justify the investment? Soon after the multiplex opened in June 1990 (showing *Dick Tracy* and *Total Recall*), the answer became clear. Not only did the new seats fill, but there still weren't enough of them to meet the demand.

Three years later, in June 1993, County Amusement added four more screens to the Richland Mall Cinemas, expanding from eight to twelve. The gamble was a success and continued to draw strong audience support.

Photo by Chuck Mamula

Photo by Ed Troll

Years later, when the theater finally closed, it wasn't for lack of business. The Richland Mall Cinemas only ended their run because the Richland Mall closed around them.

121

Friends to the End

When the Richland Mall Associates closed the Mall's midsection on March 31, 1998, the Richland Mall Cinemas was one of the few tenants that stuck around and stayed in business. The Cinemas didn't abandon the Mall, in fact, until the Mall finally ceased to exist.

At the time of the Mall's closing, the company that owned the Cinemas underwent its own ending, followed by a new beginning. County Amusement ceased to exist, and a new company called Richland Mall Cinemas Inc. came into being. Everyone who'd been a County Amusement stockholder became a stockholder in the new company, including members of the Troll and Collins families. By then, Charles Sheftic Sr. had died, and his shares went to his children, Charles Jr. and Mary Lee. (Years later, when the Sheftic children died, Ed was able to acquire their shares; otherwise, the only non-Troll shareholder at this writing is a Collins family nephew who remains a silent partner.)

By the time the property's new owners started tearing down the Mall in 2003, Richland Mall Cinemas Inc. had struck a deal to be part of the new Richland Town Centre that would replace it. The new Richland Cinemas would occupy a new outbuilding on the former Mall site, not far from the location of the Richland Mall Cinemas that had preceded them.

Actually, because of the terms of its latest lease, Richland Mall Cinemas Inc. was able to play a pivotal role in negotiations for the entire Town Centre project. "The lease for Richland Mall Cinemas signed in 1990 was a 20-year lease. Under the terms of that lease, whoever bought the Mall would still have an active lease with us and had to negotiate with us as a side deal to get the complete package," explains Ed.

"There were at least three developers who talked to us and tried to convince us to sign a deal. The final ones had a desire to keep some local color, and I am one of the more colorful local businessmen you will find.

"We actually sat down and negotiated a deal that worked for both parties…but a few weeks before we started to dig the footers for our new Richland Cinemas building, my new landlord asked if I wanted to take on a partner – Wallace Theatres, who had been looking around between downtown and the Galleria for a site for a new theater.

"I passed. The Town Centre people had known that would happen, but as they worked with Wallace in other locations, they were obligated to ask. Two days later, one of the Zamias boys called and asked if I wanted to move my deal to the Galleria. I passed on that as well, and the rest is history," says Ed.

Hooray for Hollywood High Tech
The Richland Cinemas opened on November 4, 2003 with a showing of *The Matrix*. They became Richland Mall Cinemas Inc.'s biggest success yet and are still thriving, bringing in around a quarter-million customers per year.

These cutting-edge theaters incorporate some of the latest film screening technology, with upgrades in the works every year. They finished the conversion to all-digital projection in February 2011, and that was just the beginning.

"All our rooms now have Dolby 7.1 digital sound systems," says Ed. "One of our rooms features a Dolby Atmos sound system. We are the only theater in Pennsylvania with one of those.

"That same room can also play the new High Frame Rate movies in 3D, like Peter Jackson's *Hobbit* trilogy.

Photos by Ed Troll

"Coming up on the horizon are new laser projectors, along with Dolby Vision, which is a combination of Atmos Sound and the new High Def movie images which have a black-to-white contrast range that's 100 times greater than current colors," says Ed.

"We try to upgrade some portion of our business every year. My father taught me you have to spend money to make money."

A Family Affair

These days, Ed continues to run Richland Cinemas. His son, Isaac, is Chief Technical Officer, overseeing all technology in the building, and Isaac's wife, Donna, is Chief Financial Officer. "Donna is my right arm in operating the business. She's been working side by side with me since 2002," says Ed. As laid out in Ed's will, his three children – Isaac, Ryan, and Bronwyn – will someday assume full control and ownership of the Richland Cinemas.

Looking back to the Richland Mall days, Ed says he's glad he got to be a part of the Mall and watch it all come together. "I got to watch every stage of construction, from tearing down the drive-in to building the Mall. I got to watch trucks drive inside the Mall as they hauled materials to each site. It was great fun."

When it comes to feeling nostalgic about the Mall, he takes a philosophical approach. "I don't really miss it, because it brought me to where I am today. It was the stepping-stone to the cineplex I got to design and build, which we now operate.

"I'll always be grateful for the difference the Mall made in my life, but we've moved on now to the new and better things it made possible," says Ed.

Photo by Philip Balko

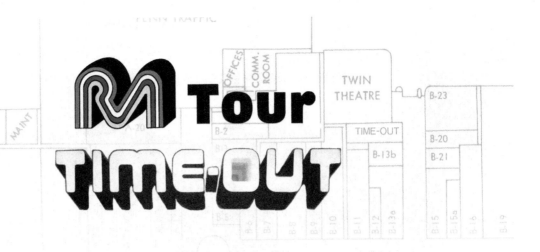

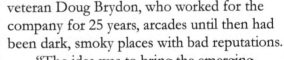
Where have you gone, Pac-Man, Donkey Kong, Q*bert, and Frogger?

Once upon a circuit board, these videogame superstars appeared daily at the Time-Out Family Amusement Center in the Richland Mall. Kids and teens spent mountains of quarters battling for bragging rights on beeping, flashing consoles, testing their dexterity and reflexes against what were then the fastest and wiliest programmed characters to hop, jog, or chomp across a screen.

Time-Out is gone today, along with the Mall, but its impact on a generation of videogame jockeys in search of the ultimate prize – initials at the top of a high-score list – must never be forgotten.

Even if the initials on the list changed a few minutes later when someone else got top score on the game.

Pac-Man and Mario Don't Smoke

No food, no drinks, no swearing, and no smoking. Those were the rules of the Richland Mall Time-Out, and all Time-Outs, wherever they were located.

For the mid-1970s, it was a revolutionary approach. According to Time-Out veteran Doug Brydon, who worked for the company for 25 years, arcades until then had been dark, smoky places with bad reputations.

"The idea was to bring the emerging video and entertainment industry out of the shadows and into the light and make it a family entertainment center," explains Doug. "That was the dream of the company's founder, Tico Bonomo."

Tico sold his candy company, Bonomo's Turkish Taffy, to Tootsie Roll in 1970, then opened the first Time-Out in the Northway Mall in Colonie, New York in the same year. The arcade, with its wholesome image and emphasis on family fun, was a smash, quickly followed by additional Time-Outs elsewhere... though Tico met with some resistance along the way.

Doug Brydon

125

Courtesy peterhirschberg.com

"He was turned down by some malls because of the stigma that gaming still had," says Doug. "That's why remaking the image was so important and always on the minds of Tico and his team."

The Richland Mall store was the twelfth to open, and it matched Tico's vision to the letter. The rules were the same as in all the other stores: no food, no drinks, no swearing, and no smoking.

"Back then, everyone smoked. There were fewer places where you couldn't, but Time-Out was one of them. We had two garbage cans on either side of the store entrance, and that's where the cigarettes would go," remembers Doug.

The 25¢ Tour of Time-Out

The design of the Richland Time-Out followed the company guidelines, staying true to Tico's concept. "They called it the Time-Out Tunnel," says Doug. "It was an arched tunnel with a lot of colors on the storefront. The idea was that as you stood outside and looked in, you didn't see too many of the games, but you had prefabricated fins in there and mirrors in the back at an angle that gave the illusion that it was never-ending. The walls were painted black.

"We didn't like that it was dark when you walked in, because we were fighting to present a family image – but the dark environment didn't seem to hurt us. It might have helped by bringing out the bright lights on the game screens."

Video games were always located in the front of the store, with new games set up in the middle to increase visibility. One or two bill changing machines were also set up in prominent locations in the center area.

The store was carpeted, but the carpeting had to be changed often because of the heavy foot traffic in the arcade. Signs on an easel out in front of Time-Out advertised whatever new game was being promoted.

Pinball machines, skee-ball games, and the basketball free throw game were all set up in the back of the place.

A Lot of Quarters in 25 Years

Doug was hired as an attendant at the Richland Mall Time-Out in late 1974, working nights while finishing high school. It turned out to be the start of a quarter-century career with the company.

"The fun thing about the company was that it was so young, so new and vibrant and exciting, and it had so much opportunity, that I wanted to keep being a part of it. I put my planned college education on hold to stay with Time-Out," says Doug.

As an attendant, Doug walked through the arcade, providing change, answering questions, and solving problems as needed. During his shifts, he wore the official Time-Out uniform, which had an interesting history.

"In the early days of the company, Tico hired uniformed security guards to operate the stores. He needed to convince the Mall owners that Time-Out wasn't going to be a smoky, dirty, dingy game room that was going to attract all kinds of trouble.

"In '74, they switched from contract security to hiring store managers, assistant managers, and part-time attendants, but a version of the uniform stayed. The official uniform was a blue security guard type of shirt with badges, dark pants, a belt, and dark shoes. It was supposed to make an employee look like a security guard, even if he or she wasn't a guard at all," says Doug.

"The uniforms made us look like authority figures to the little kids," recalls Paul Mastovich, who also worked as an attendant at the Richland Mall Time-Out. "We were like fake cops with big key rings, and the little kids were afraid of us. They didn't give us any trouble.

"But the teenagers and twentysomethings were a different story. If you weren't nice to them all the time, you'd get harassed," says Paul. "Sometimes, if you pissed someone off, they'd even wait for you outside."

Video Game Wizards

In addition to providing change, answering questions, and solving problems, Doug and Paul had to tend the machines, keeping them clean and repairing them as much as they could.

"Coins would get stuck," recalls Paul. "Sometimes, the games would just break. The kids were pretty rough on them, and we would have to fix them all the time."

According to Doug, Time-Out contracted with a local technician to fix the equipment. Doug got some training, however, and eventually was able to make repairs on his own.

Keeping the games running was absolutely vital to the dedicated – even obsessed – players who spent their free time and quarters in Time-Out. If a popular machine had stayed out of action for too long, they might have had a riot on their hands.

Courtesy peterhirschberg.com

"We had people walking around there who became so obsessed, they would scour the floor for one more quarter that someone might have dropped, just to get another chance to beat the high score," says Paul.

"If someone did beat the high score, they would write their name on a card and tape it up on the machine (in addition to their initials and score appearing onscreen after a game)...which, basically, was about bragging rights. They would bring their friends in and point at the card and say, 'You have to beat this score now.'"

Paul remembers there was a lot of excitement in Time-Out when a challenger went after a high score. "People would gather around the game. It would happen a lot. People got so used to the games, they knew what the scores to beat were. If someone made it past one of those scores, they would gather around the game really fast."

Certain players had a reputation for being difficult to beat, and their names tended to top the high score lists often. "There was this one guy, I think they called him Doc. He was a big guy, and he was in Time-Out all the time. He was one of the best players I have ever seen at any game he ever touched. People used to follow him around just to see the scores he could rack up," remembers Paul.

"We also had a guy I went to high school with, and his initials were MVP – Martin Victor Podvojsky. He would rack up incredible scores, and you would see his initials and think he was full of himself, because MVP stands for 'Most Valuable Player' – but actually, they were just his real initials," says Paul.

Employees had to beat high scores sometimes, too, because Time-Out wanted their names posted as competition for the customers. Sometimes, employees like Paul would walk around and tease the players about beating their high scores, just to keep the action going.

"There was a quest game called Dragon's Lair which was kind of like Dungeons and Dragons. There were four players, and you had to keep pumping quarters into it to finish the game. By the time you were done, you'd probably put six to eight dollars into it. That was one we employees would play, and we'd get a lot of people who would mob around and watch as we racked up the high scores. Then we'd watch as other players tried to beat us," says Paul.

Red Quarters and Gold Tokens

While on the job, Doug and Paul had to handle a lot of quarters – and two special kinds of coins that became iconic Time-Out mainstays: red quarters and gold tokens.

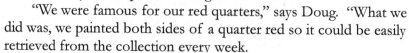

"We were famous for our red quarters," says Doug. "What we did was, we painted both sides of a quarter red so it could be easily retrieved from the collection every week.

"We used the red quarters if someone put their money in a machine and said they lost it. We opened the door of the machine and looked in the coin return to make sure the player's quarter wasn't jammed, which sometimes happened. If we didn't see it there, we would reach into a pouch and put a red quarter in the machine to start it up so the player could have the game he or she had paid for.

"We also used red quarters for promotions, or if there was a new game and someone was looking at it and needed a sample play to get hooked. We would use the red quarters to grant free games for a variety of reasons," says Doug.

The gold tokens came along as game makers urged Time-Out to charge more for playing their games. "It was difficult to raise the price from 25 cents to 50 back then because you could still buy a gallon of gas for 50 cents. Fifty cents was worth more than it is now.

"That changed when we switched the machines from accepting quarters to tokens. Time-Out could assign any value to tokens. Players would put a dollar in the change-maker and get whatever number of tokens Time-Out decided a dollar was worth. That was a big deal, a good and necessary move for the business," says Doug.

"Those tokens were a pain and got stuck in the machines all the time," says Paul. "No one liked them. If parents dropped off their kid, and the kid traded his money in for tokens and didn't spend them all, they were out of luck if they didn't come back to use the rest."

Shopping Carts Full of Quarters

In the days before tokens took over, just gathering up all the quarters and getting them to the bank took a lot of work.

"We collected the money from the machines every week," remembers Doug. "Every Monday morning, the store manager would come in two or three hours before it opened, and he would go to every machine and collect the quarters inside. Then, he'd feed them into a high-speed counter and record everything.

"Next, he'd put the quarters in bags. Each bag held 2,000 quarters, which totaled $500. Finally, the bags of quarters were all taken up to Somerset Trust. We used to put the bags in a Kmart shopping cart and wheel it to the bank around mid-morning. We never gave it a second thought.

"Eventually, the federal government changed the bank holidays to Mondays, and we had to change our collection days to Tuesdays. Otherwise, the process stayed the same for as long as we used quarters," says Doug.

The Time-Out Draft

Choosing the right games to keep the shopping cart full of quarters was always a challenge – complicated by a company pecking order that saw the most successful stores rewarded with first dibs on limited supplies.

"The higher revenue stores got the new games first," recalls Doug. "As the games aged and got less popular, they'd be moved to lower revenue stores like ours. We were below average in terms of earnings, though we still managed to increase our revenue every year."

In the early days of the Richland Mall Time-Out, basic games like Pong were featured in the store. "Everyone would stand around and watch, even though it was just two paddles and a ball going from one side to the other," says Doug.

As games evolved, picking the ones with the most potential was an ongoing struggle...especially since most of them had short life spans. "There was so much talent, and new games were being made all the time. The technology would change every four or five weeks. There were so many popular games that outdid each other that games would become obsolete in six months, because something else would come around and be popular," explains Doug.

There was constant pressure to rotate the game lineup and maximize the earnings from every square foot of the store. According to Doug, there were a few games that were so popular, they lasted a long time – but they were the exception, not the rule.

"Pac-Man and Galaga were big for a while," remembers Paul. "Then there was Space Invaders, Defender, and Cyberball, which was about robots playing football. People loved that one. The fighter pilot games with the seats and joystick were always packed, too."

Taking a Lickin' from a Chicken

The rotating cast of games was occasionally joined by special novelty games that only lingered for a limited time. For example, Doug remembers Hercules pinball, a giant pinball machine that used pool balls as pinballs.

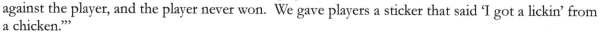

"We brought in another game called Bird Brain, which had a live chicken inside," says Doug. "The idea was for players to play tic-tac-toe with the chicken, which was inside a glass box.

"The player had a string on the outside, and the chicken had one on the inside. It seemed like the chicken was playing tic-tac-toe, but really, a light would come on, and the chicken was trained to peck at the light to try to get a bit of seed. The pecking would trigger the chicken's 'selection,' but it was actually a computer that played against the player, and the player never won. We gave players a sticker that said 'I got a lickin' from a chicken.'"

According to Doug, there were actually two chickens that came to the store to "play" Bird Brain, due to possible Humane Society concerns over treatment of the animals. "One was the day chicken and the other was the night chicken, so neither bird was overworked. We had an elaborate swimming pool set up in the back for them, and they got fed and bathed. We had all the provisions the chickens needed and made sure they were happy."

Time-Out also sponsored non-game promotional events, including a Go Kart track. "We set up the track in the parking lot and ran it for two or three weeks at a time. We did it in coordination with the Mall," says Doug.

Ticket to Paradise

The constant alteration of the game lineup wasn't the only change that Time-Out underwent through the years. The introduction of ticketed machines, for example, was a major shift in the arcade's approach.

"Somewhere around the middle of my career, we started using tickets and prizes," says Doug. "The skee-ball games would dispense tickets based on the points earned by a player. We had cases of merchandise, and each item had a value in tickets. Players could trade the tickets for merchandise, which was a big change for us and something much different than what we'd done before. That's when our revenue really increased."

Paul had an eye-opening experience with the ticketed games and prizes once. "I thought I was going to get fired. The district manager was in, and he pulled me into the office and said, 'A customer told me that you told her son that he didn't have enough tickets to get a prize, and you told him that you find tickets on the floor all the time and gave him a prize anyway.' I thought I was going to get fired over this stuffed toy, but the district manager said, 'The customer happens to be my sister-in-law, and she had a bad day, and you helped out her son, thank you.' I was like, oh man, I thought I was going to get fired, and I ended up getting complimented," says Paul.

A Polygraph Is Not a Video Game

As Paul discovered, careers at Time-Out could sometimes be rewarding in unexpected ways.

Traditional rewards could be won, too, as Doug found when his career trajectory propelled him into management.

After a promotion from attendant to store manager, he became district manager in 1977 and regional manager in '79. The regional manager job kept him on the road a lot, selecting store locations and opening new Time-Outs. "Often, I had to determine how big a game room would be in terms of annual revenue. I had a lot of experience in that and was asked to put a revenue number on a corn field once in Iowa, because they were opening a mall there," remembers Doug.

He also participated in the hiring process, which always involved the use of a lie detector. "Tico wanted to keep the family image and make sure every employee had a thorough background check," explains Doug. "Every applicant who went through the interview process had to take a polygraph test. Even if you just wanted to work ten hours making change, you had to take the polygraph.

"The test administrator asked about drug and alcohol use. It was very intensive. The closest polygraph we could find was located in Pittsburgh, so every time I hired someone, I had to put them in my car and drive them out to Pittsburgh and have them take the polygraph," says Doug.

The care taken in selecting the best job candidates paid off in the long term. According to Doug, he and the other managers strove for excellence and formed a bond that stood the test of time.

"As I came up through the company, the other managers and I all stayed with Time-Out for 15-20 years. We became a close-knit group of guys, a real band of brothers.

"We had a week-long regional managers' meeting at the end of each year, and that solidified our camaraderie. We worked together for the betterment of Time-Out," says Doug.

Who Got the Last High Score?

By the time the 90s rolled around, Doug had four district managers, more than 100 employees, and over a million dollars in management under him. Thanks to the popularity and success of Time-Out, he was able to buy a home and stay in the Johnstown area with his family. He also got extensive training and education, paid for by the company.

But things soon changed...and not for the better. Tico sold Time-Out to a company called Edison Brothers. That company, in turn, filed for Chapter 11 bankruptcy in 1995 and sold Time-Out to Namco, the Japanese game manufacturer that owned the Cyberstation chain of arcades.

Time-Out, which had spawned more than 100 stores coast-to-coast and in Puerto Rico, was out of time.

The sweet ride was over, and Doug knew it. He got out in 1999 after 25 years with Time-Out. Today, he works for Garnell Packaging in Geistown, where he's been since 2001.

Paul left, too, and works in tech support for a cable company these days. He has also performed in a number of Shakespeare productions staged at Stackhouse Park by the Band of Brothers troupe.

Both guys realize they were part of a unique organization at a singular point in time, when videogame arcades were at their peak, and every mall had one. These days, most gaming is home-based, and brick and mortar malls are fading as shopping goes in the same direction.

But for Doug and Paul, and all those players who cheered and laughed as they hammered out high scores on battered consoles in the dark arcade, Time-Out will remain forever blinking and beeping in their dreams and memories. And there will always be someone ready with a red quarter to spring for a free game.

Courtesy Jim O'Roark

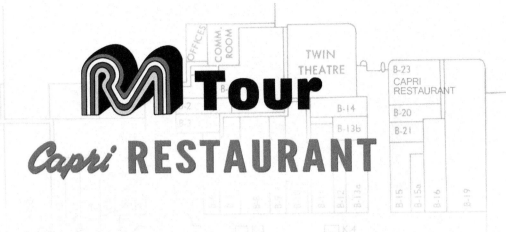

Of all the businesses that were once part of the Richland Mall, only one still operates under its original name on the site once occupied by the Mall: Capri Pizza.

The owner, Shirley DiRosa, still runs the show after all these years, serving the same menu items that she did in 1974. Her restaurant keeps the Richland Mall spirit alive and well in the Richland Town Centre, as she continues to serve the same customers that she did 43 years ago.

Late Bloomers

The Capri story started in New Castle, Pennsylvania in '74. Shirley and her husband were running a Capri restaurant in the New Castle Mall when they found out about the new Richland Mall opening in Johnstown. They drove out to look at the space and ended up making a deal with Jim Streeter and the Unimich partners to open a restaurant.

That was the easy part. Because of the many complications that came with getting a restaurant up and running, Capri wasn't ready for the Mall's grand opening on November 4th, 1974. Most of the other stores opened on time, while Capri remained shuttered.

"It's easier for other businesses to launch," explains Shirley. "With clothing stores, which they call shoeboxes, employees can go in and set up and be ready relatively quickly. With a restaurant like Capri, though, you have gas lines, water lines, and special electrical lines to worry about.

"We had to have high-voltage electricity running into Capri – around 480, I think. Everything had to be put in special, so it took a little longer for us to open than other businesses in the Mall."

No Wine with Dinner

The new Capri finally opened to the public in early November 1974. The restaurant was 3,200 square feet in size, with seating for 125 people. It included tables and booths, four pizza ovens, a large kitchen, and a back stockroom.

Courtesy Shirley DiRosa

To run the place effectively, 30 employees were needed – a mix of full-timers and part-timers. During operating hours, it took two workers just to man the pizza ovens.

The owners worked as hard as the rest of the staff, getting the restaurant up to speed and keeping the customers happy. Shirley prepared lasagna, manicotti, stuffed shells, and other dishes, helping to fill orders as they arrived.

The menu included Neapolitan and Sicilian pizzas, which were available by the pie or slice. Pasta dishes included spaghetti, shells, and rigatoni with meatballs, Italian sausage, tomato, meat, mushroom, or clam sauce. There were baked specialties such as lasagna, ravioli, manicotti, and veal or eggplant parmigiana. Capri also served a selection of hero sandwiches and a variety of salads, including an Italian salad, antipasto salad, chicken salad, and tuna salad, which turned out to be one of the most popular menu items.

One thing Capri did *not* have was alcohol. "We chose not to bring in beer and wine because we were so close to Time-Out and the movie theaters, which would attract a lot of young people," says Shirley. "According to PLCB rules, if we had offered alcohol, we wouldn't have been able to have open doors, which we did. We couldn't have had young people in the restaurant by themselves...and young people were important to our business. So we made the decision to leave out alcohol and welcome every age group. We decided we wanted to be a family restaurant."

Happiness Is a Warm Mall

The Capri team's choices paid off, as the restaurant attracted steady business from the start. It became a gathering place for kids and teens who congregated at Time-Out and the Duke and Duchess theaters, and a meeting place for Mall employees.

"Workers from the different stores would come by for lunch," remembers Shirley. "I got to know a lot of them, and they were really nice. I developed some lasting friendships with those people. If they needed something, I would help them, and vice versa."

Shirley also found friendship among the Mall's management team, including General Manager Bob McConnell. "I had a good friendship with all of them. Even when times were bad, they tried to help us as much as they could.

"Like we all said, 'We're a family.' We tried to help each other and do the best we could," says Shirley.

At the Richland Mall in those days, there was plenty of friendliness and support to go around. "Everybody was always happy. We looked out for each other and made the Mall a safe and pleasant place. You could walk around and not worry about any kind of safety issues.

"My two children, for example, grew up at the Mall, because I worked every day. They would come in, and I didn't have to worry about them. They would go over to Sears, sit on the couch, and watch TV with the guys who were selling furniture there. Then, they'd walk clear to Kmart, which was on the other end of the Mall,

and the guards and tenants would see them and keep an eye on them. I didn't have to worry.

"Today, on the other hand, forget it. I don't think I would even let one of my children out of my sight, if they were that age today," says Shirley.

Catered To

Ten years after Capri opened in the Mall, Shirley and her team stumbled upon a new opportunity. Employees of Penelec liked Capri's food so much, they approached Shirley about catering an event. She decided to give it a try…and it led to a whole new line of business for Capri that's still cooking today.

"We ended up catering lunches for Penelec's training school. We catered events for them for the next 30 years.

"Our catering business took off from there, as more and more clients ordered our food. It's still a huge part of our business, catering for companies, organizations, hospitals, doctors' offices, you name it.

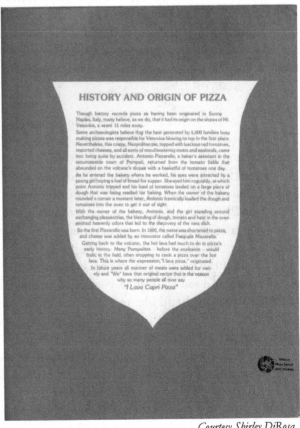

Courtesy Shirley DiRosa

135

"We still have at least three delivery vehicles on the road every day, traveling to local clients. Filling all those orders is a lot of work, a lot of cooking and preparing, because I still make everything fresh, the old-fashioned way," says Shirley.

Back in the Richland Mall days, Capri also catered holiday parties for Mall staff and tenants, sharing the job with the Encore. The relationship between the two catering and restaurant operations was always a friendly competition, free of animus.

"We were all friends," says Shirley. "I always got along well with Larry Mummert, who owned the Encore. We were part of the same Richland Mall family."

Bye, Bye, American Pizza Pie

Between its table service and catering businesses, Capri might have cruised along forever in the Mall location. Unfortunately, that option ended in 1997.

"I got a certified letter on October 8th. It said I had to have my doors closed within 30 days," recalls Shirley. "It was sad. It was like being thrown out of my house after 20 years.

"We built that store from the ground up. In the beginning, it was just dirt and steel beams. We built it ourselves, and now we were being told we had to get out."

The midsection of the Mall was closing. Capri had to vacate its space, like all the other tenants in the midsection area.

During the restaurant's last 30 days in the Mall, Shirley and her team used up the last of their stock, serving their last customers in the Mall location. At the same time, they made arrangements to break down their equipment and furnishings and get out.

At the end of the 30 days, Capri's doors closed for the last time in the Richland Mall. It took another month and a half after that to disassemble everything and clear it out.

When the place was finally empty, there wasn't much left to do. "I closed the door and gave them the key. That was the end of it. There was nothing we could do about it."

At least, by then, Shirley had a Capri location in downtown Johnstown. She could continue to make a living, though it seemed she was done with running restaurants in Richland Township.

Emphasis on *seemed*.

A Little Piece of the Richland Mall

For a while, Shirley lived her life according to the new status quo. She put all her energy into Capri downtown, running her table service and catering business lines out of that one location.

Then, in 2003, she got wind of the new Richland Town Centre development planned for the Mall's former site. So did lots of other people.

"I had five people in one day ask me to come back to Richland. 'Are you gonna go in the new shopping center?' 'Are you gonna do it?' 'Well, I'll see,' I told them...and I started thinking it might be a good idea.

"I called the people who were developing the plaza and talked to them. They got all my information and said, 'We'll let you know if we're interested.' A couple of weeks later, they called me back and said they'd like to have me in their plaza," says Shirley.

Years later, Capri in the Richland Town Centre is a success story...and a throwback to the glory days of the Richland Mall.

The recipes are still the same, though there are more choices on the menu than in the old days. One item, in particular, is a tribute to the Mall years and one of Shirley's good friends from then until now. "Gil Demos of Hush Puppies (and, later, C. Gil's Shoes) had a heart attack, and he had to go on a special diet. When he came in for lunch at Capri in the Mall, he said, 'I need a special salad. Would you make it for me?' So I made this salad for him. It was all fresh vegetables: broccoli, cauliflower, carrots, celery, and lettuce with cheese. People would see it and say, 'What's that salad?' I told them, 'It's a Gil Salad.' And people started ordering it by name. It's still on our menu in the Town Centre Capri – 'Richland Mall's Original Gil Salad.'"

Other friends and fans of the Mall continue to frequent Capri, often reminiscing about the good old days. For them, Capri in the Town Centre is like a little piece of the Richland Mall that survived the closing and demolition. "Customers will come in and sit down, and someone will start talking about the Richland Mall, and others will join in from two or three tables away.

"You could come into my store probably any day, and if you start talking about the Richland Mall, people across the aisle will tell you, 'Oh, it was so great, it was one of the best malls, I really miss it.' And you'll see people who worked in the Mall. They'll just join in talking to you and say, 'Oh yeah, I worked here or there, it was so good.'

"We have folks who come in and say, 'Boy, they should have a Time-Out across from here. Then it would really be like the Mall, because we already have Capri and then the movie theaters behind it," says Shirley.

Photo by Philip Balko

137

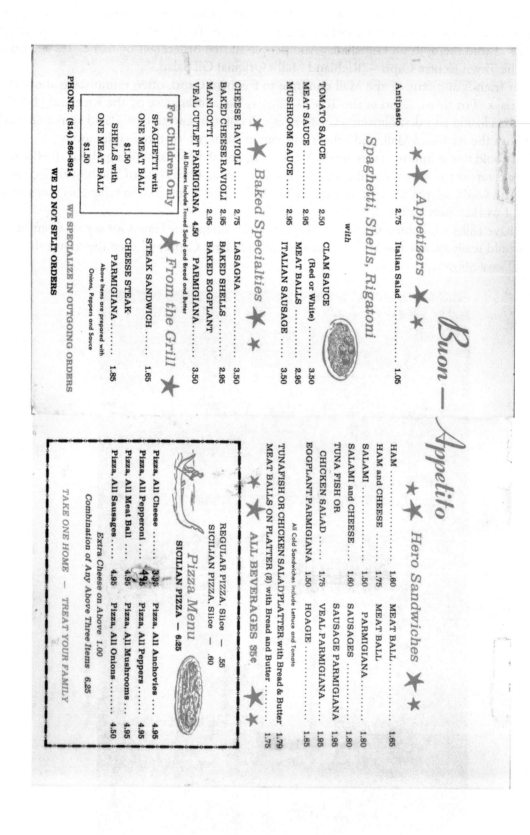

Buon — Appetito

★ ★ Appetizers ★ ★

Antipasto .... 2.75   Italian Salad 1.05

Spaghetti, Shells, Rigatoni

with

TOMATO SAUCE 2.50	CLAM SAUCE
MEAT SAUCE 2.95	(Red or White) 3.50
MUSHROOM SAUCE 2.95	MEAT BALLS 2.95
	ITALIAN SAUSAGE 3.50

★ ★ Baked Specialties ★ ★

CHEESE RAVIOLI 2.75	LASAGNA 3.50
BAKED CHEESE RAVIOLI 2.95	BAKED SHELLS 2.95
MANICOTTI 2.95	BAKED EGGPLANT
VEAL CUTLET PARMIGIANA 4.50	PARMIGIANA 3.50

All Dinners include Tossed Salad and Bread and Butter

★ From the Grill ★

STEAK SANDWICH 1.65

CHEESE STEAK
PARMIGIANA 1.85

Above items are prepared with
Onions, Peppers and Sauce

For Children Only

SPAGHETTI with
ONE MEAT BALL
$1.50

SHELLS with
ONE MEAT BALL
$1.50

PHONE: (814) 266-8914

WE SPECIALIZE IN OUTGOING ORDERS

WE DO NOT SPLIT ORDERS

★ ★ Hero Sandwiches ★ ★

HAM 1.60	MEAT BALL 1.65
HAM and CHEESE 1.75	MEAT BALL
SALAMI 1.50	PARMIGIANA 1.80
SALAMI and CHEESE 1.60	SAUSAGES 1.80
TUNA FISH OR	SAUSAGE PARMIGIANA 1.95
CHICKEN SALAD 1.75	VEAL PARMIGIANA 1.95
EGGPLANT PARMIGIANA 1.50	HOAGIE 1.85

All Cold Sandwiches include Lettuce and Tomato

TUNA FISH OR CHICKEN SALAD PLATTER with Bread and Butter ... 1.79
MEAT BALLS ON PLATTER (2) with Bread and Butter ... 1.75

★ ★ ALL BEVERAGES 35¢ ★ ★

REGULAR PIZZA, Slice — .55
SICILIAN PIZZA, Slice — .60

Pizza Menu

SICILIAN PIZZA — 6.25

Pizza, All Cheese 3.95	Pizza, All Anchovies 4.95
Pizza, All Pepperoni 4.95	Pizza, All Peppers 4.95
Pizza, All Meat Ball 4.95	Pizza, All Mushrooms ... 4.95
Pizza, All Sausages 4.95	Pizza, All Onions 4.50

Extra Cheese on Above 1.00

Combination of Any Above Three Items 6.25

TAKE ONE HOME — TREAT YOUR FAMILY

Courtesy Shirley DiRosa

Tour
Sweet William

If you were hungry for a Nero Gyro or wanted a clown sundae, there was only one place to go in the Richland Mall: Sweet William.

Beloved by Mall customers and employees alike, Sweet William featured an ice cream parlor, a full menu of breakfasts, lunches, and dinners, and two sisters and a sister-in-law who made the biggest orders and busiest days seem like child's play.

Send in the Clown Sundaes

Dorothea Stephens went to work as a waitress at Sweet William in the Richland Mall in 1980, and ended up staying 12 years. Her sister, Pamela, worked alongside her, and their sister-in-law, Jan, managed the restaurant. Whether scooping ice cream, serving meals, ringing up customers, or joking with the regulars, they made Sweet William a fun and delicious place to be.

"I really loved working there," says Dorothea. "Those were the best times of my life."

According to Dorothea, Sweet William was extremely popular back then, drawing steady traffic from shoppers in the Mall. The busiest time was during the height of shopping, from 10 a.m. to 7 p.m. on Saturdays. "We really packed 'em in during that weekly surge. The place was really jumping," remembers Dorothea.

Some customers would just stop in for the hard-packed ice cream, which was known for its quality. "We had 25 flavors at any given time, and it was all Sweet William brand. People said it was the best ice cream in Johnstown, and I agree. My favorite flavor was black cherry, which was beyond delicious."

Since the ice cream was hard-packed, Dorothea and her co-workers had to scoop it out of tubs by hand, then place it in cones — or use it for other sweet treats.

Photo by Robert Jeschonek

139

"Customers could order cones or milkshakes made from whatever flavors we had in the case," says Dorothea. "The shakes were all hand-dipped and served in tall glasses."

Sweet William's famous clown sundaes were all the rage with kids. "We used candy buttons for the eyes and sugar cones for the hat. Kids just loved them. It was a great treat for them to look forward to while shopping with their parents."

One Nero Gyro, Coming Right Up

While many customers had ice cream on their minds, others came to Sweet William in search of a hearty meal.

Early bird shoppers and Mall employees looking to start the day right came in for breakfast specials like omelets, bacon and eggs, and pancakes.

Courtesy Ben Baldwin

For lunch, there were plenty of sandwiches, salads, and other selections on the menu. "We had Reubens, tuna melts, and pita pockets," recalls Dorothea. "The Nero Gyro was a popular item, too, and my favorite. It was a pocket bread stuffed with ham and cheese and onions, plus a special sweet and sour sauce. It was grilled on one side, then flipped and grilled on the other."

When it came to dinner, customers often ordered hamburgers and French fries, meat loaf and mashed potatoes, or liver and onions. Sweet William had an extensive daily menu, plus holiday specials including a turkey dinner at Thanksgiving and ham dinners at Easter and Christmas.

"Those holidays were the busiest times of the year for us," says Dorothea. "We got huge crowds of holiday shoppers stopping in for a break and something to eat."

Photo by Jason Pozar

From Sweet William to Joe Paterno

After spending so much time in Sweet William over the years, Dorothea remembers the layout of the place as if she were there only yesterday.

"The ice cream station was up front," she says. "Next, there was a horseshoe-shaped lunch counter with 15 seats. That's where people sat for coffee, breakfast, or lunch. There was a gang of regular customers from Sears, for example, who always sat there and joked around at lunchtime.

140

Photo by Robert Jeschonek

"Along the windows, there were four booths. There were four booths on the other side of the counter, as well.

"If you walked further back, you came to the dining room, which seated about a hundred people. From front to back, it was a pretty big restaurant, really."

It was big enough to keep 13-14 employees busy every day, including waitresses, cooks, dishwashers, and the manager. For Dorothea, that meant 3-4 days per week on the schedule, working a typical shift from 8:00 a.m. to 3:00 p.m.

"My sister Pamela and I would get $125 to $150 per day in tips," says Dorothea. "We were good waitresses, and it paid off for us."

Keeping an eye on her future, Dorothea spent her tips on nursing classes, eventually leaving Sweet William for a new career. She moved to State College in 1992 and found a job as a Certified Nursing Assistant at a nursing home.

While there, she helped care for the mother of Penn State University football head coach Joe Paterno. She became a friend of the family and even got to attend Joe's 70th birthday party.

Another job led her to Mount Nittany Hospital, where she continued her career in the medical field. These days, she's retired from the healthcare world and works as a receptionist at the offices of the American Association of Retired People in downtown Johnstown.

But she still looks back on her days at Sweet William as a happy time spent with good friends and family.

"It was really nice working there. My sister, sister-in-law, and I got along great. The whole crew was great. We worked hard and helped each other get through the day. It's good to know we made so many people happy at Sweet William," says Dorothea.

Courtesy Steve Grimes

mall and tenant data

richland mall fact sheet

PART I   THE PROJECT

Project Name: Richland Mall

Opening Date: October 9, 1974

Location: Richland Mall is located in sub-urban Johnstown, Pennsylvania approximately 75 miles east of Pittsburgh.

Major Access Highways: Traffic Route 219 running north/south, and State Route 756 running east/west.

Tentative Improvements To Major Highways: Improvements on 756 from Geistown to 219. 219 will go south from Somerset to the Maryland line and north from Ebensburg to Interstate 80 to New York.

Owner/Developer: A development of Uni-mich Development Corporation.

Size Of Project: 650,000 square feet.

Gross Leasable Area: 550,000 square feet.

Total Number Of Planned Phases: One

Population Within Primary/Secondary Markets: 364,000.

Average Family Income Within Primary/Secondary Markets: $10,378.

Number Of Parking Facilities: 2670

Financing: American Fletcher, Indianapolis, Indiana

PART II   THE STORES

Major Department Stores:

Penn Traffic
a. **Total square footage:** 70,000 square feet
b. **Architect:** Steenwyck and Thrall, Grand Rapids, Michigan
c. **Engineers:** Progressive Engineers of Grand Rapids, Grand Rapids, Michigan
d. **Contractor:** Robert E. Fryling, Grand Rapids, Michigan

Sears
a. **Total square footage:** 117,000 square feet
b. **Architect:** Allen B. Mitchell, Pittsburgh, Pennsylvania
c. **Contractor:** Wilson Construction Company, Johnstown, Pennsylvania

K-mart
a. **Total square footage:** 84,180 square feet
b. **Architect:** Steenwyck and Thrall, Grand Rapids, Michigan
c. **Engineers:** Progressive Engineers of Grand Rapids
d. **Contractor:** Robert E. Fryling, Grand Rapids, Michigan

Smaller Stores and Specialty Shops
a. **Number:** 85
b. **Total square footage:** 243,310 square feet

Just for you-

Yes, the entire shopping experience of Richland Mall was determined with you in mind. The architectural designs of circular and half-circular columns highlighted by bright reds, blues and yellows were carefully chosen to enhance the beauty of the area. On the interior the natural look is dominated by beautifully landscaped trees and shrubs surrounded by natural Pennsylvania boulders.

Plus three major department stores and many specialty shops all chosen to make your shopping experience a pleasant one . . . and all just for you!

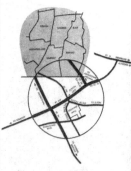

Richland Mall will serve a 6 county area and is located off traffic route 219 and State Road 756.

Courtesy Jim O'Roark

Tour
Hush Puppies
Teeks
C. Gil's Shoes

One man built five different stores in the Richland Mall, and all of them sold shoes. By the time the Mall closed in 1998, Gil Demos had built Hush Puppies, Hush Puppies for Kids, Stride Rite, Naturalizer, and C. Gil Shoes. He was also instrumental in bringing other businesses to the Richland Mall, including Cinnabon, The Appliance Store, and Schultz Waterbeds.

But before all that, his Mall career started at a place called Teeks Fine Shoes.

Courtesy Gil Demos

Malls 101

Gil was a charter member of the Richland Mall tenants' roster, managing Teeks from the Mall's grand opening on November 4, 1974. He'd been working for Teeks near Pittsburgh and in Steubenville, Ohio for years by then, and this was his chance to expand his talents.

"It had the potential to be a high-volume store, so I was excited," he remembers. "My wife, Deborah, and I came up when they were building the store, and it was inspiring. I thought it was a great opportunity."

When the Mall and Teeks were finished, Gil was ready for action – though not everyone who paid him a visit was on the same page. "Back in those days, in this town, people didn't always understand the concept of a mall. It was surprising to me, coming from Pittsburgh, because I'd grown up with malls, but there was sometimes a bit of a learning curve.

"In the Mall's early days, for example, an older gentleman came in and wanted to purchase a pair of shoes from me. He handed me a Sears credit card, and I said, 'Oh, that's a Sears credit card, you can't use that here.' He said, 'Oh, I thought the whole *Mall* was Sears.' Folks like him were just used to places like Glosser Bros., where everything was under one roof, but purchases were made from a single company. I said, 'No, this is a separate store. These are all separate stores in the Mall.' I had to explain the concept of a mall to him," says Gil.

People got the idea soon enough, though, and business at Teeks picked up after a slow start… but no one foresaw how the store would get its biggest boost.

Making It Rain

"I must have jinxed it," says Gil. "Three of us guys were standing in the Mall, talking about how business was finally improving a little. I was saying, 'We're really going to do well here, I feel it, I sense it. There's not much that can stop us now.'

"The next morning, I woke up and got ready to go to work. I walked outside, and my neighbor asked me what I was doing. 'I'm going to work,' I told him. 'You're not going to work,' he said. 'Johnstown is completely flooded.'

"It was July 20th, 1977, the day of the Johnstown Flood. True story," says Gil.

It was a disaster that left the city and surrounding area in ruins. The Mall was relatively unscathed, however, and tenants like Teeks experienced an unexpected impact that altered their long-term outlooks.

"People started bringing in vouchers to pay for purchases," recalls Gil. "I called my boss and asked if we could accept them, and he told me I could. People could use them to buy shoes, and we would get reimbursed.

"All of a sudden, the Mall took off. That's when things really started to happen. The sales volume almost doubled overnight. There were no stores left downtown, so shoppers were forced to come to the Mall, and it was like Christmas every day for years.

"I think the same thing probably would have happened without the flood, but it wouldn't have been as quick. But that flood came, shut everybody else down in the city, and shoppers had to come to our Mall," says Gil.

Courtesy Gil Demos

It's Only Naturalizer

Business at Teeks continued to increase through the years, and so did Gil's responsibilities. Eventually, he was promoted to overseeing all 30 stores in the Teeks chain.

But over time, his frustration with Teeks grew. "They wouldn't change their merchandising and marketing. They were stubborn and wouldn't change with the times," says Gil.

In 1981, he decided to find out if another company, Naturalizer Shoes, would be interested in opening a store in the Richland Mall.

The answer was yes. Naturalizer Shoes seemed like a perfect fit. "Naturalizer liked the location, and I liked what they had to offer. Concept stores like theirs were popular at the time, offering specialty shoes, special sizes, and so on."

However, as Gil built the Naturalizer store, there were complications. Teeks found out about the new venture and sued the Richland Mall over an exclusivity clause in their contract that limited the opening of competing shoe stores. If Teeks won the lawsuit, Gil wouldn't be able to open Naturalizer, and his investment in the store would be lost.

Deciding it wasn't worth the risk, Gil sold the Naturalizer store to another party. Things worked out for the new owner, as Teeks' lawsuit failed to prevent the store from opening.

The new owner ran Naturalizer in the Richland Mall for years before putting the business up for sale. That was when Teeks ended up buying it, and Gil – who'd built the store in the first place – ended up running it for them.

Next Steps in Shoes

Gil continued to work for Teeks, but he hadn't given up hope of finding the right opportunity for his next step in the shoe business. In 1987, he stuck a toe in the water with another company, Hush Puppies Shoes, and decided he liked their style.

Again, Gil made plans to open a new store – but this time, before getting too far down the road, he offered the opportunity to Teeks. Teeks turned it down, which freed him from observing any exclusivity clause and worrying about legal action from his employer.

With Teeks out of the mix, Gil was able to finalize his deal with Wolverine Worldwide, owner of Hush Puppies, and get the new store set up in the Mall. "I got a terrific location next to my friend Joe Cohen's La Rose store. Joe sold clothing that would complement my shoes. Hush Puppies made more mature, comfortable footwear, and Joe had more mature, comfortable clothing. So we would be a real draw for each other."

Photo by Chuck Mamula

Gil quit his job at Teeks and opened the Hush Puppies store in 1988. He was committed, but the new venture was stressful in the beginning. Faced with true independence as a store owner for the first time, Gil worried about the consequences of his actions.

"Even though I had all that vast shoe experience, I didn't truly understand the concept of being on my own, being independent, and it frightened me. Thank God I had great friends like Joe Cohen and Joe Fortunato, who were independent businessmen. They told me, 'You're gonna love it. Don't worry about it.' Then there was my friend Larry Mummert at the Encore, who sat me down one evening and encouraged me over Long Island iced teas. He said, as many other friends did, 'You have to open the store, you have to open the store, you have to open the store.' So I opened the store."

Taking that leap was only part of the battle, though. There were plenty of complications at the get-go. "For one thing, I was way under-inventoried. And I'd borrowed a lot of money to open up the store, but I didn't have access to that money yet. According to the terms of the loan, I couldn't get that cash until I started making payments, which I hadn't done yet.

"So when I threw the gate open, I didn't have any petty cash on hand. I wasn't set up for credit card sales. I had nothing, and I just felt I like either I had to open up, or I was never going to do it.

Courtesy Gil Demos

145

"But then I did hundreds of dollars' worth of business in my first few hours. The Mall was really busy, people came in my store, and the sales were all cash," says Gil.

And business took off from there. Gil's Hush Puppies went on to win an award for the most outstanding new store in the company. "We went from zero to top sales, the best performance for a newly-opened store in Hush Puppies' history. The only shoe store I couldn't beat in the Richland Mall was Foot Locker, which was an athletic store and did the most sales per square foot.

"My store was so successful, I didn't even have to draw the money I'd borrowed from the bank. That's how strong that Mall was back in the day. It was really the place to shop," says Gil.

The Secret of the "C"

Once Gil had mastered life as an independent businessman, there was no turning back. He made his next move in 1990, buying a Buster Brown children's shoe store from a friend who'd opened it in the Mall.

Gil rebuilt the store from scratch, converting it from Buster Brown to Hush Puppies for Kids. The store had colorful, kid-friendly décor with neon lights and a built-in wide-screen color TV on which cartoons and other children's programming constantly played.

"We made it a fun store to appeal to kids," says Gil. "It was such a beautiful store, it even made it into the publication *Footwear News*."

Hush Puppies for Kids was a hit, which only encouraged Gil to try another venture. In 1991, he talked Joe Cohen of La Rose into going in with him on a new shoe store to take the place of Teeks, which had closed.

Joe didn't want his name to be part of the store's name, but Gil convinced him to at least contribute an initial.

"We used the first letter of his last name, Cohen, followed by my full first name. That's how 'C. Gil's Shoes' was born," explains Gil.

Unfortunately, this latest business didn't start strong, thanks to intense competition from the Galleria. "When we opened C. Gil's, it didn't go as planned. It was a little bit sluggish at first. The reason is, Boscov's in the Galleria had opened two months earlier and just sucked the shoe-buying economy dry. I was getting reports that their shoe department was doing record numbers, as in hundreds of thousands of dollars. I know that to be true because it was my business to know what was going on.

Photo by Chuck Mamula

"They just took all the shoe dollars, so we had a very slow start. We were like walking zombies for a while as the business almost flatlined. But finally, we put out a good advertising campaign, and that brought the store to life."

Eventually, Gil bought out Joe, and another plan took shape. Sensing there was room to grow sales on the kids' side of the business, Gil opened a Stride Rite store next door to C. Gil's Shoes. He combined the two into one big store under the name Stride Rite Shoes.

What would Gil do next? How many more stores would he build at the Mall?

Photo by Philip Balko

The answer became clear in late 1997. It was zero.

Mall Things Must Pass

When the Galleria arrived in 1992, business at the Richland Mall began to slow down. The gradual fade continued over the following years, in spite of efforts to stay afloat.

Courtesy Gil Demos

Courtesy Gil Demos

Courtesy Gil Demos

"The Mall Associates remodeled the place and brought in a carousel. We did lots of promotions, and we were doing all right, but we couldn't attract any new stores. Brand-name stores all wanted to go to the sexy new mall. They didn't want to come to our Mall," remembers Gil.

"I would meet with Jim Streeter and Bob McConnell on a weekly basis. We would have lunch and talk about what we could do to improve and save the Mall. We did everything. We even had outside consultants come in to help us compete and so on, but it didn't work because we just didn't have the power to draw in new stores. We just couldn't get new stores in. And we could get none of the chains. They were all going to the Galleria. So it got pretty bad. It got really slow."

Finally, in '97, the word came down that the main section of the Mall would be closing. All the merchants in that section, including Gil, would have to vacate the place by March 31st, 1998.

As slow as things had gotten, Gil still hated to leave. "They had to push me out," he says. "I'd spent half my life in that Mall. I didn't want to go."

He was out of options, though. On the advice of Jim Streeter, he arranged to move C. Gil's Shoes and Hush Puppies to the Galleria.

He knew he had to do it to survive, but the process of closing up shop and getting ready to move was still painful. "We were just very disappointed. None of us wanted to see this happen.

"But certain people helped make it a little easier. The Zamias family, for example, was very receptive to my relocating to the Galleria. They made the transition easy for me.

"Also, Waste Management cut me a break. As I was closing my Richland Mall stores, I generated a huge pile of garbage. It was *huge*. It took I don't know how many trucks to haul it away. And I figured it was going to cost me a lot of money to get rid of it all. But when I called Waste Management about the bill, they told me they weren't going to charge me. They forgave the bill. What a first-class outfit," says Gil.

Not a Love Connection

Soon, C. Gil's Shoes and Hush Puppies were open for business at the Galleria. Many customers followed them from the Richland Mall, so the money kept flowing…but the Galleria was a different world than the Richland Mall had been.

"There weren't many independents at the Galleria at that time, just national chains," says Gil. "It's a huge difference, less of a family of self-employed and independent merchants. The Richland Mall had 30 or 40 independents at any given time, which helped create its unique character.

"It was harder to make friends at the Galleria, too. Maybe it was because I was so much older by then. Many of the managers were younger, as I'd been during my early days at the Richland Mall.

"I didn't even know my neighbors at the Galleria. The Richland Mall, on the other hand, had been smaller, more intimate, and more like home."

The fit wasn't great, and Gil moved when he got the chance. Rejecting a lease renewal at the Galleria in 2004, he closed both stores and opened C. Gil's Shoes at a new location in the East Hills Plaza on Scalp Avenue. The new store was a success from the start, and Gil is still running it today.

"My business went up fifty percent the first year," says Gil. "It really did well, because I was more of a destination store. Customers knew me and sought me out. Plus this location has easy access. You can park close to the door and get in and out quickly."

Still Getting His Kicks

According to Gil, his formula for success still applies to today's footwear market. "We carry better, comfort footwear. We carry brand names. My prices are around a hundred dollars and up. Customers seek out the better footwear I carry for better quality and fit.

"I'm dealing with probably fifteen or twenty percent of the population in this area, and I probably only get five to eight percent of that, customer-wise. That works out to about sixty five hundred steady customers."

He says he loves his customers and is grateful for their support through the years. "They've been loyal to me. They've followed me from location to location, and I have a very good rapport with them. I'm a lucky, lucky man, to be honest with you."

Gil's current customers include children and grandchildren of his original customers from the Richland Mall days. "After all these years, I've waited on four generations of some families. When the original customers come in, some of them are in their eighties or nineties now...though I'm no spring chicken myself these days.

"When those customers come in the store, if I'm not busy, sometimes we'll just sit and talk for half an hour. They'll just sit, and we'll talk and catch up."

Sooner or later, the Richland Mall comes up in conversation, and the memories are always good.

"The Richland Mall was right-sized, right everything," says Gil. "Had that other mall not been built, the Richland Mall would be thriving today.

"Going to that Mall was like a social event. Customers would come in, they would sit down, and we would talk. It was more of a community social event for them.

"Not to mention, the Mall gave many of us our start in life. The Richland Mall provided us with opportunities, and we ran with them. I appreciate all of it and every minute of the time I spent there.

"I feel like the richest man on Earth because I've made a lot of friends and know a lot of great people. You don't get wealthy in this business, but I've made a comfortable living for 52 years, enjoying what I do. I've absolutely loved it through good times and bad times alike, and I'll never forget that the Richland Mall helped make it all possible," says Gil.

Courtesy Gil Demos

Tour

spencer gifts

Jim White

Everything you wanted but nothing you needed. That's what you could always find at Spencer Gifts in the Richland Mall, according to former store manager Jim White.

When Jim worked there, Spencer carried everything from lava lamps to posters to incense. It was a microcosm of 70s pop culture and a haven of "cool"...plus the only place in the Mall where you could buy certain "adult" goodies (if you were old enough and could prove it).

If one place in the Mall could be said to push the boundaries of taste and social mores, Spencer's was it. But it also pushed the boundaries in another way, as well.

It was one of the first stores in the Richland Mall to be managed by an African-American.

Trailblazing Boss

When Jim transferred from Spencer Gifts in the Monroeville Mall in 1978, he was "kind of a novelty." According to Jim, there was just one other African-American working in the Richland Mall, in a clothing store. Jim isn't sure if he was a manager or an employee.

"Both black and white people were curious," he remembers. "Once they found out I was at the Mall, I'd see people who'd walk by the store and then two minutes later walk by the store again, looking in. I'd always say 'Hey, come on in and visit.' My personality was the same back then, always friendly. I never had any problems with anyone."

The Mall, and Johnstown itself, turned out to be a great fit for Jim. He got to know the area thanks to co-workers of his wife, who worked at Sears, and he joined the Mall Merchants Association. He often had lunch at Sweet William with his fellow managers and business owners.

Meanwhile, in Spencer Gifts, he presented his curious clientele with a wide-ranging variety of products, which in most cases could not be found anywhere else in the Mall.

Hey Kid, You Can't Go Back There

According to Jim, Spencer Gifts started as a mail order company, selling novelty items through a magazine. The novelty concept continued when the company moved to brick-and-mortar stores like the one in the Richland Mall.

"We had a gag department, a blacklight department, and a poster department," recalls Jim. "Many of the posters we sold were from Universal Studios movies, since Universal owned Spencer Gifts.

"We sold a lot of incense, which you could smell as soon as you walked in the store. We sold a lot of t-shirts, too. We used to print logos and graphic tees. We would do it right there, next to the poster and blacklight sections.

"We also sold a line of unique lights. We had something called a lava light that balanced on a platform and contained glowing waves that moved like an ocean. We had fiber optic lights called sunburst lights that were popular items. When I was in Monroeville, I sold one to Manny Sanguillén once."

Spencer's also featured a selection of costume jewelry and a department of adult merchandise. No one under 21 was allowed in that department, which was the only place in the Mall where customers could buy grown-up toys for the bedroom.

Then there was the scary stuff, which came out around Halloween. "We sold a ton of Halloween costumes every year. We had a whole wall of them, and they were all related to movies from Universal Studios. Universal had a trademark on those, so only Spencer's could sell them. We had Frankenstein and Wolfman costumes that looked like the versions of those characters from Universal horror movies. We also had masks of characters from popular Universal movies made between 1975 and 1980."

Out of all these items, what was the most popular? "We had this little train toy, and all the train did was go around the tracks, flip over, and go back around the tracks. That thing was the most popular item in the store. It sold for $7.99, and we couldn't keep it in stock, especially during Christmas. We were always backordered on that one at Christmas time."

The Merry Prankster

Jim worked at Spencer's in the Mall for two years before changing career gears, but he made the most of his time at the store.

He especially got a kick out of teasing kids when he got the chance.

"The office was in the back behind a two-way mirror. I could see into the store, but customers could only see their reflections. Once in a while, I'd be back there, and I'd see kids cutting up in the back of the store, and they didn't know I was there. Then I'd jump out scare the heck out of them," remembers Jim.

He also put the Halloween costumes to good use, dressing up and standing in front of the store like a mannequin. "We had these things called Flippies, and they were like popsicles that pushed up. When you flipped your hand, the Flippie would flip four or five feet in front of you. I would flick it just as kids were walking by, and they would jump.

"Once in a while, I would stand out there, and the kids would come up and didn't realize I wasn't a mannequin. Sometimes, I'd flick the Flippie at them, and they'd jump. Other times, they'd be checking out my mask, which had an eye hanging out, and I'd say 'How you doing, buddy?' and scare them. I loved seeing how people would react to those kinds of jokes," says Jim.

Looking Back…with One Eye Hanging Out?

Though sales rose 3-5 percent annually under Jim's leadership, he left Spencer's after two years and went to work as a salesman for a company that sold energy-saving lightbulbs. After that, he moved to the steel industry, working as a structural steel fabricator for Griffith Custer Steel for 12 years. Next, he became Director of Community Development for the City of Johnstown, a job he retired from in 2012.

These days, he occasionally meets Gil Demos, Joe Fortunato, Joe Cohen, and Frank Koscis for breakfast and talks about the old days at the Richland Mall. Though he went on to bigger and better things, he still treasures his time at the Mall.

"I enjoyed working there. It was a great experience and helped prepare me for other challenges. Plus, it was so much fun!" says Jim. "I wonder if I still have that mask with the one eye hanging out."

Photo by Chuck Mamula

Mall's $3 million to $5 million project includes redesigned entrances.

MALL

Continued from Page 1

include Sender Ornamental Iron Works and Chapple Bros. Roofing, both of Johnstown, and Morocco Electric and Berti Excavating, both of Somerset.

Additional changes at the mall will include the Richland Mall Cinemas expanding to 12 theaters and an additional anchor store to replace Sears, which will relocate to the Galleria Mall in October. Streeter said final talks are ongoing with a new anchor store. He expects a decision by early fall.

A new shoe store called C. Gil's Shoes will set up shop in the former Teeks Shoe Store, and Wall to Wall Video & Sound will remodel the former National Record Mart store.

Other tenants planning to remodel will include Family Pantry, Franks 'N Stuff, Hushpuppie Shoes and Watchmaker Jewelry. The mall information booth will also undergo some face-lifts.

Mall officials are referring to the overall renovation project as a "renovation compensation" to past loyal customers.

"The stores will offer some unbeatable deals to the public," McConnell said. "This will be one way tenants will be able to participate in this renovation project."

McConnell said the project will be completed in 15 weeks.

"We anticipate the smallest amount of disruption," he

Richland Mall stores

AAA Mid-State Auto	Kay Bee Toys
Altmeyers	Kay Jewelers
American Outfitters	Kinderfoto
Bermans	Kinney Shoes
Brooks Fashions	Kwons Jewelers
Burtons Men's Store	LaRose
Campus Hairstyling	Lane Bryant
Capers	Life Uniform
Capri Pizza	Linda's
Century-21	Long John Silvers
Chess King	McDonald's
Chic Wig	Millers Flowers
Cinderella Showcase	Mommy & Me
Cinnabon	Motherhood Maternity
Claire's Boutique	Musselman Jewelers
Commercial Credit	Natural Compliments
Crown Jewelers	No Name
Dreams Unlimited Travel	Only One Dollar
Duke & Duchess Theatres	Ormonds
Encore Restaurant	Oswald's Music
Family Pantry	Pearle Vision Center
Fashion Bug	Ponderosa Steakhouse
Fines Men's Shop	Radio Shack
Foot Locker	Regis Hairstyling
Foxmoor	Richland Mall Cinemas
Franks 'N Stuff	Sears
GTE Phone Mart	She
Gallery Cards & Gifts	Shoe World
Gardners Candies	Somerset Trust Co.
General Nutrition Center	Spencer Gifts
Gordons Jewelers	Susie's Casuals
Great Ideas	Sweet William Restaurant
Hanover Shoes	That Pet Place
The Hello Shop	The Earring Tree
Hess's	Things Remembered
Hot Sam	Thom McAn
Household Finance	Thrift Drug Store
Hushpuppie Shoes	Time Out Amusements
Hushpuppie Kids' Shoes	Vitamin World
John V. Schultz Waterbeds	Waldenbooks
Johnstown Savings Bank	Wall to Wall Video & Sound
K-mart	Watchmaker Jewelry
Karmelkorn	Zack's Frozen Yogurt

said. "The mall hours will remain the same."

The Richland Mall is owned by Richland Mall Associates of Grand Rapids, Mich., and has been at its present location for 18 years. The mall's 650,000 square feet houses 90 stores, which employ approximately 1,700 people.

Elizabeth Zilch Barto

An avid reader, Elizabeth Zilch Barto loved spending time at Waldenbooks when she was growing up. Naturally, she was moved to apply for a job there in the spring of 1984 after graduating from Richland High School in '83. Her love of books and reading shone through, and she was hired as a part-time bookseller at the store.

The hours were limited at first, but working with books and magazines was a dream job for Elizabeth. She loved talking books with customers and helping them find what they wanted on the shelves...or in the dumps and gondolas.

Dumps are cardboard display bins with books stacked inside and some kind of poster-like artwork on a standup backing behind the bin. As for bookstore gondolas, they are "freestanding bookshelves that are set up in the middle of the store," according to Elizabeth. "Ours had three shelves apiece, and customers could see over them if they chose."

Books were also displayed on taller freestanding shelves, wall racks, and end caps, though some were put on carts and wheeled into the entryway to draw the attention of passersby. There were also books in the display window out front, often arranged around a theme or featuring a particular author or genre.

Break Out the Microfiche

Processing and putting stock on all those shelves and displays was part of Elizabeth's typical day at the store. "After signing in for my shift, I would start doing freight, unpacking books in the back and putting them on the cart to take them out front and shelve them," she explains.

The shelving process was mapped out in detail in advance, with no room for improvisation. The use of in-store display space was all carefully planned by Waldenbooks' corporate office to maximize sales and revenue.

155

"Books by bestselling authors like Stephen King and James Patterson went straight to the front of the store." Elizabeth remembers that Stephen King's *It*, Garrison Keillor's *Lake Wobegon Days*, and *Men Are from Mars, Women Are from Venus* by John Gray, Ph.D. all received prominent placement during their days as bestsellers in the 80s.

Other books were placed elsewhere, based on what part of the layout might yield the biggest sales for each genre. "General fiction was in the front area. Moving back through the store, we had science fiction, romance, and mystery. Teen novels were between the science fiction and romance. Non-fiction books like religion and psychology were on the other side of the store," says Elizabeth.

Even with all that shelf space supporting thousands of books, however, customers often wanted titles that weren't in stock. That was where the store's microfiche reader device came into play – a low-tech solution for finding and ordering out-of-stock books in the days before online data and "the cloud" made it easy to tap into vast data systems from any location. With microfiche, documents are photographed and stored in miniature on a flat piece of film, then magnified and viewed by a reading device.

"The microfiche reader was located on the 'cash wrap,' or checkout counter, alongside two cash registers," remembers Elizabeth. "Every week, we would get a new set of microfiche that listed the current books we had in our warehouse. The purpose of it was to locate any books that weren't in the store but could be found in our warehouse, for special orders. It usually took about a week for them to come in.

"The volume of special orders depended on what people were looking for or what the topic of the day was. It depended on what was in the top 10, and sometimes we didn't get all the books that were in the top 10. That could have been because we were a little store, compared to a bigger store somewhere else like Pittsburgh," says Elizabeth.

Say Yes to Pre-Orders

For a small bookseller, Waldenbooks in the Richland Mall racked up some pretty big numbers. During Elizabeth's time there, it became a million-dollar store, making at least a million dollars in annual sales.

A high percentage of those sales happened during the fourth-quarter holiday season. "It would start at the beginning of November. Actually, mid-October is when authors would start pushing their new releases for the Christmas sales. The big push would last right up until Christmas and beyond.

"Sometimes, sales would drop after the holiday, then pick back up around the first of the year. We sold calendars, and everyone would be in buying them around New Year's," recalls Elizabeth.

At any time of year, new hardcover titles by bestselling authors gave sales a big boost. Some authors' work was so in demand, customers pre-ordered copies so they'd be sure to get them as soon as they went on sale.

"When a big author like Stephen King had a new book coming out, lots of people pre-ordered it," explains Elizabeth. "When the book arrived at the store, we would grab the first couple copies and sell them to the customers who'd placed pre-orders. Those customers were assured of getting the discounted sale price, which was typically 15-20 percent off the cover price. The discount would last about six weeks, and then we changed the pricing to 10 percent or so. Pre-ordering was a great way to guarantee you'd get your copy as soon as possible, and at the lowest price."

Angel Was a Centerfold?

Though Elizabeth worked extensively with books, she also did a lot with magazines on a weekly basis. Waldenbooks carried an extensive selection, and it was up to her to put them on the shelves near the front of the store.

"Every Tuesday, we got our magazines from the distributor, and I was in charge of shelving them. That's all I would get done that day, because I also had to watch the cash wrap and ring up customers."

Waldenbooks sold everything from *Good Housekeeping*, *McCall's*, and *National Geographic* to *Playboy* and *Penthouse*. "The adult magazines were wrapped in brown paper, and we had to keep them on a high shelf in the back where the teenage boys were less likely to get hold of them. Lots of people still bought them, though."

Not everyone in the store was a paying customer, however. "There were people who came in and couldn't afford what they wanted, so they would read a book or magazine right there in the store," says Elizabeth.

"They would stand there for an hour or an hour and half, reading. We just let them stand there. We didn't chase them out of the store. We let them do their thing and worked around them. Sometimes, they would go and buy a different book, other than what they were reading, or sometimes they'd come back another time and make a purchase. But not always."

Just a Reader Now

Elizabeth left Waldenbooks after nine years, in 1992. These days, she's a civilian reader, not a bookseller, but Waldenbooks will always be close to her heart.

The same goes for the Richland Mall. "I really liked the Mall. It was one floor and very well-lit and taken care of until the end. I made some great friends there, like Twila from Hot Sam and a couple of the girls from Hickory Farms. I still keep in touch with Twila on a regular basis, in fact.

"It was a nice Mall, full of nice people, and I'm glad I got to work there when I did," says Elizabeth.

RICHLAND MALL TOUR

©The Tribune-Democrat

158

Tour
Richman
BROTHERS

Joe Fortunato was an original member of the Richland Mall Board of Directors. Invited by Mall General Manager Bob McConnell, Joe joined the managers of Sears, Kmart, and Penn Traffic, plus the promotions director and other tenant representatives and members of the Mall staff, in working out issues affecting the Mall.

Photo by Philip Balko

"We met in the conference room, which later became the community room," says Joe. "We would just talk about what the Mall needed, problems that were going on, and what we needed to promote."

The rest of the time, Joe managed Richman Brothers, a men's clothing store specializing in affordable, quality business suits.

If I Were a Richman

A Pittsburgh native, Joe went to work for Richman Brothers in Pleasant Hills in 1972, after graduating from Allegheny County Community College. From there, he was transferred to the Monroeville Mall store, then to the store on Main Street in downtown Johnstown.

When Joe heard that Richman Brothers would be opening a store in the new Richland Mall, he made a play for a managerial position there…and got it. That was when the *real* work started.

"The Mall just provided the space and concrete flooring," explains Joe. "Every store's personnel had to build out their own unit from there.

"I went up when the downtown store wasn't open, which was every evening except Mondays and Thursdays. I watched the workmen build the shelving and lay the carpet. I got to see them assemble the custom-built suit racks and customer service counter. It was magical, watching our store come together."

As the store took shape, Joe turned his attention to building a team to man it. Extra staff would be needed to meet the requirements of the grand opening, so he enlisted members of the downtown Richman Brothers crew. He also interviewed and hired new employees in the downtown store and Richland Mall location.

He didn't waste any time putting them to work. Getting ready for the grand opening was a challenge, but everyone pitched in and got the job done in time.

When opening day arrived, all was in readiness, and Joe was thrilled. "I remember Jim O'Roark talking to all of us managers and owners in center court that day about how exciting this was and how great it was to bring something like the Mall to this little community."

After the opening ceremony, as the general public poured in, life at Richman Brothers was a whirlwind of activity. "The Mall was an instant success. We were busy from day one. Everybody just loved that place."

Suited for Success

The success of Richman Brothers didn't stop after opening day or week. Joe's store made waves on a regional level.

"Out of my boss's 18 stores, I was his number two highest percentage store profit-wise. I did about $400,000 in a year, which was a lot, and the Monroeville store did about $600,000…but Monroeville was a lot bigger and had a lot of expenses," says Joe.

The price and quality of Richman products kept customers coming back for more. "That particular store had the best garment you could buy for the money. There was no question about that. You could buy a really nice men's suit for about $60 or $75.

"Richman Brothers would sell a suit that had two pairs of pants that matched. That was one of their claims to fame. All the pants were cut to length and tailored to fit, strictly dress pants. The girls did all the tailoring in the back," says Joe.

A Real Customs Agent

Richman Brothers in the Mall also hit it big in the custom suit business. "If someone didn't like anything on the rack, I would ask him to come take a look at the custom suit book and see if there's anything he liked. Say a fella walked in and needed a 42 short or a 42 short stout, and he only had four suits in the store to choose from and didn't like any of them, that's when I would suggest custom ordering.

"To order a custom-made suit, I started by taking all the measurements, then helped the customer select a style from a special order book and a swatch to go with it. Then, I sent the measurements to Richman Brothers' home office in Cleveland. Three weeks later, the custom suit would be delivered to the store. At that point, I'd call the customer in, and we'd do the final fitting. Everything was done to what was ordered," explains Joe.

Joe's work was so good, and there was so much demand for it, his Johnstown store became the number one custom order store in the entire Richman Brothers chain. "I was constantly ordering suits for people. There were about 400 stores in the chain, and mine was number one. The other managers just didn't promote it like we did, even when I was in Monroeville. Of course, in bigger stores like that, they probably had twice as many suits as I had in Johnstown, so it was easier for a customer to walk in and find something he liked.

"All I know is, the custom ordering did really well for us in the Richland Mall. It was a unique service the Richman Brothers chain offered back then. No one else had anything like it, and we made the most of it in Johnstown," says Joe.

That Sunday Feeling

It's safe to say Joe loved the Richland Mall. To this day, he gets together for breakfast on a weekly basis with some of his buddies from those days.

"It was like family," he remembers. "When I left the Monroeville Mall after working there for a year, no one cared, but working at Richland Mall, I became part of an instant family.

"Everyone was friendly and genuinely concerned about how you were doing and how your store was doing. We were all concerned with each other's lives as well as the numbers. Everyone was genuinely interested."

If the Richland Mall was so great, why did Joe bail out after just four years? It had to do with Sundays.

"People laugh when I tell them why I left, but when Pennsylvania started to do Sunday retail sales, and the Mall started opening for business on Sundays, I was like, 'I'm not doing that.' I said I didn't mind working evenings, and I didn't mind Saturdays, but now they were trying to take my Sundays.

"I was a big skier. My family had a cabin in Hidden Valley. I remember walking into the Mall on a beautiful January Sunday, and I knew my whole family was on the slopes, and I was like, 'Why am I doing this?' Not to mention, if I worked a Sunday, I didn't get to take another day off to compensate.

"So I put in my resignation early in '78. My boss said that out of his 18 managers, he never expected a resignation call from me. I loved my job, I really did, but when they started to do Sunday sales, I drew the line," says Joe.

Little did he know that his destiny would someday intersect with that of the Mall again.

Déjà Mall

After leaving Richman Brothers in '78, Joe went into the insurance business, starting the American Insurance Marketing agency. Around the same time, he joined forces with fellow Mall notables Joe Cohen and Bill Heim to purchase the Pup Hut in the Richland Mall, which he and his partners renamed Franks 'n Stuff.

In '87, he opened a salon called Locks Off/Tan On in the building where his agency was located. That salon did well enough that he decided to open another under the same name in the Richland Mall in 1990. Continuing his association with the Mall appealed to Joe, but he did take steps to avoid a bad outcome, convincing Mall General Manager Bob McConnell to let him out of his lease if the store underperformed. Ultimately, that proved to be a smart business move.

"The Mall salon had 10 chairs and 15 stylists," says Joe. "But it didn't deliver the target numbers I needed to justify its existence. I went to Bob after 18 months and asked to be let out of the lease. Good friend that he is, he agreed, and I stopped doing business at the Mall a second time."

After his second exit from the Mall, Joe focused in on the insurance business, and he's kept it going ever since. His company, American Insurance Marketing, is a life, health, and annuity agency with a special focus on group and individual health products. He runs a walk-in center called The Health Insurance Place where customers can find help navigating the convoluted world of health insurance coverage.

Meanwhile, almost every Saturday morning, he meets his Mall buddies – Gil Demos, Joe Cohen, and Frank Kocsis – for breakfast. When the four of them get together, it's like the Richland Mall comes to life again for an hour or two.

And the family that Joe came to love so much is as close-knit as ever.

Richland Mall Merchants Association

It sure doesn't taste like TOMATO JUICE!

I'll start my diet tomorrow?!

The Richland Mall Merchants Association held its initial meeting August 8, 1974, at the Sunnehanna Country Club in Johnstown, Pa. This was the first meeting of all the tenants and everything from the theme "Richland Mall Just For You," to the entertainment, to the order of business was planned "just for you."

The evening started with a cocktail hour followed by a delicious dinner and ended with a program of business and entertainment. First on the agenda was the welcome by Jim O'Roark who told the tenants that Richland Mall was going to reach consumers in the six county area of Cambria, Westmoreland, Blair, Indiana, Somerset and Clearfield Counties, and who explained how our advertising plans would saturate this market. The Articles of Incorporation and the By-Laws of the Richland Mall Merchants Association were distributed and discussed.

Mall Manager, Bob McConnell, also gave a hearty welcome and stressed how "we're all in this together." He discussed the 10:00 a.m. to 10:00 p.m. mall hours and announced the Merchants Association Board of Directors. They are: Bill Adams of Sears, John Hanley of Penn Traffic, Bob Brallier of Matchmaker, Joe Fortunato of Richman Brothers, Dick Halbritter of Framing Hut, John Jones of Our Furniture, Steve Heller of Ormonds, Richard Weaver of Somerset Trust, Jim O'Roark and Bob McConnell of Richland Mall Associates and the K mart manager, to be announced.

The next order of business was publicity. Jim O'Roark informed the group of the fantastic publicity Richland Mall has received from the local media and introduced our first guest, Ron Stephenson--news director of WJAC-TV. Ron did an excellent job of narrating a film he put together based on highlights of all the news events concerning the mall that had been shown of WJAC-TV. What a SMASH!!

John Twomey, legal counsel for Richland Mall Associates, was our next guest. Aside from composing those 100 page leases and those 20 page by-laws, John is also the world's only manualist. For those of you who missed his performances on the Johnny Carson Show, John plays music (real songs) with his hands and we were honored to have him perform for us. Let me tell you, he really had everyone rolling from his seat!!!

Finally, the featured guest of the evening was introduced to the group. Our lovable, sweet and only...Richie the Pook!!!!!

What was the punch line?

Let's pause for station identification.

SO BIG !!

"Name That Tune"

Courtesy Bob McConnell

Tour

Watchmaker's
DIAMONDS & JEWELRY

Only one store in the Richland Mall had a mezzanine and 200 clocks of every description: Watchmaker's Jewelry, located between center court and the Mall's main entrance.

Watchmaker's opened in 1975 in the spot originally occupied by the Craftsmen II leather shop – a prime, high-traffic location, according to owner Dennis Petimezas. It didn't hurt that it was near the center court nature area, with its stream full of live trout.

"When I first moved to Johnstown, I didn't have much money in my pocket, and my paychecks had yet to be forwarded from Arkansas," remembers Dennis. "What do you do when you're the manager of a jewelry store, and you have no money and you have to eat? I occasionally caught and cooked a fish from that stream. They were delicious. You do what you have to do, right?"

Courtesy Dennis Petimezas

Flight of Destiny

Dennis might never have become a part of Watchmaker's without a fateful meeting on a plane to New York City.

A graduate of the University of Arkansas with a degree in marketing and economics, Dennis suffered a setback when an accidental shooting left a bullet lodged near his spine. Though doctors removed the bullet, his medical history caused potential employers to shy away from hiring him. He finally got a job at a Gordon's Jewelers store in Little Rock, Arkansas, and that gave him his start in the jewelry industry.

Eventually, Dennis was enlisted to open a Gordon's store in the Richland Mall. He traveled to Johnstown to watch the build-out of the store and decided he liked the area enough to want to stay there. "The year before, Johnstown had won the All-American City award, which was impressive. The steel mills were very active, coal was king, and everybody was working," remembers Dennis.

But moving to town and getting the store rolling had its hardships. In the first few weeks, money was tight (which was where the center court trout fishing came in), but the store did well and kept the Gordon's corporation happy.

The same wasn't true for Dennis, though. "With chain organizations, you're limited in what you can learn about the actual manufacture and supply side of the business," he explains. "My job was more geared to management, sales, and marketing within the individual stores. I moved from store management toward district management, but my future was limited, and I acknowledged early on that I wasn't learning the closely guarded inside aspects of the jewelry business."

That all changed when Dennis took a chance and jumped ship in 1975. Resigning from his position with Gordon's, he flew to Brazil and spent his life savings on several parcels of emeralds. He planned to resell that investment in New York to start his own business...though he still had a lot to learn about how it all worked.

To seek guidance, he flew to New York City – and found the support he was seeking before he even got off the plane. The owner of Watchmaker's Shop in the Richland Mall (a direct competitor of his previous employer, Gordon's) was on the same flight, and he and Dennis struck up a conversation. By the time the plane landed, they had also forged an alliance. "He introduced me to people in New York, some of which I still do business with today," says Dennis.

Most importantly, the two agreed to join forces in the Richland Mall and in the Greengate Mall in Greensburg. Dennis agreed to buy into the Watchmaker's Shop business and become the new co-owner. "It was an opportunity to go into business with someone who was actually on the inside of the business." He got his emeralds appraised in Pittsburgh (free of charge, as a favor he later repaid) and used them as collateral for a loan to cover his buy-in.

Behind the Name

When Dennis joined Watchmaker's, the store truly lived up to its name, specializing in timepieces. "Watchmaker's carried Rolex, Piaget, and Corum watches, and fine grandfather clocks," says Dennis. "It was more a watchmakers' specialty shop at that point, not a jewelry store."

That all changed later in 1975 when the original owner left, and Dennis became the sole proprietor of Watchmaker's. By then, there were three Watchmaker's locations, all focused on selling timepieces. Soon after the change in ownership, Dennis added more jewelry to the stores...though he decided to keep the name and brand that had been built.

"When I introduced diamond jewelry, I wanted to emphasize its inclusion without losing the value and name recognition of the established Watchmaker's brand. I just added on to the original name, making it Watchmaker's Diamonds and Jewelry," explains Dennis.

As Dennis expanded the diamond jewelry line and updated the name, he brought his brother, Basil, from Arkansas aboard as a full partner to help with further changes and expansion. Basil formulated a plan that led to stores in in three states.

Eventually, the Petimezas brothers owned seven stores in the U.S., though the Richland Mall store was always the hub of the enterprise. "Richland Mall was always our home base. It was the backbone of everything we did. It was our main store and our main office. It was where everything happened."

When the Richland Mall started Sunday hours, the main Watchmaker's store became a seven-days-a-week business. "Originally, the Sunshine Laws prevented the Mall from being open on Sundays. Eventually, those laws went away, and we could be open on Sundays. My brother and I looked at it from a business standpoint, realizing we had four more days a month to do business. As an employee, you might not want to work on a Sunday, but as an employer, you're paying another day's rent either way, so you want to capitalize on it."

Courtesy Dennis Petimezas

Shots with the WWF

The expansion of business hours wasn't the only thing they capitalized on at the Richland Mall location. Dennis and Basil were quick to participate in Mall activities and special events, gaining publicity for their store while helping to amplify awareness of the Mall in general among shoppers.

"When Richard Simmons the workout guru visited the Mall, he used our upstairs room as a changing room," recalls Dennis. "Two famous wrestlers, George "The Animal" Steele and Bruno Sammartino, also came to the store during Mall visits. We did shots of whiskey with them, and it was great.

"Another high point was when we sponsored the Miss Laurel Highlands pageant. The judge of the pageant was a former Miss America, Elizabeth Ward, who was a cousin of my college roommate, Guy Gardner. Being an Arkansas Razorback, she posed for a photo wearing a hog hat we had. She also demonstrated hog calls on stage, and the audience was wondering, 'What the hell was that?' When her chaperone was called away unexpectedly, I drove Elizabeth back to her plane. It was cool showing her the real Johnstown along the way, starting with breakfast at Coney Island, of course," says Dennis.

Goat Poop on the Mezzanine?

Then there was the goat that made a run for the mezzanine.

Celebrity guests like Richard Simmons and Miss America came around every once in a while, but visits by a traveling petting zoo were more frequent. One time, the animals from the zoo decided that if Watchmaker's was good enough for George "The Animal" Steele, it was good enough for them, too.

"They would set up the petting zoo down by Ormond," recalls Dennis. "At the end of the day, they would bring all the animals out through the Mall, following a lead animal. The lead animal would run down the corridor from Ormond, turn the corner at my store, and go out the doors by Somerset Trust and into the vans that were waiting in the parking lot. That's where the animals would sleep for the night.

"One night, something went wrong. The lead of the pack was always a goat, and regrettably, he didn't make the corner. Instead, with our doors still open so we could watch the nightly exit of the animals, the goat turned too sharply and ran right into the store, followed by all the other animals – goats, fawns, sheep, and ducks. We had about twenty animals run into the store before their handlers could stop them.

"We went for the goat first because he'd run halfway up the mezzanine, and the others were trying to follow. Oh my gosh, it was a hysterical nightmare. And yes, we had poop patrol for twenty minutes after that."

The petting zoo animals weren't the only strange creatures Dennis encountered at the Mall. Another attraction called "the Missing Link" also provided a surprising adventure.

"The Missing Link was an eight-foot tall thing in a human form, frozen in a huge block of ice. You'd pay admission and could walk up into the display and look down into the area that housed the block of ice. It was big and scary-looking.

Courtesy Dennis Petimezas

"Now, this was in my very early days at the Mall, when I couldn't afford the admission to the Missing Link. I remember my burglar alarm went off one night, and the police came to my store, but it was a false alarm. We got to talking, though, and decided to go peek at the Missing Link. It was closed off, but we were able to sneak in and take a peek.

"Just as we were peeking at the Missing Link, a janitor came by and yelled at us. My police friends and I all jumped up like little boys, as if the Link had come to life. It was crazy, because there I was with two armed policemen. What did we have to be afraid of?"

Not-So-Sweet Hangover

Dennis had an even more "alarming" experience one morning in the store, thanks to his mischievous brother, Basil.

"We had over 200 clocks of every description in the store," says Dennis. "There were cuckoo clocks, wall clocks, grandfather clocks, mantle clocks, you name it. And we intentionally set them all to different times so the chimes and cuckoos would be staggered and wouldn't go off all at once.

"Except this one Sunday morning, when I came in after a night on the town. I'd come home very late, maybe intoxicated, and got up late that morning with a gigantic headache. I got to the store about five minutes till noon.

"As it turned out, my brother Basil was aware of my late and boisterous night. Actually, I'd awakened him in the wee hours of the night when I'd returned home and asked if he would work my shift for me. (The answer had been "no.")

Jewels & Gems

By Dennis & Basil Petimezas

DIAMOND FACTS: HARDNESS — The diamond is 85 times harder than the nearest contender, corundum, of which sapphires and rubies are composed. This means the diamond's facets can be polished to a luster and cut to an accuracy unequaled by any other gemstone, thus adding to its incomparable brilliance.

WATCHMAKER'S JEWELRY. You will find us conveniently located in the Richland Mall. Your VISA, Master Card and Watchmaker's Jewelry charge cards are honored. Phone 266-9653.

Open Daily 10 to 9:30 and Sunday 12 to 5

© The Tribune-Democrat

Before I got to the store, Basil had gone up ahead of me and set every one of those clocks to go off at the same time – 12 noon. The chiming, clanging, and donging was definitely not good for my giant splitting headache! Needless to say, I called Basil up as soon as the clocks stopped blasting and had a few choice words for him!"

Courtesy Dennis Petimezas

One Mall, 18 Competitors

To say the least, Dennis had lots of fun and memorable experiences at the Mall. They only helped cement Watchmaker's connection to the place, and Dennis' connection to the people who worked there.

"There was a camaraderie at the Mall that you don't find much today," he says. "The friendships I developed are still a part of my life today."

Dennis would often join his friends Gil Demos, Joe Fortunato, Joe Cohen, Frank Koscis, and Bob Enos for breakfast at Sweet William and lunch at Capri or the Encore. They became a kind of workplace family, just as the Mall was a kind of home away from home.

"It was like we were all in this together. Even your rivals were pals. I was always friendly with all my competitors...and there were plenty of them. At one point in the early days, there were 18 competitors, including full-line jewelry stores, department stores that had jewelry counters, specialty shops selling jewelry within other stores, and kiosks selling jewelry. And for quite a long time, everyone was successful."

There was plenty of business to go around, and it grew over time as younger generations followed their predecessors' buying habits. "As we grew and built Watchmaker's with outstanding personal service, many of our customers' children and grandchildren also became customers. It's a great feeling when someone comes in and says, 'You might know my dad,' or 'Do you remember my mom?' or it's the grandchild of someone we served in the past," says Dennis.

Courtesy Dennis Petimezas

Unfortunately, Watchmaker's successful run in the Richland Mall was destined to end. By the late 90s, after the coming of the Galleria, Dennis could see the end was near. "We could tell things were cycling down. We could see that stores were leaving, and no new ones were coming in to replace them."

In late 1997, when the Richland Mall Associates announced the closing of the middle portion of the Mall, Watchmaker's got a notice to vacate and was suddenly on the verge of being homeless.

With the beloved Richland Mall folding around them, Dennis and Basil decided that until they found a new home, the logical step was a move to the only other mall in town: the Galleria.

Shoot the Alarm

Making the move a reality was relatively easy with the help of past and future landlords alike. "The Richland Mall Associates were among the most fair people we'd ever dealt with. They were helpful when we were making our move.

"George Zamias helped a lot with his counsel and direction. We had stores in his other malls, so we were already in business together. We were very lucky to have the Zamias family – not just Mr. Zamias, but also Sammy and Steven Zamias – to make the transition easy and make us feel comfortable and welcome moving there."

That isn't to say that leaving the Richland Mall went off without a hiccup. A problem with the store alarm led to one last crazy incident for Dennis, Basil, and the gang.

"When we cut the final power to the store, and the Mall was virtually in darkness, our burglar alarm went off, triggering a ringing so loud it was deafening. We cut the power cords, but it wouldn't stop ringing. It drove us and the poor guards crazy for two days.

"We couldn't open the alarm case, so we hit it with sledgehammers, even iron bars, and it wouldn't break. Since the mall was vacant, we even tried to kill it with firepower. Basil shot it twice with a .45, but it wouldn't pierce the plating on the cover. It continued to ring until it finally ran out of backup battery power and went dead. There was a certain finality to it. We did, literally, go out with a bang," remembers Dennis.

Galleriazation

Watchmaker's operated at the Galleria for five years. "We were located on the upper level, the first store out of Boscov's, next to the bathrooms by the food court. It was a strategic spot, the best location in the Mall. It was, in fact, the spot George Zamias had previously chosen for his real estate company. If it was good enough for George Zamias, it was good enough for Petimezas."

Any worries Dennis might have had about losing business after the move were quickly put to rest. Loyal customers followed Watchmaker's to the Galleria, and the sales numbers continued to improve steadily.

"What happened is that our base of clients stayed with us," explains Dennis. "As they matured, their incomes increased, so what was spent had a natural increase as a percentage of their greater income."

This steady spending could be attributed to the predictable nature of customer demand in the jewelry industry during strong economic times. "In my business, we have certain guarantees. It's guaranteed that people will get engaged, people will get married, and these same people will have birthdays and anniversaries. Those are things that are fixed, and they don't change. There was also another surge of customer demand when second marriages became more common. This led to strong spikes in sales because in a second marriage, the engagement ring is always bigger.

"Those guarantees helped fuel our continued success at the Galleria and beyond. We also kept a clear focus on the three things that jewelry provides that no other commodity, gift, or service can: it conveys an emotion, has continuing and increasing value, and you can wear it. Do you know who told me that? Harry Gordon of Gordon's Jewelers (at the time about 2500 stores strong) himself told me that in his office in Houston, Texas," says Dennis.

Scalped

Though Watchmaker's was a success at the Galleria, the store moved to new digs on Scalp Avenue in Richland after five years. According to Dennis, the new free-standing location was something that had been on the radar for many years.

"Even when we were successful at the Richland Mall, we always wanted to have our own free-standing location, but we could never find the appropriate site. As our five-year contract at the Galleria expired, however, we found what we were looking for: a perfect location and lots of space with a property purchase from Mike Beaver, a friend and business partner from an investment group I belonged to.

"We weren't unhappy at the Galleria, but we wanted a life outside Mall hours. We were moving toward having our own families. Having solidly established ourselves in the market, we were ready to break free with our own building.

"We had reestablished ourselves with the move to the Galleria from the Richland Mall. We felt that moving from the Galleria to the high traffic volume of Scalp Avenue would be a smooth transition.

"Would our customers again migrate with us to the new location? The answer was 'yes.' We actually never missed a day's business from moving to either one of the new stores. We always orchestrated the moves from the close of business one day, to moving all night long and opening at the new location the following day," says Dennis.

As expected, business remained consistent for Watchmaker's after the move. A pattern of steady growth continued, which Dennis attributes in part to the nimble nature of his small company.

"We were able to adapt to the market as it changed and adapt quickly. A national chain of jewelry stores is like an ocean liner; it takes a long time to make a left or right turn. A small, independent jeweler like Watchmaker's is like a speedboat, however, able to cut in and out quickly.

Courtesy Dennis Petimezas

169

"That's the advantage an independent jewelry store has over a big box chain jeweler," says Dennis.

The Scalp Avenue store is still in business today, another Watchmaker's success story. The permanent staff includes longtime employees such as store manager Ron Tomak, who started working for Watchmaker's over 30 years ago; Larry Bertino, the "diamond concierge" of Johnstown, another 30-year staff member; Judy Scott, a 35-year jewelry veteran, who left and returned to Watchmaker's; and Toni Baker, Connie Huff, and Nina Crichton.

Dennis has no regrets about the road he's traveled, though he still misses the Richland Mall sometimes. "With the exception of the hours, all my memories of the Richland Mall are good, happy, and positive.

"We enjoyed many holiday and birthday celebrations at the Richland Mall store, and we shared them together. It was always a family feeling among the staff and those who worked there. It was always enjoyable going to the Encore and its Red Lady Disco after work. It was a meeting place for Mall employees after hours.

"From a business standpoint, it was the right place to be at the right time. All the experiences I had there were building blocks that led me to where I am now.

"But it's true that the mall business model seems to be fading these days. In the beginning, shopping in an enclosed mall was a family experience. Families don't seem to have those type of group experiences as much anymore, and I think it could be among the many factors of why regional malls are closing or being repurposed. It's not the shopping experience it once was. Nowadays, people want to get in, shop, and get out quickly, which might be why hybrid strip centers are so popular now.

"But we still have the memories of the Richland Mall to treasure. We remember the good times and the people who made us happy, and the Mall lives on in our memories and, occasionally, our dreams," says Dennis.

Photos by Robert Jeschonek

Tour
Somerset Trust COMPANY

A smart robber could have made off with a lot of money back in the Richland Mall's heyday. All he would have had to do was follow a tenant manager as he or she toted bags of cash, undefended, to the Mall merchants' longtime bank, Somerset Trust.

It was a different time, as they say, and the threat level at a small town shopping center like Richland Mall just wasn't that high. The really big tenants – the anchor stores Sears, Kmart, and Penn Traffic or Hess's – delivered their proceeds via armored car, but the smaller tenants sometimes just toted them through the Mall on foot.

And Somerset Trust, right from the beginning, was always happy to deposit them.

Flipping the Cash

Bob Enos was there from the start, too. He helped open Somerset Trust's branch in the Mall in the Fall of 1974 – the first branch office ever for the state-chartered commercial bank.

Bob, whose father was a residential mortgage officer, had been working as a teller at the bank through high school and college. After graduating from UPJ, he got the offer to help open the Mall branch from bank president George Cook, and quickly accepted.

171

"It was an all-hands-on-deck situation, since the company had never opened a branch before," explains Bob. "We all just worked together to set everything up and get the doors open."

The Richland Mall branch opened in November 1974. It was extremely busy from the start, though the inner Mall wasn't full yet, and most business was coming from the three anchor stores.

After helping launch the Mall branch, Bob transferred to the main office of Somerset Trust in '75. He returned to the Mall in 1977 as branch manager, just in time for the latest Johnstown Flood. It was a difficult time for the city, but the Mall continued to thrive, and so did Somerset Trust.

There were still challenges, though. According to Bob, it was tough to handle all the cash that the anchors brought in. "The anchors' deposits came via an armored carrier complete with guards. So that all came at one time, you know. The challenge was just being able to get all the cash counted and the deposits made on a daily basis. At that point in time, we didn't have cash counters like we have today. We had some mini-cash counters, but they couldn't handle the volume. Back then, credit cards weren't that big, so a lot of transactions were done in cash."

God Bless the Little Guy

The influx of cash from the anchors didn't necessarily guarantee the branch would be a success, however. Anchor tenants didn't leave their cash in the hands of Somerset Trust for long.

"That's one thing we didn't realize at first," says Bob. "We were saying, 'Why aren't we growing more if we've got these big business accounts?' After we thought about it and looked at it, we said, 'You know, these big chain stores deposit and transfer out into their main bank pretty fast.' Cash comes in one day, and it's gone the next because they transfer everything around.

"These were pretty big players, and they had their transfers down pat. What they deposited today was gone tomorrow afternoon," says Bob. On the other hand, smaller, local tenants kept their funds in place at Somerset Trust instead of flipping them to other, bigger banks like the big guys did. Bob favored those accounts because they helped his bank grow over time.

"We still work with some of those same loyal local customers, like Gil Demos, Dennis Petimezas, and Joe Fortunato. Thanks to our time in the Richland Mall, we made inroads with merchants in the Mall and in the Richland area, which was important to us. It helped us grow beyond our base in Somerset."

Old Faithful Vacuum Tubes

Though the Mall branch of Somerset Trust had it made in some ways, *parking* was one issue that had no easy answer.

"Everybody thought 'man, they have a lot of parking' because of the big Mall lots outside, but we didn't. People who want to go to a bank want to go right to a parking lot and park. During the day, we didn't have any problems with this, but on a busy Friday or Saturday night, the parking lot was full. Customers had to find a parking space just to walk in to go to the bank, and that was one of the problems we fought," says Bob.

One proposed solution, using the fire lanes for bank parking, was rejected. "People would definitely take advantage of that. The fire department didn't want to set a precedent, and then have those lanes blocked when they needed them."

Instead, Somerset Trust decided to install a drive-up station in the parking lot near the main doors of the Mall, just beyond the primary access and fire lanes. They buried a vacuum tube system under the parking lot, so tellers in the office could send and receive cash, receipts, statements, etc.

The vacuum tubes were accessible at the drive-up, where customers could communicate via a microphone and speaker system.

It seemed like a good idea…until water started spurting out of the tube system.

"The tubes weren't installed properly. They'd get flooded under the parking lot, and water would shoot up. We could never get it fixed, so we closed the drive-up after a couple of years," remembers Bob.

Photo by Chuck Mamula

Friends to the End

The drive-up had its problems, but the bank's relationships with tenants at the Mall never did. According to Bob, a lot of it had to do with Somerset Trust's approach to banking.

"My theory has always been, give the customer service, be honest with them, be up front with them, and you'll probably keep them for as long as you want them. I think merchants at the Mall appreciated that over the years. We serviced them, and they took care of us, and the relationships turned into friendships. It was good for both parties," explains Bob.

Whenever possible, Somerset Trust tried to help tenants in the Mall keep going. Bob and his staff also participated in activities outside work hours with the staff and management of Mall businesses. "We went to baseball games together," recalls Bob. "We had holiday parties. We went out after work and had drinks or met at the Encore restaurant for dinner and drinks. We met for breakfast at Sweet William and lunch at Capri. We got to know each other's families. It was a very close-knit community."

Those bonds made it all the harder when the Galleria got rolling and the Richland Mall started having financial troubles. A facelift in '92 wasn't enough to stop the loss of business and defection of tenants.

"The downward trend really picked up speed when Sears signed the agreement to move to the Galleria. A lot of the merchants followed Sears."

Somerset Trust ended up being one of the last tenants to stay in the Mall, but it didn't last. After a few years, the Mall closed its midsection, and the bank had to make a decision. Did Somerset Trust want to stay in Richland and maintain the business it had worked so hard to build at the Mall?

"The handwriting was on the wall. The Mall had no future…but we definitely wanted to stay in Richland. Fortunately, we found the perfect new location – the Bob Evans restaurant on Scalp Avenue, which had gone out of business. We moved down there, and it was a great fit for us," says Bob.

The branch on Scalp Avenue is still going strong, though Bob isn't based in Richland anymore. After 42 years with Somerset Trust, he's now Senior Vice President, Senior Commercial Lender, working out of the head office in Somerset.

But he still has fond memories of his days at the Richland Mall. "It was a pleasant time. It was a good time. I got a good start there and met a lot of very good people there, many of whom I've kept in touch with. It was a special place for so many of us."

Rise & Stride Walking Club

The Rise & Stride Walking Club is designed to offer a new way to gain physical fitness through a unique walking program developed by the Richland Mall and the Keystone Chapter of the American Red Cross.

The program offers access to Richland Mall from 6:30 - 9:30 a.m., Monday through Saturday before the stores open. This offers you an opportunity to walk in a safe, temperature-controlled environment.

Participants must pick up a registration/information packet at the Rise & Stride kiosk, located beside Household Finance in the mall. All new members will receive a identification badge after the proper forms have been completed and processed. All members must fill out the waiver releasing Richland Mall from liability in order to participate in the Rise & Stride Walking Club. All members must wear the badges. Membership is free.

Exercise can and should be enjoyable and beneficial. Physical activity is an essential factor in every fitness program, along with a balanced diet and plenty of rest. By gradually increasing you exercise, you will help improve your muscle tone and increase the heart's ability. Please consult your doctor before deciding to join the Rise & Stride Walking Club.

For additional information, contact the
Keystone Chapter of the American Red Cross
Health Services
533-2777 or 533-2779
or contact the Richland Mall Management Office
266-5876.

Walking Distance Chart

JANUARY							FEBRUARY						
M	T	W	T	F	S		M	T	W	T	F	S	

MARCH							APRIL						

MAY							JUNE						

JULY							AUGUST						

SEPTEMBER							OCTOBER						

NOVEMBER							DECEMBER						

Rise & Stride Walking Club

Safe, Uncrowded
Walking Environment
at Richland Mall
Elton Exit, Rt. 219

Monday - Saturday
6:30 a.m.- 9:30 a.m.

sponsored by

richland mall

America.
Red Cross

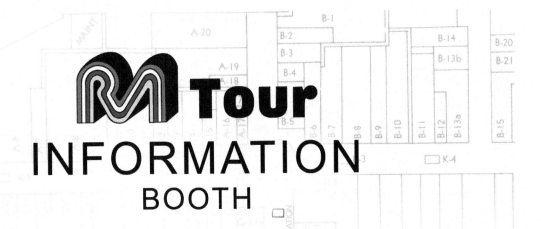

Tour
INFORMATION
BOOTH

Connie Hayes was as much a "Dear Abby on the corner" as she was the operator of the Richland Mall's information booth.

A fixture in the booth at center court for 20 years, Connie helped visitors find their way, sold newspapers and lottery tickets, and dispensed friendship and advice to Mall regulars who came to see her as part of their Richland Mall family.

And she loved every minute of it.

"Where Everybody Knows Your Name"

After working as a member of "Team Pook" before the Mall's grand opening, Connie was hired as Information Manager in 1975. Her early duties included handing out maps of the Mall and renting wheelchairs and strollers to customers. Eventually, she also sold newspapers and lottery tickets.

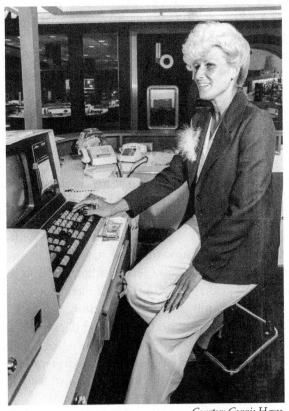

Courtesy Connie Hayes

She was a perfect fit for the job from the get-go. "I love people, and it was great fun dealing with so many of them. I especially loved seeing folks I'd known from before, from other jobs or activities. It was a wonderful experience right from the start."

In those days, the booth was cylindrical and covered in blue bricks like those on the exterior of the Duke and Duchess Theaters. It was situated in the center court area, near Watchmaker's and Kay Jewelers, and close to the Mall's main entrance.

It was the ideal location for greeting visitors and became a hub for the Mall's community of regulars. Those regulars, many of them retirees, would come in every day just to spend time with Connie and each other.

175

Courtesy Connie Hayes

She would listen to their problems, offer advice when she could, and generally joke around and chat with them as much as she could.

"A lot of folks would stop and pick up a newspaper in the morning," recalls Connie. "Some would buy a lottery ticket, playing their lucky numbers, and some would just stop and say 'hey.'

"They would meet there on those benches in front of the information center, have their coffee, and chat with me. Often, I'd do a crossword puzzle to get my brain working in the morning, and they would help me with that.

"We all got to know each other quite well and helped each other when we could."

Some of the older regulars even brought Connie gifts from time to time. She repaid their kindness with respect and made sure others did the same.

"I always told the other people who worked in the information center, 'You might be the only person some of these folks speak with today. Please make it a really pleasant experience because some of these people go home and shut the door and have no one to keep them company.'

"I do believe that meeting at my booth was probably the highlight of the day for some people. I really do. And I'm glad I could be there for them," says Connie.

The Walk of Life

Connie got to know the Mall staff and tenants as well as the regular customers. She spoke often with everyone from General Manager Bob McConnell to the cleaning crew to the security team. She also chatted with the Unimich partners when they were in town, especially Jim Streeter.

Her own family got in on the action, too, as members of the Mall's decorating committee. Each year, Connie and her kids helped decorate the Mall for Christmas, Easter, and other holidays and events.

"For Christmas, we put up the big Christmas tree and decorated it," remembers Connie. "We helped set up Santa's throne in center court, too. It was a lot of fun getting everything ready for the festivities."

Fun was a big part of another of her responsibilities – managing the carousel that was installed in center court during the 1992 renovations. "It was a beautiful, beautiful carousel. People came from near and far to see it because it was quite outstanding. I think that was a real drawing point."

Connie also had fun running the Rise and Stride walking club. Connie was one of the founders of the group, which was inspired by walking clubs in other malls.

It was another perfect fit situation, as Connie had been a fitness enthusiast for years. Before coming to work at the Richland Mall, in fact, she had taught aerobics three mornings a week.

Drawing on her fitness instructor background, she set up the club and acted as its leader, recruiting members at first from the community of Mall regulars she knew so well. The club caught on quickly and became a popular feature at the Mall, attracting a steady influx of new members who enjoyed the daily routine.

"Rise and Stride started every morning at seven," explains Connie. "We did our laps until nine, when I had to open the information booth for the day. Along the way, we chatted and laughed a lot and watched the merchants getting ready to open their businesses.

"I really enjoyed it, and so did the members of the club. Most of them were retirees from Richland or nearby, and they wanted to get a little exercise and have some fun and companionship. We developed a lot of nice friendships in that group."

Richland Mall Proud

After twenty years in the information booth chatting with the retirees, Connie retired herself. She left the Richland Mall in 1995 and moved to Indian Shores, Florida, between Clearwater and Saint Petersburg.

A cancer survivor, she still pursues a healthy lifestyle – and fondly remembers her time at the Mall.

"It was my home, and it really made me feel that I was quite well accepted. I had the freedom to enjoy and help others at that Mall, and I consider it a privilege," says Connie.

She does miss the Mall, and wishes for the sake of retirees like her regulars that it hadn't closed and been demolished. "I think it was one of the friendliest places around. A lot of people were very heartbroken when the Mall closed, because that really was a wonderful meet-and-greet place, especially for the elderly. As a single-floor Mall, it was easy for them to get around in, and the tenants were quite lovely."

These days, Connie regularly sees one of her Mall friends who also moved to Florida. The friend, Debbie Hill, worked at Foxmoor; she and Connie go to a movie and have lunch once a month. Naturally, they talk about the old days at the Mall.

"I'm proud that I was part of it. I feel like, from the ground floor up, I experienced all the growth of that place, and I felt privileged that I had that opportunity," says Connie.

Courtesy Connie Hayes

Walker's Notes

* Start at any entrance
* Follow the arrows
* Walk on the right side
* Finish at starting point = 1 lap
  (approximately 3,600 ft = 2/3 mile)

1 lap = 2/3 mile
3 laps = 2 miles
6 laps = 4 miles
9 laps = 6 miles
150 laps = 100 miles

Tips On Walking

1. Wear comfortable, loose clothing.
2. Wear good supporting, comfortable rubber-soled shoes and socks.
3. Start off at a casual pace and distance then, gradually increase to a moderate pace and distance. Later you may want to walk briskly.
4. Your doctor may recommend an appropriate starting distance goal.

Customer Service Symbols

▲ Official Starting Point/Kiosk
✚ Information
☎ Telephones
⌐ Coat Rack

🚺🚹 Restrooms
⛲ Drinking Fountains
Lockers

*Lockers are available for $.25

Eating Establishments

Cinnabon
Franks 'N Stuff
Hot Sam Pretzels
Karmelkorn
McDonalds
Zeke's Diner

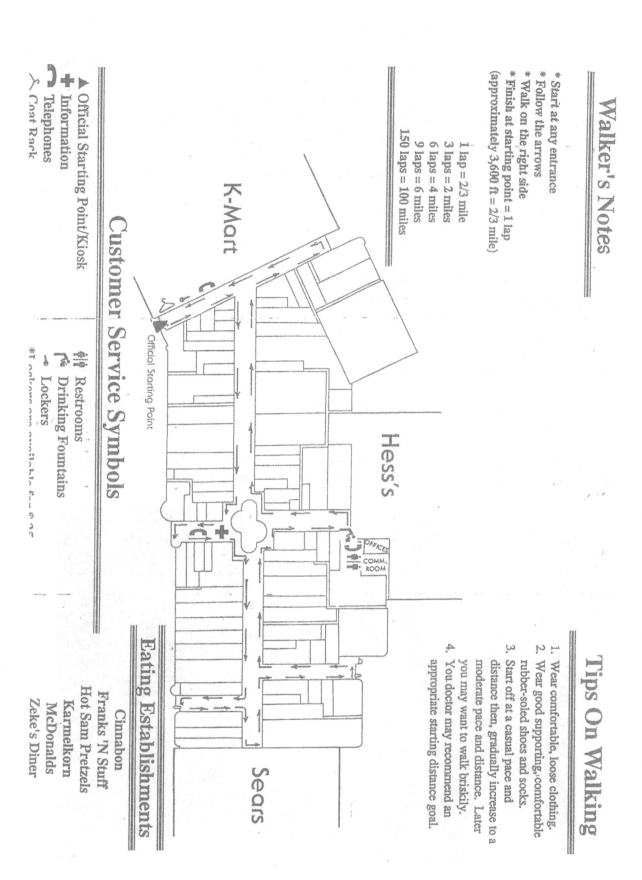

K-Mart

Official Starting Point

Hess's

OFFICES
COMM. ROOM

Sears

Photo by Philip Balko

Before Frank Koscis sold shoes at Thom McAn, he made plenty of feet tap as a rock 'n' roll musician.

Frank played his first live gig in a bar at the age of 14, then went on to perform with two popular local bands – the Silvertones and the Bluejays. With Frank on rhythm guitar at first, then lead, the bands played all the local bars, clubs, and events, plus a steady string of weddings. Fans loved them, and they made decent money.

But Frank got off the circuit in 1962 at age 18 and went to work for the Thom McAn shoe store on Main Street in downtown Johnstown (in the storefront currently occupied by the Fish Boat restaurant). Little did he know it at the time, but it was the start of more than two decades in the shoe business.

Frank on the Run

Frank was destined to manage Thom McAn in the Richland Mall, but he had to do some bouncing around before he got there. It started with a transfer from the downtown Johnstown store to one in Hagerstown, Maryland, followed by a move to Cumberland.

Next came a jump to the Great Southern Shopping Center in Bridgeville, PA, near Pittsburgh. It was a step in the right direction, since Frank was married by then, and his wife was from Pittsburgh and attending nursing school there.

The Bridgeville stint didn't last, though. Frank was transferred to Steubenville, Ohio, where he worked as an assistant manager. His heart was still in his hometown, though, and the opportunity to return there eventually arrived.

When Frank learned that his former boss in Johnstown, Paul Benson, was terminally ill with lung cancer, he reached out to Paul about coming back. Paul welcomed him with open arms, and Frank wasted no time wrapping up his Steubenville assignment.

When Paul stepped away from the store, his assistant manager became manager, and Frank was also promoted. He worked as assistant manager at the downtown store until 1974, when his new workplace started to take shape up the hill in Richland.

The future of Thom McAn, and Frank, was all about the under-construction Richland Mall.

Overture, Curtain, Lights

"My district manager told me I was going to get the store in the new Mall, and I was thrilled," says Frank. "My years of experience with Thom McAn were about to pay off."

During his time with the company, Frank had helped open and close various store locations, so he knew exactly what to expect in prepping his new store at the Mall...and he had lots of opportunities to apply it. "I was very involved with getting the store up and running. I helped set up the display racks and shelves and put merchandise on them. I ordered inventory, placed signage and decorations around the store, and hired and trained the staff."

Hiring was a big job, but Frank tackled it with his own techniques. "First, I screened prospective employees at local high schools and the University of Pittsburgh at Johnstown. I wanted smart, A-B students. They didn't have to be outgoing, but they did have to be good students who were attending or likely to attend college and would therefore be around town for a few years. I didn't want to have to train someone new every other month.

"After the screening, there would be an in-store interview. I would go through a list of what I wanted the applicant to know. After I'd gone through everything, if I decided I wanted to hire the person, I told them what time to come in on the first day.

"The first day the new worker came in, I told him or her to clean the restrooms in the back, to really make them sparkle. Why did I do that? Because I knew if the person listened to me there, he or she would follow my orders on the job.

"It was a great test of character. Out of all the people I took back there, I only had one guy say, 'I wasn't hired for this.' I told him to not let the door fall on his head on the way out," says Frank.

True "High-Tops"

With the staff in place and the store set up, Thom McAn was ready for business by the grand opening on November 4th, 1974. Shoppers flocked to the place and kept coming in droves in the months that followed.

"In the beginning, $250,000 in sales volume for the year was our break-even point," explains Frank. "Anything we did over that was profit.

"Well, from November 4th to the end of '74, we did over $300,000. So we got past the break-even point in just two months. We were so busy, I couldn't even go out to eat! I kept calling other stores, saying 'I need shoes! Help me, I'm out of shoes!'"

One particular type of shoe he couldn't keep in stock was the platform shoe. "We couldn't get in enough men's platforms – the ones with the thick sole and big heel, what we used to call elevator shoes. I had two sections of platforms, and I couldn't keep them in the store."

Thom McAn hit shoppers' sweet spots with its selection of shoe styles for men, women, and children. There was an emphasis on women's fashion (though women's shoes hadn't even been sold at Thom McAn until the mid-60s) and perfect fit for kids.

"Whenever a sales associate sold a pair of kids' shoes, before the associate rang them up at the register, he or she either called myself or an assistant manager to check the fit. If the fit was right, we gave the customer a signed certificate indicating that we'd guaranteed the fit. Most stores didn't do that in those days," says Frank.

Clown Sundaes for Breakfast?

As Thom McAn hit its stride, Frank settled into the Mall community, making friends among his fellow merchants. His best buddies included "the three Joes" – Joe Fortunato of Richman Brothers, Joe Cohen of La Rose, and Joe Balogh of Tiffany's Bakery – along with one of Frank's main competitors in the footwear business, Gil Demos of Teek's Fine Shoes.

"We would go over to Sweet William every morning and just have a ball, laughing and carrying on," recalls Frank.

"The Mall opened to the public at 10 a.m. on weekdays. I'd get there around 8:45, flip all the lights on in the store, and get everything ready to go. I'd have the gate down and do all the paperwork and make sure everything was ready for the day. Then, up went the gate, and I would be over at Sweet William, which would open early for us to get breakfast."

Students of Shoebiz

Thom McAn's success continued in years to come, in tandem with the Mall's good fortune. After a while, the store was doing $550,000 in sales in just one year, more than double the break-even amount of $250,000.

According to Frank, the great numbers were all thanks to his great staff. "If you don't have good help, you can't do it yourself. Your help is the most important part of your store."

In return for his staff's hard work, Frank went out of his way to give them the best possible training in the business world. "I taught them well. I taught them how to make money, and they stayed with me. I very rarely had anyone leave before they were done with college."

Lots of success stories developed from Frank's staff over the years, going on to bigger and better things after leaving the Richland Mall store. "Most of them got out of college and moved on to a career. Six of my employees became managers at other stores, and one even became a district manager. So a lot of managers came out my store, and they did really well."

Mid-Career Crisis

As well as the staff and store were doing, however, Frank became disenchanted after a while. The rewards didn't always make up for the downside in the world of retail. "Retail made me a good living, but it *just* made me a good living," he says.

When the Mall added Sunday hours, requiring all tenants to be open from noon until 5:00 p.m., Frank's disenchantment grew. "My job wasn't so great when it became seven days a week. Thom McAn certainly didn't give me any more money for working the extra day.

"None of the merchants were happy when the hours changed. All we did was spread our hours out. It didn't really have an impact on the amount of business we did.

"In the old days, we were busy on Saturday nights. When we started opening on Sundays, we just took that business from Saturday night to Sunday, and it didn't even compare to Saturday nights. It was a trade-off from Saturday to Sunday."

As Frank's general level of satisfaction with mall retailing faded, he started looking for other opportunities – and ended up helping create one. He and some partners turned the old Skateland building on Bedford Street into a family fun center called Grand Slam USA.

Hitting a Home Run

Grand Slam catered to kids and featured batting cages, a miniature basketball court, video games, and other activities. When it launched in 1986, the positive response was immediate and strong.

"Kids from first through eighth grade came to Grand Slam," remembers Frank. "When the first and second graders were playing, you couldn't get in the building. When those little ones were playing, the place was packed with moms and dads, grandparents, aunts, uncles, brothers, and sisters."

Though Grand Slam's focus was on sports and games, the place also hosted dances for young people. "We hired the D.J. from Chuck E. Cheese, and he brought the crowd with him. Those dances were very popular."

The new chapter in Frank's life was underway – but it was soon interrupted by misfortune. Frank suffered injuries in two car accidents that left him unable to effectively run the business.

He and his partners decided to close Grand Slam after his second accident in 1997. Frank turned his focus to recovery and retirement, plus staying upbeat with weekly breakfast get-togethers with his Mall buddies Joe F., Joe C., and Gil. (Joe Balogh passed away in 2011.)

Memories of the Richland Mall still make him laugh. "I had a great time there," he says. "I had a great store that always did well, a great team that helped me succeed, and great friends who knew the secret to keeping the stress from getting to you is never taking yourself, or anyone, too seriously."

Photo by Philip Balko

The Michael Jackson glitter gloves didn't sell so great. Michael was a megastar, so La Rose store owner Joe Cohen thought replicas of his famous glove would really move…but they didn't. It's a good thing he can laugh about it now.

Because he usually made the right decisions when it came to La Rose – like opening a store in the Richland Mall.

Planting La Rose
La Rose was founded in 1923 in downtown Greensburg by Joe's grandfather. Decades later, the Cohen family opened a second store in the Greengate Mall, which was where Joe became friends with Greengate Manager Bob McConnell.

Later, when Bob moved to the new Richland Mall, he approached Joe and the Cohens about opening a store there, too – and the Cohens didn't say no.

Photos Courtesy Joe Cohen

Jim Streeter negotiated a deal to their liking, and La Rose joined the Richland Mall's inaugural roster of tenants in 1974.

"We had some family nearby, but I had no clue as to where Johnstown even was," says Joe. "It was a very exciting offer and time for us, though. We liked the layout of the Mall and the plans they had to market the place."

183

The store's original location was between Tiffany Bakery and Spencer Gifts in the Sears wing of the Mall. Joe moved to Johnstown so he could watch the place take shape and provide input when needed.

"We had our own architect build to our specs, and the Mall was very helpful to us in building the store of our dreams. It was wonderful.

"We had it ready to open in time for the November 4th Grand Opening. Everything was totally done, and all the staff had been hired. We couldn't wait to open the doors and welcome the public to our store," recalls Joe.

Conquest of the Coats

After the grand opening, the Cohens realized they had a hit on their hands. "Business was unbelievable. The acceptance by Mall customers was overwhelming."

One of the biggest challenges the family faced was ordering the right stock to keep up that high level of churn. "From a buying standpoint, we had to add more merchandise, and it was difficult. We had to keep testing to see what worked and what didn't. And we had to keep in mind the older end – the Missy market – because at that point, the Junior and younger markets were dominated by the major chain stores. We tried to find our niche by getting into the older market."

Joe did the legwork, traveling to New York City to do most of the buying for the three La Rose stores. He also did some buying at trade shows in Monroeville, where he could work hands-on with the individual manufacturers or reps.

All that buying took a lot of know-how and experience, as the different markets had very different styles and sizing. "The Junior market was more teenagers to women in their early twenties. The Missy market started from there and went up in age with different sizing. Missy clothes had a much different look than Junior clothes, more mature.

"What we ended up doing at La Rose in the Mall was catering to teens to early twentysomethings, then skipping to age 50 and above. It suited our clientele and kept our numbers where they needed to be," explains Joe.

The store's numbers were especially strong when it came to outerwear. "At the Richland Mall, we became known for our coats, to the point where we literally had 1,000 coats in stock during the fall/winter season. That's a lot of coats."

The success of the coat business led to a big change for La Rose.

"Specialists in Misses' and Half-Size Fashions"

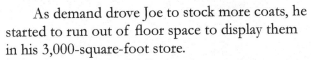

As demand drove Joe to stock more coats, he started to run out of floor space to display them in his 3,000-square-foot store.

It was time for La Rose to move.

Movin' on Up

La Rose took up residence in a big new 5,000-square-foot store in the Kmart wing of the Mall. There was plenty of room to display all the coats, and everything else besides.

Photos Courtesy Joe Cohen

Joseph and Sandra Cohen
cordially invite you to the opening
of the newly remodeled
LaRose
Please come celebrate
with cocktails and hors d'oeuvres
on Sunday, the twenty-fourth of March
Nineteen hundred and eighty-five
from six to nine in the evening
at the Richland Mall Store
Johnstown, Pennsylvania

GRAND OPENING
La Rose
NEW LOCATION IN THE RICHLAND MALL

Advance Notice Previous to General Advertising
LIMITED TIME ONLY · OFFER ENDS OCTOBER 1st

Valuable Coupon - Please Present to Cashier

15% OFF
LOWEST TICKETED PRICE
ENTIRE STOCK
Fall and Holiday Fashions!

Free Christmas Layaway * Not Subject to Prior Purchases

YOU'RE INVITED TO OUR AUTUMN FASHION SHOW

Saturday, September 30th, 6:00 PM
Centre Court, Richland Mall
...THEN ENJOY A FREE CONCERT BY THE VOGUES at 7:00 PM

"Experience the Specialty Shop Difference"

Based on existing demand and La Rose's business model, it looked like a great move. "We had coat sales all the time," says Joe. "The coat business is what held us together."

Net sales continued to grow over time. The Mall store was busier than ever, even as the Greensburg stores required additional time and effort.

Photos Courtesy Joe Cohen

186

It could have been a burden for Joe, who'd been managing all three La Rose stores since his father's retirement – but it worked out thanks to his dependable, quality staff. "My staff and employees were the best I could ever ask for, and they were loyal. I was so lucky because they enabled me to have a life.

"I remembered, as a kid, how I didn't see my dad a lot when he was running the business. I didn't want it to be that way for my kids, and it wasn't. I was fortunate enough to have the staff that allowed me to be there for my family."

Everything had come together for Joe. La Rose was a success story…he got to be there for his family…and the Richland Mall was thriving around him.

Unfortunately, the bubble finally broke.

Climate Change Killed the Coat Biz?

People stopped buying so many coats. That was how it started.

"The winters started getting warmer," remembers Joe. "Demand for coats fell. We went from keeping 1,000 coats in stock to 200."

The decline of that marquee item cost the store hundreds of thousands of dollars in business over time. La Rose absorbed the loss, but that couldn't go on forever.

Neither could the Mall. After the opening of the Galleria in 1992, business in general declined at the Richland Mall. Decreased foot traffic in the Mall further depressed La Rose's business – and it soon became clear that the situation had to change.

Joe moved La Rose to the Galleria in 1997. The store stayed in business there for three more years before Joe shut down the Richland operation for good. By then, the Greengate Mall location was long gone, and the downtown Greensburg store was also a thing of the past. La Rose was no more.

Joe went on to work in real estate and partnered with Gil Demos on his C. Gil Shoes store. These days, he's retired, spending his time tending his home and gardens in Westmont.

But he still gets together with fellow Mall veterans Gil, Joe Fortunato, and Frank Koscis every Saturday for breakfast, and he still misses the glory days of the Richland Mall.

"I feel sad that the Mall is gone. It was just an unbelievable situation, personally and for the people of Johnstown. It was a fantastic facility with great ownership. It was sad that it didn't work, but I'm forever grateful that I got to be a part of it," says Joe.

Photos Courtesy Joe Cohen

THE NEW LA ROSE WILL BE IN FULL BLOOM
ON MONDAY MORNING, NOVEMBER 4th, at 10:00 A.M.

The world of
YOUNG
IDEA
FASHIONS
in.....

Coats
Suits
Dresses
Longs
Pantsuits
Sportswear
Accessories and even Furs

La Rose

Mr. Joseph Cohen, store manager, will be here to answer any questions you might have concerning the store or the merchandise we carry. Come in and register for $500 in prizes. Free gift for everyone who registers . . . No purchase necessary. So won't you join us and discover the difference in true specialty shop shopping . . .

GREENSBURG
GREENGATE MALL
RICHLAND MALL

CENTER COURT AREA . . . **richland mall**   OPEN 10:00 A.M. TO 10:00 P.M. DAILY

Tour
NATIONAL Record Mart

One store in the Richland Mall was *always* rocking, and Karen Largent was lucky enough to work there in its prime.

"We played music *constantly* at National Record Mart," remembers Karen. "We played hit tunes all day, every day, and sang and danced along to the music. We just had a great time! I would have to say that working at Record Mart was the most fun I've ever had at a job."

Photo Courtesy Karen Largent

THE Boss Is As Important as YOUR Boss

More than any other store in the Mall, National Record Mart – NRM, for short – was all about music. The store, which was located on the corner closest to Kmart, sold cassette tapes, 8-track tapes, and of course vinyl in the form of LP albums and 45 singles. It was part of a Pittsburgh-based company started in 1937 – the first music retail chain in the U.S.

Karen was interviewed for a job at NRM in 1976 at the age of 19 by manager Paul Folk, who of course grilled her about music. "He asked me a lot about the music that was current then, the artists and albums of the time. It was important to stay up-to-date on the latest popular music."

Her knowledge of Bruce Springsteen, David Bowie, and other musicians impressed Paul enough that NRM hired her as a part-time sales associate.

"I would wander around and help people find what they were looking for. There was no pressure to sell, because people almost always came in knowing what they wanted," says Karen.

It was just a matter of finding the right record in the right rack or opening the special case where the valuable (for the 1970s) cassettes and 8-tracks were kept under lock and key.

Photo by Chuck Mamula

Quadrophonic 8-Tracks?

"We kept the cassettes and 8-tracks locked up behind Plexiglas doors to prevent theft," says Karen. "The vinyl albums and singles were out in racks in the middle of the store. There were always customers flipping through them, looking for something new."

NRM also sold quadrophonic 8-track tapes for the hardcore music enthusiasts. "Quadrophonic stereo separated sound so something different came out of each of the system's four speakers. It was way ahead of its time, a 1970s precursor to Surround-Sound.

"My dad actually bought a quadrophonic system, and he loved it. Unfortunately, it was a high-end product, and we had a very limited selection of tapes for it," says Karen.

When it came to other formats, though, NRM was well stocked. "We sold vinyl albums the most, for sure. That was mostly what people came in for."

More Than a Star Is a Feeling

Albums might have been the most popular format back then, but the genres of music featured on them varied wildly. Though NRM in the Mall was more of a rock 'n' roll store, Karen and her co-workers sold plenty of folk, disco, country, and classical records and tapes, too.

"We had a little of everything," she recalls. "But the music playing in the store was almost always rock. That's mostly what young people, including the store employees, were into in those days."

The band Boston, for example, was a smash in 1976, with a string of hits off their self-titled debut album, including "More Than a Feeling," "Long Time," and "Peace of Mind." Karen remembers playing their music a lot in the store back then, as customers poured in to buy the album.

"'More Than a Feeling' was a number one hit, and we played it constantly," says Karen. "We all sang and danced to that one, and so did the customers."

Another record that caught fire at NRM in '76 was the soundtrack to the Barbra Streisand-Kris Kristofferson movie *A Star Is Born*. "That was the big movie that year," says Karen. "To promote the album, we made a fancy display with a big papier-mâché star, and other stars hanging from the ceiling. We had one rack that was just copies of the soundtrack, and we sold a ton of them."

Every Day Was Record Store Day

In addition to vinyl records and tapes, NRM sold concert tickets. "For big shows in Pittsburgh, the lines would be out the door," remembers Karen. "The managers always sold them, not the sales people, but the ticket sales always brought a lot of business to the store."

No matter what was going on at the store, NRM's rock 'n roll style always drew a young, hip crowd. The singing and dancing were infectious – for some, more than others.

"We had one guy who would climb up on top of the record racks and dance," says Karen. "He had long, blond hair, and he worked there, and he would just lose himself in the music."

The décor was all about the music, too. According to Karen, promotional posters featuring current stars and hit albums covered the walls and lined the big windows facing Kmart. The posters would arrive with shipments of records, and employees would claim their favorites to take home when new ones replaced them.

#BringBackRichlandMall

As much as Karen loved working at NRM, she left after a year to work at Our Furniture, another Richland Mall store. NRM moved on, too, becoming the largest of 40 stores in the NRM chain thanks to a 4,000-square-foot expansion in 1978.

NRM continued to thrive in the Mall through the 80s, but in the mid-90s, it was replaced by another music store, The Wall. In 2001, the entire National Record Mart company went out of business, a victim of the declining sales of physical recordings. After 64 years and dozens of stores around the world, NRM couldn't fight the growth of online downloading and streaming.

There has been a lot of water (and music) under the bridge since then, but Karen still looks back fondly on her days at the coolest place in the Richland Mall.

"I absolutely wish that National Record Mart was still there," she says. "It was just such a wonderful place to work and hang out. The camaraderie was great, and we all had so much fun.

"I wish the whole Richland Mall was still there, in fact. It was such an important part of my life, and the lives of so many of my friends and family. Bring back the Richland Mall," says Karen.

Photo Courtesy Karen Largent

192

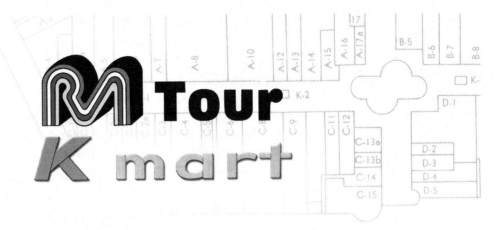

Tour Kmart

Long before Wal-Mart came to dominate Richland Town Centre, Kmart ruled the discount retail roost on the same site in the Richland Mall.

At the opposite end of the Mall from Sears, Kmart attracted hordes of customers with its low prices, Blue-Light Specials, back-of-the-store snack bar, and incredible selection of clothes, shoes, furnishings, toys, jewelry, automotive supplies, and you-name-it.

Brian Mahon remembers it well. After all, he worked there for 19 years.

Photo by Philip Balko

The Midway Man

Brian started working at Kmart in 1981 as a part-time "Midway," which he describes as a kind of stock person. "The midway was what they called the main aisle that came up through the store. They used the same name for a person who stocked the displays along that aisle.

"The manager would send me to the department heads, and they would tell me what to stock along the midway. They would show me using a map that was generated daily at the store level. Then I would bring the requested merchandise out of the stockroom and place it on the designated displays," explains Brian.

As racks or shelves along the midway aisle emptied, Brian refilled them. It got pretty busy sometimes, as shoppers snapped up featured bargains that caught their eye as they walked along the midway...but Brian always kept up with demand. And he learned Kmart's system along the way.

When a chance for promotion came along after a year, he was ready. His part-time Midway days were over as he stepped into the role of full-time hardware department manager.

193

It was a great fit, as Brian had always had a natural affinity for working with hardware and mechanical things. His father, he says, was the same way.

But running the department required a lot of paper pushing and desk work, as well. "I was responsible for the ordering, stocking, and just about everything related to hardware," says Brian. "I was constantly ordering, filling the shelves every week. I had to make sure we replaced what we sold and were fully prepared for every sales event and holiday."

Photo by Joyce Mitchell Cannonie

Blue-Light Family

During his time as hardware manager, Brian came to enjoy being a part of the Kmart family.

He and his fellow Kmart employees "all had a niche, but we all got along." According to Brian, there was more separation between departments when he first started, but that changed over time as workers were encouraged to assist more often in different departments.

"Once you started working there, you were family. People hated to leave," he says.

The Kmart staff cooked out and watched fireworks together on the Fourth of July, picnicking in the parking lot outside the store. "The view was incredible, because the fireworks were launched in a field by the Mall," he remembers.

On the day before Thanksgiving, Kmart employees had a turkey dinner in the break room at the back of the store, with all food provided by the company. "There were two break rooms, actually – one for the men and one for the women – and we used them both on Thanksgiving," says Brian.

There was an annual Christmas party, too, and a charity softball tournament. "We were just close. In fact, I can't think of a time when there was a problem between one employee and another. We just got along."

Brian also enjoyed being part of the Richland Mall community and making the most of its simple pleasures.

"I loved our location, because it was conveniently close to McDonald's, where I like to eat. There was another place nearby where I often got doughnuts and iced tea for breakfast.

"At lunchtime, my friend and I liked to go to Time-Out. We had an hour-long lunch break, which gave us plenty of time to play the arcade games," remembers Brian.

Bouncing Around the K

When Kmart merged its hardware and building supplies departments into a new Homecare Center, Brian found himself in a changed situation. Though he was still managing the hardware side of the Homecare Center, he worked more closely with the building supplies manager – Tony Tomaselli – and both of them were given a new supervisor.

Photo by Chuck Mamula

"It was a big change for Kmart, converting part of the department store to a lumber store. It was a big change for me, too, compared to what I'd been doing. I would handle the hardware, and another guy would handle the building supplies, but now we were part of one department with a new boss," says Brian.

Thanks to the great working relationships among Kmart employees, the new arrangement worked well, and the Homecare Center was a success. "I liked working there," says Brian. "Tony and I got along great, and things were good for a while."

After a couple of years, though, Brian left the Homecare Center behind and moved to managing the Stock Replenishment Crew. "Basically, we handled stocking the way that Wal-Mart does now. We had a small group of people who stocked all the departments at once around two in the morning. We tried to have it done before the store opened at 8:30 a.m., so we wouldn't be stocking the shelves when customers were there.

"There was a team that handled every department. I managed the teams and also helped to stock shelves," says Brian. "Plus I had a key to the store, to give our crew access as needed."

After four years in stock replenishment, Brian was asked to join the Receiving Department. "I had a reputation for getting things done and doing them the Kmart way. I'd worked there long enough that I understood how people wanted things done. So they made me the manager of the Receiving Department."

Complainers Back Off

As a manager, in addition to leading the Receiving Department, Brian performed general supervisory duties in the store. He was able to approve checks and handled customer complaints – though he didn't always enjoy dealing with irate customers.

"The worst complaints were on Sundays if items went on sale, and they were featured in our newspaper circulars, but we didn't have them in stock.

Photo by Chuck Mamula

It happened sometimes when a company just didn't send the items soon enough. It wasn't our fault, but I still got chewed out by customers a couple times. It was bad, and I mean bad," says Brian.

The store's policy, in general, was that the customer was right...but not always. "Sometimes, it was clear that an employee was in the right. In those cases, everyone on staff at the store would side with him. Management would never let an employee hang out to dry if that person was right."

Still, Brian always worked hard to satisfy customers when he could. "I would get special requests from customers all the time, and I would spend half the day on the phone trying to order stuff for them. Sometimes, I had to threaten companies so they would send their products sooner. I would tell them that Kmart is a large corporation, and if they didn't send their products in time, it would create big problems for them. It wasn't true that the company would hurt them, I just said it. I did it to try to get the products shipped faster and keep the customers happy," explains Brian.

Very Special K

As the years passed, Kmart continued to thrive in the Richland Mall, becoming one of the best-performing locations in the region.

"We did better than Somerset and Indiana," says Brian. "We did as well as Altoona if not better. We didn't lag behind anyone in the region at all."

Even when the Richland Mall closed its main section in March 1998, Kmart was doing well enough to stay open. Loyal shoppers kept supporting the store as they always had, though the Mall seemed to be slipping away around it.

But Brian wasn't blind. He knew it would only be a matter of time until the Mall took Kmart down with it.

He knew it was time to get out. When he was offered a job at Home Depot, he took it. One month shy of his 19th anniversary at Kmart, he left behind the Blue-Light Specials and strapped on an orange apron.

But even after all this time away from the Big K, he still bleeds blue. "Kmart was a big part of my life for almost two decades," he says. "The employees became like family to me. A lot of the people I consider to be good friends now, I worked with at Kmart. I still see them from time to time. I was even the best man at the weddings of two of the people who worked under me back in the day, Doug Ream and George Rozum.

"Kmart people are special, and they always will be. When there was a reunion of Richland Mall employees recently, in the parking lot of the Richland Town Centre, the biggest group was former Kmart employees.

"The store itself might be long-gone, but Kmart people will always come through," Brian says with a smile.

K-mart Became First to Open

K-mart held a ribbon-cutting ceremony Oct. 9 to become the first store in the Richland Mall to open for business. Officials of the S. S. Kresge Co. and local store employes participated. K-mart offers a complete line of merchandise, mostly at discount prices. They have a "Satisfaction Always" policy — and employes were told at the opening that "the customer is always right." The Kresge chain is the nation's third largest retailer and its K-mart division is the fastest growing in America. The local store is the first K-mart to go into an enclosed regional shopping mall.

© *The Tribune-Democrat*

RM Tour
SHOP 'n SAVE

In August 1977, Wendy Jeschonek interviewed for a job at Shop 'n Save supermarket at the Richland Mall. That five-minute-long interview, which took place in the canned vegetables aisle, was the start of a grocery store gig that lasted seven and a half years.

Wendy had graduated from high school in June of that year. "After the 1977 flood, area high school graduates were eligible for unemployment compensation. I didn't feel right about collecting a weekly paycheck but not working for it, especially when so many people's lives were devastated. I

Wendy Jeschonek

began applying to stores in the Mall. Then, one of my good friends who worked at Shop 'n Save told me that they were hiring," says Wendy.

Hired as a part-time cashier, Wendy mostly worked at a checkout station in the front of the store, ringing up customers' purchases. At first, she operated an old-fashioned cash register with buttons, but after a few years, the store installed scanners. "I think we might have been the first grocery store in the area to have scanners," says Wendy.

At that time, the technology was still new and not always dependable. Wendy says that there were always one or two scanners that weren't working properly.

"I preferred the old registers. After a while, I didn't even have to look at those registers when using them to ring up groceries. Also, I liked figuring out customers' change instead of having it done for me."

Paper or Paper?

In addition to analog cash registers, paper bags were the only option for bagging groceries in Wendy's early days as a cashier. Plastic grocery bags didn't come along until later.

"We didn't say 'paper or plastic' back then," recalls Wendy. "It was just paper."

Plastic soda bottles didn't exist in the store then, either. Soda was always bottled in glass, which led to frequent mishaps. "Those glass bottles were sold in 8-packs, and stores like Shop 'n Save had to stack them on the shelves and floor. As you might guess, we often heard a crash of breaking glass, followed by an announcement over the P.A. system saying, 'cleanup in aisle so-and-so.'"

The store's hours were also different in the beginning. Shop 'n Save wasn't open on Sundays or holidays then, though that eventually changed.

Store Manager Bert Bouchard decided to follow the lead of other stores in the Mall and instituted Sunday and holiday hours. Union members like Wendy were paid double time and a half for working Sundays and holidays, though she says the extra pay wasn't worth missing family gatherings.

Something else that eventually changed, but not for the better, was Wendy's uniform. "We wore smocks. At first, they were red (I think)...but then the company ordered new ones, and they were a rust-orange color with plaid on the collar. They were hideous and didn't match anything I wore!" remembers Wendy.

Copacetic Cashiers

When she wasn't running the register, Wendy did other jobs in the store, like stocking shelves, taking boxes to the compactor, and repricing items. Sometimes, in the scanner era, she would come in early and check the tags on sale items against the prices listed in the latest ad, making sure the items rang up correctly.

During breaks, she liked to grab a bite to eat at the Big Top Deli or her favorite restaurant, Super Chick. "Super Chick had the best chicken and breading," she remembers. "I was in there all the time. I loved their 'Afternoon Delight' lemonade, too, which was named after a hit song."

Back on duty in the store, Wendy found that her shifts always flew past. "We were always very busy, right up until closing time. We closed an hour after the Mall so we would get the people who worked at the Mall leaving work at the end of the night and buying things."

As busy as it was, Wendy remembers that the cashiers worked well together and got along in spite of age differences. "Young people and older people worked side by side, and we had a good time together," says Wendy.

She also has fond memories of the original store manager, Bert Bouchard. "He was really nice and easygoing. For example, there was an elderly couple who owned a small mom and pop store, and they would come and buy things to sell in their store. Bert would give them a discount so they could make a bigger profit."

Best Part of the Job

For a while, Wendy also worked at Monarch's, a women's clothing store in the Mall. In 1984, she quit both jobs so she could have more time to pursue her teaching degree at the University of Pittsburgh at Johnstown.

She went on to have a 25-year career as an English literature teacher, a position that she loved. But she still has great memories of the Mall and Shop 'n Save. "What I loved most was talking with the customers. So many of them would come in regularly. Some people would even come in daily. They would go through the express aisle and maybe get just a pack of cigarettes, but they were in there every day. I got to know a lot of them by name and got to know about their lives.

"The cool thing was, the customers would often pull up to my checkout when I had a line, and I would say 'that register is open over there,' and they would say 'I'll wait for you.' It used to make me feel so good that they wouldn't mind waiting for me," says Wendy.

These days, Wendy still sometimes crosses paths with customers and fellow employees from Shop 'n Save, and they reminisce about the old days. Nothing quite recaptures that long-gone supermarket, though one local grocery store reminds Wendy of the Shop 'n Save spirit.

"Market Basket always reminds me of Shop 'n Save," says Wendy. "The cashiers there are friendly, they talk to customers, and they joke around. It's comfortable to work and shop in a place like that. I felt that was how we were at Shop 'n Save.

"I'm glad I got to experience that place during its heyday," says Wendy. "It helped me to learn the importance of good customer service...and the convenience of plastic soda bottles."

PONDEROSA
STEAKHOUSE

When you think about classic Richland Mall restaurants, Capri, Encore, and Sweet William might come to mind – but there was a place out in the parking lot that was often the top performer in the country for its parent company.

Photo by Larry Stahl

Ponderosa Steakhouse was a "mall pad" store, located in the parking lot but not directly connected to the Mall. For years, it was one of the top three Ponderosas in the U.S., many times making it all the way to number one.

"Sometimes we were number one, and sometimes we were number three," remembers Barry Thomas, who once worked as a manager at the Richland Mall Ponderosa. "Our competition was Kissimmee, Florida, which served Orlando and Disney, and Watertown, New York. So we matched up pretty well with the big guys. We made our Ponderosa into a two-million-dollar-a-year store and ended up being the highest selling unit in the country."

Even a devastating fire in '86 couldn't keep Ponderosa down for long. It took the coming of the Galleriazilla and the death of the Richland Mall to finally close the book on that particular mall pad restaurant.

Photo by Larry Stahl

199

Photo by Larry Stahl

Tastes Like Patriotism

When the steakhouse first opened in 1976, it was all about Bicentennial fever...and it wasn't called Ponderosa.

Larry Stahl, later an executive manager of Ponderosa, worked at that original version, which was called Patriot. "The Patriot Steakhouse chain rode the wave of the Bicentennial with their concept. They had a Revolutionary War-era motif, with tri-corner hats and Colonial décor."

Photo by Philip Balko

Larry started at Patriot in 1977 as a cook, then went into the company's management training program. After completing that program, he worked in several Patriot stores as an assistant manager to learn the ropes, then returned to the Richland Mall unit. The Richland Mall Patriot was number 002, the second store in the chain to open.

According to Larry, the Patriot Steakhouses were developed by a company that owned and operated a number of Ponderosas in Pennsylvania. The two chains had similar concepts in terms of how they prepared and served food.

At both restaurants, customers came through a line where they picked up trays, silverware, napkins, and beverages. The broiler and ovens were set up alongside the line, so customers could see the cooks preparing their food.

But Patriot didn't have a salad bar or buffet, unlike Ponderosa. "At Patriot, customers got their bowl of salad and rolls in line. They also got their steak right there, since the employees cooked in advance – unless the team didn't have the right steak available. In that case, they'd give the customer a color-coded tag, and he or she would go to their table and wait. A server would bring the steak out to the customer's table in a few minutes," explains Larry.

Soon enough, the differences didn't matter. In 1980, the two chains' parent company converted all its Patriot Steakhouses into Ponderosas. The Bicentennial-inspired concept had run its course.

Photo by Larry Stahl

200

From then on, the steaks would all be cooked to order, and all salads would come from the salad bar. A Western motif pushed out the Colonial style, and employees switched to uniforms with lots of brown in them.

It looked like a smart play as the months and years went by, and sales continued to rise by leaps and bounds. Barry attributes the increase, in part, to the buffet installed in the early 80s as part of Ponderosa's business model.

"People in Johnstown wanted value. They appreciated the opportunity to get a lot of food at a low price. I think the quality, quantity, and atmosphere were what drew people. When you tried to get into the place, the line was out the door most of the time," says Barry.

Years after the changeover, a group of investors brought back the Patriot concept, opening the Five Patriots Steakhouse across Theater Drive from the Mall. It didn't last, though. In the end, Five Patriots was converted to a Hoss's Steakhouse, which occupies the same building to this day.

Photo by Philip Balko

Larry, Barry, and Terry Unite (and Rhyme)

In 1984, as the Richland Mall Ponderosa was booming, Terry Miller became the newest manager to join the team. It was the start of 13 happy years with the company.

Prior to Ponderosa, Terry had worked his way through the ranks of the Burger King chain for 11 years, bouncing from Johnstown to Utah to Wisconsin. Returning to Johnstown in '83 to give his young son roots in the area, Terry went into business as a co-owner of Zak's Tap Room between Shop 'n Save and Kmart at the Mall. When that venture folded, he heard Ponderosa was looking for a manager, and he applied and was hired...starting the tradition of managers whose names rhymed with Executive Manager Larry's.

"I loved working at Ponderosa," says Terry. "It was the best job I've ever had. We had the best crew, and the people cared about what they did and the service they gave. They were some of the most enjoyable years of my working career."

Barry Thomas, who started as a manager at Ponderosa in the spring of '85 (and had the perfect rhyming name for it), agrees with Terry about the quality of the staff. "There is no substitute for hiring good people. I still see some of them to this day, and they are proud and really good people."

"Johnstown had a very good work ethic," says Larry. "You could count on people to show up for work and do a good job. That doesn't mean it was totally problem-free, but by and large, it was excellent. It was the same with management. You could trust people to do what they were asked to do."

Photo by Philip Balko

"We treated our people right, and as a result, had the lowest employee turnover in the entire company," says Barry. "We took a significant amount of pride in that, because we had a great plan for hiring and retaining employees, and the fact that people weren't leaving said we had a pretty great environment to work in.

"We had people calling from other parts of the country, asking what we were doing to recruit and retain so effectively, and we said it's not that hard, you just have to hire good people and treat them right."

According to Barry, Ponderosa hired a lot of young people – especially high school students who planned to attend UPJ. "That way, we'd have them for five or six years instead of just one or two." Ponderosa also hired veterans and special needs employees.

Whatever a worker's age, capabilities, or background, the management team always strove to treat them fairly and with respect. "We asked what they wanted, and we tried to understand where they were coming from," says Barry. "Larry is a guy who works hard and has great ethics, and I think that was the backbone behind the philosophy of treating employees right. He's a Christian who really lives his faith and works hard and sets an example."

Larry, Barry, and Terry tried so hard to look out for the staff that they were even determined not to let them down when there wasn't a steakhouse for them to work in anymore.

Burnt to a Crisp

In November 1986, Barry was living in the Roxbury section of town when he got an early-morning call from an employee. She told him there had been a fire at the Ponderosa.

He drove straight to the steakhouse and found a scene of stunning destruction. The flames were out, the fire crews were cleaning up, but the Ponderosa had been burned from within.

Photo by Larry Stahl

Photo by Larry Stahl

Photo by Larry Stahl

When it was safe to go inside, Larry and Terry toured the ruins with him. The roof had collapsed over the dining room, leaving a heap of blackened timbers and cinders. Equipment was melted and charred; furnishings had been reduced to ash. Their precious Ponderosa Steakhouse was a singed and smoking husk.

Photo by Terry Miller

Photo by Larry Stahl

Photo by Terry Miller

Photo by Larry Stahl

It was truly a life-changing experience. As the shock wore off, the consequences of the blaze became clear to the management team.

"It was devastating," recalls Terry. "We were worried about what was going to happen. We were one of the top three stores in the U.S., and now we were going to close for an indefinite amount of time. Everything we'd worked so hard to build was in limbo."

The fate of the people who worked at Ponderosa also weighed heavily on their minds. "We knew the company would rebuild the store, but what would happen to the crew in the meantime?" asked Terry. "We had such a fabulous team. Would we lose them while the store was closed?"

Though the future was uncertain, Larry, Terry, and Barry pledged to do their best to keep the crew – and their own management team---together.

Bravo, Encore!

As the ashes settled, investigators combed the rubble of the Ponderosa, trying to determine the cause. The closest they came was to report that the fire had started in the dining room. Damage was estimated at between $600,000 and $700,000.

Photo by Terry Miller

Insurance claims were filed, corporate paperwork was processed, and reconstruction was soon underway. Until it could be finished, the three managers were deployed to other locations – Larry to Altoona, Terry and Barry to Indiana, PA.

But they made it a point to keep their employees in the loop. "We had periodic meetings at the Richland Mall to let our crew know what was going on," says Terry.

Photo by Terry Miller

203

"The employees were eligible for unemployment, and of course they were able to get jobs elsewhere," says Barry. "But we made it clear we wanted them all to come back."

"Larry Mummert, who owned the Encore, really came through for us," remembers Larry.

"Without asking for anything in return, he let us meet with our employees at the Encore for these progress updates. He was one of the most supportive people from the Mall during a challenging time, letting us use his facility since ours was being rebuilt."

The managers' efforts paid off. When the new Ponderosa was finished in May 1987, most of their employees from before the fire came back.

"I don't recall any hourly employees going anywhere else," says Barry. "The family stuck together."

And it grew, as well. The pre-fire staff of 40 employees was more than doubled, pushing 100 employees.

Photo by Terry Miller

Pajama Game

The reconstructed steakhouse was new and improved in every way. The damage had been so extreme that the builders had had to replace everything.

"The footprint of the store was about the same, but they enclosed what had been a porch slab and added about 20 more seats," explains Larry. "Everything in the dining room and kitchen was brand new, of course. The old equipment all had to be replaced. We were starting over with an all-new store."

A grand opening event was held in May '87, publicizing the restaurant's fresh start. "Big Jim Burton, the TV and radio personality, was out in a bed in the parking lot, wearing pajamas. Customers could get a free breakfast if they showed up in their pajamas, too," remembers Terry.

"The local community was excited about us reopening," says Barry. "I get emotional thinking about it, because they really accepted us back."

"We served about 10,000 people that first week we were open. Business was better than before. It doubled, I think. It helped that the

Photo by Terry Miller

new store had more seats, better design, and was updated. The seating and kitchen area were definitely made for high volume and high efficiency," says Terry.

Photo by Terry Miller

Photo by Larry Stahl

It was the start of a new era for Ponderosa, the beginning of the good new days for the popular steakhouse. Back then, in 1987, there were no signs of additional danger on the horizon.

But when the Galleria opened in '92, the winds of change started blowing.

Photo by Larry Stahl

Ponderosa's Secret Ingredient

In the years that followed, business at the Richland Mall dropped off, and tenants jumped ship. Ponderosa hung in there, as the restaurant's numbers were still good, but the future of the Mall was looking grim.

"It was sad," says Barry. "I remember walking around the Richland Mall with the Ponderosa district supervisor at the time, who was visiting from Pittsburgh. Almost everything was closed or closing by then. There was a store here, a store there, but there wasn't much life left in the place. It was a part of the community, and it was dying."

In March 1998, the bulk of the Richland Mall closed, and it became clear the rest of the Mall wasn't long for this world. Something had to change for Ponderosa to stay in business in Johnstown.

"I remember telling people at corporate that they should consider a site at the Galleria, because the shopping habits of people were shifting in that direction," says Larry. "Our Elton Road location was still a pretty busy spot, but we had a window of time in which to consider moving before it was too late."

Larry was right. Ponderosa moved to a Galleria outparcel in 2000 (and closed for good on December 6, 2015). The entire Richland Mall, including the original Ponderosa location, was demolished by July 25, 2003.

Though the Ponderosa team had moved on by then – some to other jobs or locations out of town – the demolition was a bitter pill to swallow.

"When they were tearing the Mall down, I kept seeing pieces of it fall, and I knew it was the end of an era and you could feel that change," says Barry. "When they started to build something new there, it just didn't fit and was maybe not as efficient.

"Back when we were in high school, everyone said 'let's go to the Mall.' You did lose a piece of yourself when they started to tear that down," says Barry.

"Tear-down was sad. It was done," recalls Terry. "I would look at it every time I drove by. I definitely paid attention to the progress. I watched the interior of the Mall become the exterior, and remembered different things about each of the stores, and what I'd experienced in those 30 years since it first opened."

As for Larry, it's the people of the Mall Ponderosa he thinks about most. "I miss the employees and repeat customers, the regulars. I could almost think of those people as family, because I spent so much time with them in that particular work environment. They were our secret ingredient. They were what made Ponderosa at the Mall so special."

Photo by Philip Balko

206

I am 36 and was raised in Seward, PA. I used to go to the Richland Mall once or twice a week with my parents and family or with friends. Seward was about 20 minutes away from the Mall, though it seemed a lot longer when I was young.

I remember we would always park at the Kmart end of the Mall. I had an aunt who worked there, so that is where I would end up after making my rounds. I normally had about an hour or so before I had to meet my mom there. Yes, this was before I could drive.

My rounds started at Kay Bee Toys. They always had a ton of stuff out in front of the store. I loved spending the small amount of money I had on some stupid toy off the clearance rack. Moving on, I visited the pet store beside Kay Bee. You could buy a cricket for a quarter from a vending machine in front of the store, then watch it drop down and get eaten by a lizard.

At the time, the Mall seemed huge. The middle of the Mall had plants and a pond, and I loved walking through it with that smell of humidity in the air.

Staying on course, I would walk past Foot Locker and the flower store (can't remember the name) and end up at Waldenbooks. That's where I would check out my favorite comics and the latest issue of *Fangoria* magazine and see if any new role-playing games had come out.

Food was not big on my list at the Mall. I think I ate once or twice at Sweet William, maybe once at Hot Sam (I know, "for shame") and a handful of times at Capri. I was never in the Encore or had Karmelkorn. Cinnabon was there later, and I would get food there, but most of the other fast food places, like Long John Silver's and McDonald's, were few and far between.

I never ventured too far past Waldenbooks into the Hills/Oswald's/Family Pantry/Thrift Drug area. I remember there being an offshoot that had a stamp machine and PO boxes, and at one time, later in the Mall's life, I had a part-time job at the Video Game Exchange that was on the corner there.

After Waldenbooks would come Time-Out. I spent *way* too much money there as a kid. I loved it there, but I was always "scared" of that area. No offense to anyone, but when it was close to the Mall's closing time, the people outside Time-Out, Pockets, Capri, and the movie theaters always scared me. I saw too many denim jackets with big heavy metal back patches on them there.

After dropping $5 or so (a lot for me at the time), I headed back to Kmart to meet up with my parents. I would stop to see my aunt at the checkout line, enjoy the smell of the popcorn, have a Slush Puppy, and watch my mom and grandma sift through all the Blue-Light Specials.

While they were checking out, I would stop off at National Record Mart and look at all the cassettes behind sliding glass, and the new CDs in their long boxes. If there was still time, my dad and I would sit on the curved stone window rails outside Kmart and watch the people go by.

I never really "hung out" at the Mall as I got older. I would drive to it to go to work (for a brief period of time) or buy something, but never with the intention of hanging out. I lived in Seward and always thought it was "so far to drive" to the Mall. I never cruised it, but always saw people cruising.

I never appreciated that Mall until they started closing it down. It was sad to see the stores closing, and the Mall being empty. I was working out of the country when they closed it up completely (minus the theaters) and when I came back for vacation, it was already being torn down. I have a few videos and photos of the inside, but I never got to see the inside myself before it was demolished.

It's sad to think that it could have been saved (though I'm sure it would have been very costly), that it was torn down to build a Wal-Mart, and that the Galleria is still standing, but at least we can talk and reminisce about it. There are 1,272 members on a Facebook page that all have the same love for the Mall that is no longer there, and only 12 on a Johnstown Galleria Facebook page (at this writing).

Jason Pozar

chapter nine

along came
a galleria

1988 - 1992

If quantum physics theories are correct, and multiple alternate realities can branch out from a single triggering event, there must be a parallel world where the Richland Mall expanded in 1989. After all, that was the longtime plan of Jim Streeter and Richland Mall Associates, confirmed by *The Tribune-Democrat* in December 1988.

In that other world, the Associates erected a 156,900-square-foot addition on the Eisenhower Boulevard side of the Mall. All three major tenants at the time – Sears, Kmart, and Hess's – got extra square footage to expand. A fourth major, J.C. Penney, occupied 85,000 square feet, bringing new life and shopping opportunities to the Richland Mall.

It's not hard to believe that crowds of shoppers still swarm the Richland Mall in that parallel reality. You can easily imagine it all still being there, sprawling over that massive property instead of Wal-Mart and the rest of Richland Town Centre.

Walk up to one of those passing shoppers and ask about the *other* mall in town, and they'll answer you with a question, completely oblivious.

What Galleria? That's what they'll ask. And then they'll hustle off to grab a quick bite at Sweet William or the Encore before continuing their Christmas shopping at Hess's, Sears, or any of the 100-plus stores filling the interior of that ever-popular, first-and-only Mall.

J.C. Penney at the Richland Mall

It's easy to imagine a world where the Richland Mall expanded and brought J.C. Penney into the fold because that world *almost* happened. We came a lot closer to having that reality than you might know, in fact.

According to Streeter, J.C. Penney had already committed to occupying a fourth department store space in the Richland Mall when the expansion project was announced. J.C. Penney was *so* on-board that the Richland Mall Associates had designed and laid out the new store as part of the project. "We had engineered it and were ready to go with construction," remembers Streeter. The end of a long quest to bring J.C. Penney to the Richland Mall was finally in sight.

There was just one catch. The deal with J.C. Penney was subject to Sears renewing their lease at the Richland Mall. J.C. Penney wanted to be sure of a certain level of foot traffic likely to generate a certain level of business, and such levels just weren't as likely with fewer than three majors in place.

At the time, though, Sears seemed to be doing fine at the Richland Mall. There seemed to be no real danger signs to indicate the retail giant might want out.

Unless you counted the brand spanking new mall up the road, that is.

Galleria Rising

Developed by the George D. Zamias company and located just off the Route 219 Industrial Park interchange, the Johnstown Galleria opened for business on October 22, 1992. With 894,646 square feet of space on two levels, the new mall was significantly larger than the single-story, 625,0000-square-foot Richland Mall.

The Galleria also included a sprawl of outparcels for the development of additional commercial properties. Between the mall complex and these properties, the Galleria represented a retail behemoth with extensive room in which to grow.

The level of its threat to the Richland Mall could not be overstated. The Galleria's location itself – the first Johnstown exit reached by drivers heading south on Route 219 from the direction of Ebensburg – was a huge advantage.

Zamias, a major mall developer located in Johnstown, had previously adopted a neutral posture toward the Richland Mall raking in cash in its backyard. Those days, clearly, were over.

Though it took a little while for the full impact of this new shopping center giant to rattle its chief competitor down the road in Richland. That all changed when the Galleria stole one of the Richland Mall's longtime major tenants, and a new one that never made it through the door.

Photo by Chuck Mamula

Showdown in Sears Tower

When it came time for Sears to renew its lease at the Richland Mall, things did not go as expected. What might have been considered a foregone conclusion suddenly became a lost cause.

"Sears basically said they were going to the new mall because it was new," recalls Streeter. "They were not staying in the Richland Mall."

It was a pivotal decision, to say the least. Just like that, our reality sheared away from the one in which the Richland Mall expanded and J.C. Penney became its fourth major tenant. Without Sears, J.C. Penney pulled out of its Richland Mall deal, choosing instead to follow Sears to the new Johnstown Galleria.

Streeter went all the way to the headquarters of Sears in the Sears Tower in Chicago to try to avert disaster, but it did no good. "The real estate rep at Sears said, 'We're just going to go with the new deal at the Galleria, and we really don't care what happens in the community because we're Sears.' I asked him what he meant by that, and he said, 'Don't you understand we're one of the largest retailers in the country, and no matter what we do, it won't affect us negatively at all?' I told him, 'I hope you're right and I'm wrong, but if I'm right, with this kind of attitude, you're going to become a second or third tier retailer.'

"I might have been on to something. Look what's happened to that company since then," says Streeter.

He had a similar experience with Kmart executives when he confronted them about Wal-Mart, which opened a store on a Galleria outparcel. "I asked the vice president of real estate for Kmart about it, and he said, 'Don't worry about Wal-Mart. They're just a little company building big stores in secondary markets, and they'll never be able to survive with that concept. Kmart's going to stick with the major markets and let Wal-Mart have all the little markets because we know they'll never survive.'

"Look at them now, and you'll see where arrogance gets you. Kmart invented the concept of discount department stores, and now Kmart's hanging on by its fingernails. Wal-Mart marched into the big markets and took on Kmart nose to nose, and they won," says Streeter.

Taking a Stand

Suddenly, the future of the Richland Mall looked a lot less certain. As Zamias continued to scoop up more tenants for the Galleria, dire consequences became more of a possibility.

"We always believed that the Johnstown market could only support one major shopping complex," says Bob McConnell. "As long as we had the only shopping complex, we were going to survive. But once Zamias got both Sears and J.C. Penney under contract, and we realized the Galleria was definitely entering the market, we knew the ending was somewhere in the future for the Richland Mall."

That didn't mean the associates were going to surrender to their perceived fate, though. Sears and J.C. Penney might have been lost, but Jim Streeter, Bob, and the rest of their team had not yet begun to fight.

Upon learning of Sears' defection to the Galleria, they immediately mounted a search for a new major tenant to fill its spot in the Richland Mall. Their diligent efforts soon paid off, as Hills Department Stores announced it would open a new location in the site once occupied by Sears.

The Richland Mall Associates also quickly filled the vacant out-building that had once housed Sears Automotive. A Michael's store opened there, replacing tires and fan belts with arts and crafts.

The holes, for the time being, had been plugged, but the bleeding had not been stopped. Other Richland Mall tenants were soon lured to the Galleria by the promise of new facilities, better terms, and bigger profits.

ROBERT JESCHONEK

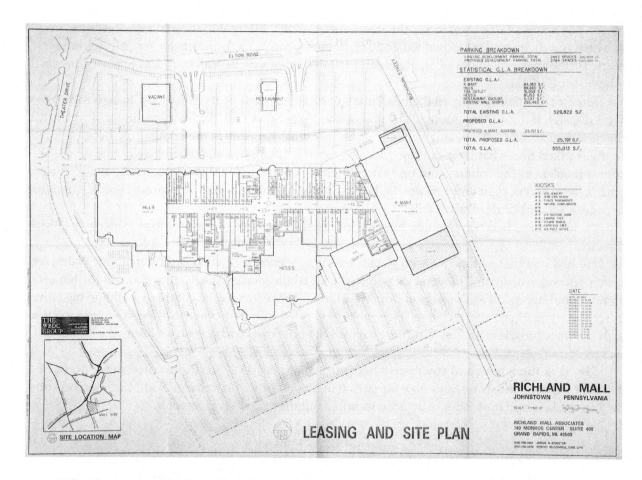

"What happens with the national retailers in these kinds of situations is, they always go. They want to go to whatever's the newest thing," explains Streeter. "Some of them open two stores, and if both stores do great, they keep them both, and if they don't, they close the one in the older center. It happens all over the country, and that's what happened at the Richland Mall, too. That's what happened with Hess's, eventually.

"Meanwhile, the core of the local tenants made their commitment and stood their ground at the Richland Mall. Joe Cohen and La Rose were part of that group. So was Dennis Petimezas and Watchmaker's Jewelry. They all made their stand at the Richland Mall," says Streeter.

Sprucing up the Joint

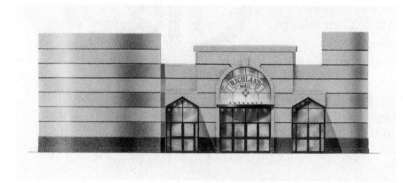

It was one thing for the Mall's core tenants to make a stand – but the Mall Associates knew they still couldn't survive without making some big moves, fast. Even as a shiny new mall courted tenants and customers alike, the Associates had to give those people a reason to stay loyal to the good old Richland Mall.

All Courtesy Bob McConnell

212

It was time to loosen the purse strings before there wasn't anything left in the purse to spend.

In July 1992, the Richland Mall Associates launched a sweeping new renovation plan budgeted at several million dollars. "We tried to freshen our Mall up to meet that new competition," says Streeter.

The project would change many of the Richland Mall's trademark design features, creating a look that was meant to be sleeker and more modern. For example, the multicolored glazed brick on the exterior walls and turrets was encased in monochromatic plaster panels, swapping the rainbow color scheme for more of a beige and beiger palette.

All Mall entrances were redone with glass vestibules and doors, replacing the dark metal framing with turquoise metalwork. Inside the Mall, new lighting and a ceramic-tile floor were installed.

Perhaps the most instantly noticeable change to the interior was the removal of the nature area in center court, where it had stood since the Mall's grand opening in 1974. Workmen hauled out the vegetation and boulders, drained the water feature, filled in the central well, covered the space with flooring – and topped it all off with a carousel. Built by Chance Rides of Wichita, Kansas, it was an authentic reproduction of a turn-of-the-century carousel with seats for 26 riders.

From the new exteriors to the carousel, the renovation was the biggest project to impact the Mall since its original construction. It was such an extensive effort it took a designer (TL Horton Design Inc. of Dallas, Texas), a general contractor (Jendoco Construction Co. of Pittsburgh) and four subcontractors (Sender Ornamental Iron Works and Chapple Bros. Roofing of Johnstown, plus Morocco Electric and Berti Excavating of Somerset) to complete all aspects of the work.

Americana 28' Carousel with Bradley & Kaye Horses
Chance Rides, Inc., Wichita, Kansas

213

The result? After 15 weeks, the place looked like a brand-new Mall. Mall tenants performed their own renovations, changing their individual stores as part of the makeover. Even the logo and color scheme were new, projecting the Mall's image makeover in ads and promotional materials throughout the community.

But would the facelift be enough to save the Richland Mall? Could the place hold its own even as the tide of retail business continued to favor the Johnstown Galleria? Or would changing the Richland Mall so dramatically actually work against it, making it feel less familiar and welcoming to longtime supporters?

Shoppers, analysts, and the media could only speculate as shopping patterns shifted, numbers were tabulated, reports were compiled, and the future of retail in Johnstown took shape around them.

Photos by Chuck Mamula

I have so many memories of the Richland Mall! I remember when it was near Christmas one year, maybe 1984, and Care Bears were so hot that they couldn't be found anywhere. I was at the Mall with my parents, and we found Cheer Bear behind the counter in Circus World. My dad bought her and kept her from me until Christmas. I know he was probably disappointed that he had to buy her with me standing right there. He has no clue that it made it an even better memory.

I also remember going to Super Chick after my kindergarten graduation. The chicken on a stick made for an awesome celebration! I'll also never forget being in complete awe of Gus (and completely terrified of him, too!). I remember him as being *huge*, but I'm sure that's just because I was so small.

Amanda Oswalt

I managed Motherhood Maternity Shop. Every morning, I would go to Somerset Trust to pick up my money for the day. Cinnabon was right across the hall. The smell of fresh-baked cinnamon rolls was the greatest start to my day.

Jane A Stiffler Hagerich

One day in the late 70s, my friend Cheryl Hill and I got out of Richland High School early due to snow and headed to the Mall. We were quite surprised when they announced the Mall was also closing due to snow.

Amy Wise Petrillo

Photo by Larry Stahl

In 1986, at the age of 13, I was allowed to pick out one item of back-to-school clothing on my own. I went to an iron-on t-shirt place across from National Record Mart and chose a Beastie Boys design showing the group sitting in a baseball stadium. I had it put on a black t-shirt, which I wore until the design faded away.

Doug Custer

I remember getting a glue-in tail in my hair at Chic Wig in 1991 when I was 12 and thinking it was the coolest thing ever.

I was terrified of Gus and Melanie when I was little and wouldn't go to that part of the Mall because they freaked me out so bad.

I remember going to the Mall and walking around aimlessly to get a pretzel on a stick slathered in cream cheese or a Cinnabon at the end of the evening. I also remember going to eat with my mom at Sweet William for girl time. We would get our meals and a sundae afterward. Oh, and my family would eat at the Encore for special occasions. I remember they had pennies in the tables. Good times!

Jamie Courter

I worked at Somerset Trust in the Mall. I was the manager there in the late 70s. I don't remember exactly when I left the Mall office, but I retired from the company in 2011. I was Senior Vice President at the time.

Somerset Trust was important to the Mall because it was the primary banking institution in the Mall, and we had to satisfy the deposit and cash needs for the businesses to keep running there. Most of the tenants used the bank, though the larger stores used their own outside interests, as well.

Richard Stern

I think it was probably the best mall I've ever been in. It was small, but I loved that place. I got to know the people who worked there. I used to just sit and read in Waldenbooks, and they let me do it. They got to know me and didn't mind me sitting on the floor. My parents used to take me to get ice cream at Sweet William all the time.

I loved the Mall and walked around it often. I worked five years down in the corner at the Duke and Duchess and Time-Out, plus a year at Wilsons Leather part-time, on and off.

Paul Mastovich

On Fridays and Saturdays, there'd be thousands of kids roaming the Mall – literally thousands. We just had to go around and try to control them, but it wasn't easy, because there were *thousands*. Too bad we don't have that problem today at the malls.

Gil Demos

Photo by Chuck Mamula

chapter ten

the two-mall town

1993 - 1997

People said it couldn't last. A town the size of Johnstown couldn't support two malls indefinitely. Experts and laymen alike agreed on that.

But what did they know? As 1993 became 1994, and '94 became '95, the status quo continued. The balance remained stable.

Photo by Chuck Mamula

There were two malls in business a mile apart, competing for the same limited pool of consumer dollars.

The underdog Richland Mall, though smaller and without as many national-level draws, was keeping its head above water since the renovation.

Photo by Philip Balko

Though no longer the big local success story, it was keeping the lights on.

The Galleria, meanwhile, just kept chipping away at it, peeling away tenants and reeling in scads of shoppers with its unbeatable lineup of under-roof and outparcel attractions. The giant complex couldn't go wrong with an onsite Wal-Mart, plus a ring of big-box stores and eateries.

It didn't seem possible that this lopsided competition could go on for long. People constantly speculated about the Richland Mall's impending demise.

Yet there it still stood, with shoppers coming and going as they always had. There were more vacant storefronts every year, but the Mall soldiered on, marking its twentieth anniversary in 1994.

Even when the Hess's department stores were sold to Bon Ton in 1995, the Richland Mall stayed afloat. A Bon Ton store replaced the Richland Mall Hess's, ensuring there would continue to be three major tenants in the center.

Maybe the two-mall model could continue to work, after all. Maybe the Richland Mall and Galleria could continue to coexist in harmony, without further significant setbacks.

Or maybe the Richland Mall would end up on the auction block in 1996.

Going Once, Going Twice

Even as the Richland Mall kept holding on in the face of the Galleria's challenge, a ticking time bomb was about to threaten its very existence.

On July 25, 1996, the story hit *The Tribune-Democrat*. The Richland Mall would be auctioned off at a September 9th tax sale unless its owners paid hundreds of thousands of dollars in back taxes to the Richland School District.

Apparently, though the Mall had looked marginal but viable on the surface, its tax debts had been mounting in the background. It hadn't helped that the Richland School District had raised taxes by 13 mills that year, further deepening the Mall's outstanding debt.

By July '96, Richland Mall Associates was in the hole $307,579 for taxes and costs from 1994 and another $455,762 for 1995. By the time of the tax sale in September '96, the bill would total $773,376.

Just like that, any illusion of stability went out the window. The two-mall paradigm that had seemed to be working so well was suddenly, irrevocably undermined, and the Richland Mall was *not* looking like the winner.

Not that it was going down without a fight. The Richland Mall Associates and their landlord, County Amusement Company, filed an emergency petition appealing the Mall's listing in an ad for the tax sale. According to the petition, listing the Mall in the ad would have "a devastating and irreparable adverse effect" on the Mall's tenants.

Photos by Philip Balko

Judge Timothy Creany agreed to consider the petition, but Richland School District's solicitor, Richard Williams, opposed it because the Mall had rejected a proposed payment plan.

Meanwhile, the Mall Associates were appealing an assessment, hoping a win might make their whole tax problem go away. The assessment appeal was scheduled for trial on August 21st and 22nd before Judge Norman Krumenacker.

One way or another, the Richland Mall's fate would be sealed by September 9th. Was the end near, or would the Mall receive a reprieve?

Photo by Chuck Mamula

By the Skin of Their Teeth

On Friday, July 26, 1996, the Richland Mall Associates and County Amusement Co. crossed their fingers for luck – and it didn't work. The emergency petition hearing was a flop. Judge Creany wasn't going to cut them any slack.

According to Creany, the assessment appeal filed with the state court prevented the county court from ruling on the matter. Since the case was out of the county's jurisdiction, the Mall's tax debt couldn't change until the state hearing in August. Therefore, Creany couldn't remove the Mall from the tax sale ad.

Faced with disaster, the Richland Mall Associates did the only thing they could. They made a down payment of $94,141 – 25% of what they owed in 1994 taxes to the Richland School District – and got the Mall off the auction block.

For a while, at least. They still had to make three payments of approximately $76,900 over the next year to clear the remainder of that '94 tax debt...which didn't even touch the $455,744 in 1995 taxes that it owed to the school district, Richland Township, and Cambria County. If the '95 taxes weren't paid during the next year, the Mall would be up for auction in 1997, according to Cambria tax-claims director Sam Runzo.

In other words, the Richland Mall would live to fight another day...but the writing was on the wall. Unless something changed dramatically, and soon, the Mall would be unable to pay down the mountain of tax debt it owed, and the auctioneer's gavel would swing.

The Tax Man Taketh Away

As scheduled, the Richland Mall's tax bill came due again in September 1997, and the auction block loomed. In fact, the Mall was actually put on a list of properties that would be auctioned off at Cambria County's annual delinquent tax sale at 10:00 a.m. on Monday, September 8th.

Three weeks earlier, the Richland Mall Associates had tried to get a court order to take the Mall off the list because the assessment appeal was still in progress. When Judge Normal Krumenacker rejected the request, the Associates knew they had to pay up or lose everything, so they found the money once again. They paid $151,537.65 to the Cambria County tax claims bureau as the first payment on the $1 million dollars in back taxes they owed. Three more payments were scheduled over the course of the next year, though each close call made it seem less and less likely that the Mall could stay a step ahead of disaster indefinitely. It felt like luck was running out for the place, if it hadn't run out already.

Like it or not, barring anything short of divine intervention, the days of the two-mall town were numbered. The Richland Mall was as good as gone already, and now everybody knew it.

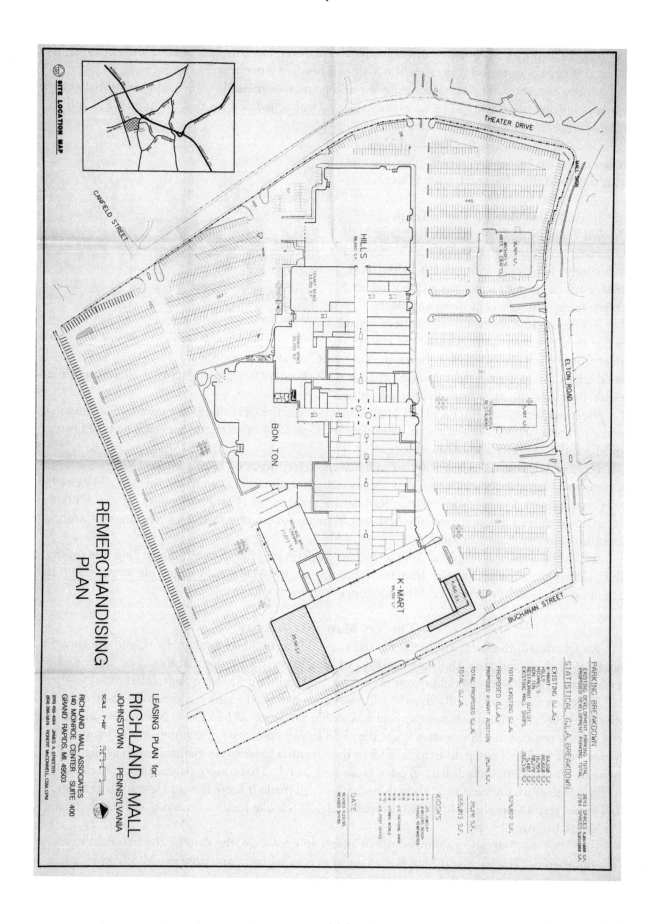

The Richland Mall is a place that will always be very special to me. From some of my earliest memories, I can remember going to the Mall with my mom, and the place was packed. Some of my friends and family still call the main section of the Mall the "Blue Part," as that was a phrase I coined around age 4 or 5. I still remember thinking that the main ceiling of the Mall looked blue as you entered through Sears or other stores and made your way to the main part of the Mall.

I distinctly remember being with my mom, my sister, and friends of our family while they shopped in many stores, especially Ormond. I remember sitting with my sister on the steps beside the mirror in Ormond (where patrons could look at themselves while holding up the latest fashions). It felt like it took forever while they shopped; they loved it, and we hated it. Now, thirty years later, it is a great memory to look back on.

I also remember eating the great ice cream at Sweet William while we sat in the booths near the windows. As a young teenager, I often went to Time-Out and The Wall. I have lots of great memories of the Mall that I'll never forget.

Jeff Cerula

I remember when the Johnstown Chiefs would sign autographs at the Mall. My dad would take me to see them, and we would stand in line for what seemed like hours to get autographs. I guess I was about seven or eight years old, and this probably happened around 1988. My dad had season tickets to the Chiefs games, and those players were stars to me. I still have some of the memorabilia that the players signed in my old bedroom at Dad's house.

Brenna Mock-Durst

I worked at McDonald's back in the day, and I remember that the Mall had a great Christmas party. You were able to go to Capri Pizza to eat, play as much as you could at Time-Out, and see a free movie at the Duke and Duchess movie theaters. Those were really good times that you don't see nowadays.

Shawn Beam

I loved the merry-go-round in center court! They held fashion shows there, too, showing clothes etc., from stores in the Mall. I wore a beautiful fur coat in one of them.

Margaret Pebley Roth

I started at Sears in the Richland Mall in 1977, right after the Johnstown Flood. I worked there for 24 years and retired in 2001. I started in what was called housewares, but they discontinued that and moved me into hardware and paint. We would sell paint out of there like crazy. On Saturday mornings, people would be lined up by the door for paint, and we mixed it as fast as we could. Later, I worked in Customer Service, then in Catalogue.

I loved to eat at Capri and Sweet William. You could go to Capri and get pizza and a drink for $2 or less! It was quick, so you could get lunch and get back to the store in half an hour.

Becky Kakamor

I remember dressing like the Easter Bunny and talking to the children while they had photos taken. The children were sweet, but the best part of the job was waving and blowing kisses to the teenagers walking by. Some of them would get so shy.

Cheryl Shirzad

The Richland Mall opened in 1974 when my son Ronnie was three, and we went Christmas shopping there that year. We stopped for lunch at McDonald's, where there was a riding horse that cost a nickel per ride. Ronnie wanted to ride it so bad. His father told him, "We have to eat first. If you eat all your food, you can ride it." When Ronnie had one bit of cheeseburger and a few fries left, he looked up and said, "Daddy, I'm all done. Can I ride the horsey?" His father said, "You have to finish." Ronnie began to cry and needed to go to the bathroom. His father took him, leaving me to wait for them to return. As I sat there, an African-American woman sitting nearby said to me, "Honey, 25 years from now, it won't make any difference whether he ate the rest of that food. Remember, life with him is as long as the white of your fingernail." After hearing that, when Ronnie came back from the bathroom, I gave him a nickel to ride that horsey after all.

Diane Olenik

Photo by Chuck Mamula

chapter eleven

walled off

1997 - 1998

When is a mall no longer a mall? When all the small interior tenants are gone, for one thing. When the two remaining major tenants are walled off from what used to be the hallways, for another.

Also, when all you have left are those two majors, a bank, a movie theater, and a Michael's and Ponderosa Steakhouse on outparcels. That's when you know for a fact, after 23 years, that your mall isn't a mall anymore.

The Ides of March

The announcement by Jim Streeter on October 14th, 1997 was no surprise. After the coming of Galleriazilla, the loss of Sears, the cancellation of the expansion, the exodus of tenants, the closing of Bon Ton (in '96), and the tax troubles out the whazoo (barely held at bay by a $150,000 payment in mid-'97), everyone but everyone had known this day was coming. The exact details were the only things that had been in doubt – and now those details were made public.

Photo by Chuck Mamula

The not-so-much-of-a-secret was out. The Richland Mall was mostly closing on March 31st, 1998.

As if to underscore the terrible news, a sniper opened fire on the Mall on the day of the closing announcement. Windows were shot out at Hill's, Michael's, and several other businesses, part of a spree that extended throughout Richland Township.

It was only fitting. The Mall had been under fire for a long time already. Sooner or later, the shots were bound to hit home.

Wanted: Bailout by a Major Player

"The writing's on the wall," Bob McConnell told *The Tribune-Democrat*. "We just can't hack it anymore. The bottom line is, it's over."

Hill's and Kmart, located at opposite ends of the Mall, would stay open. So would the Richland Mall Cinemas, Somerset Trust, Michael's, and Ponderosa. But the vast interior wings and center court of the Mall would be shut down and walled off, closed to pedestrian traffic.

It was a move that would free the Richland Mall Associates from maintaining the Mall's common area, saving over $1 million annually. No special access or services would be needed for the remaining businesses, since they all had their

own utilities and entrances. No Mall personnel would be needed to maintain them, as they were all self-sufficient.

So some of the Mall would stay open, keeping the legacy of the place alive, maybe buying enough breathing room for the Mall Associates to finally come up with a plan that would somehow salvage or revive the property. There were rumors that a major player would yet step in and bring the Mall back to life. Home Depot, for example, was rumored to be a white knight in the making, interested in opening a big new store on the Richland Mall site between Kmart and Hills.

People wanted to believe it was possible, that Home Depot or some other big fish would rescue the Mall. As pessimistic as they had been since the Galleria's opening, as often as they had speculated about when exactly the Richland Mall would finally die, it seemed that most of them didn't want it to bite the dust. It seemed there was still a lot of love in town for that Mall, and a real reluctance to let go of it forever.

Even as the crowds continued to pour into the Galleria the way they'd once poured into its now-terminal predecessor, spending money in some of the same stores that had once occupied that earlier center. By the time the closing was announced in October '97, C. Gil's Shoes, La Rose, Bon Ton, Kay Bee Toys, Foot Locker, Gardners Candies, GTE Phone Mart, and others already had their new locations up and running in the Galleria. Some, like Kay Bee and Gardners, still had open stores in the Richland Mall, too, but all of them had chosen to put their futures in the hands of the Galleria.

And by then, no one could blame them. The Richland Mall had gone from the dominant retailer to the longest of long shots. No one seemed to have much faith in it anymore.

The Big Goodbye

At the time of the closing announcement, the Richland Mall had 45 tenants – a far cry from the high point of 105 during its glory days. With the decision made to close the Mall's interior, it was up to Jim Streeter to conclude those tenants' business with the Mall.

"I went around to each of the 45 tenants and negotiated termination agreements with them," explains Jim. "As part of those agreements, I made sure they all had enough time to prepare to move out before we closed the interior of the Mall. In some cases, I provided rent-free months so our tenants could wind down their businesses without undue pressure. I tried to be as fair to everybody as I could."

The leases of 21 of those tenants were set to expire at the end of 1997, which simplified matters somewhat. But there were other issues that Jim had to address, of course, before the closing in March '98.

For example, he had to release most of the 30 employees who worked for the Mall organization... including Bob McConnell.

"A few employees stayed with us to work on the remaining functional components of the property. As for the rest, I informed them as soon as I knew for sure that they'd be leaving their jobs at the Mall," says Jim. "I didn't leave them hanging, wondering what was going to happen. I told them all when their last day would be in March, so they could plan accordingly."

Until that day arrived, the men and women of the Richland Mall set out to spend one last holiday season in the place that had once been Christmas Shopping Central for all of Johnstown.

Photos by Chuck Mamula

One Last Christmas

There was no sign of Richie the Pook that Christmas season – but Santa Claus, at least, made an appearance. Saint Nick showed up on November 28th, the last time he would ever visit the interior of the Richland Mall.

Hickory Farms also came to the Mall that year, setting up its annual holiday store. And the Mall was decorated as usual for the season, almost as if the closing wasn't about to happen. Almost as if it wouldn't be the last Christmas ever celebrated at the Mall in its intact state.

Though the word "celebrated" didn't really come to mind much in those days. Tenants were too focused on finding a new location – or in some cases, closing up shop for good. Employees were too focused on finding new jobs. And Jim and the Richland Mall partners were too focused on figuring out some kind of future for their dying shopping center.

Suggestions and speculation on the subject abounded in the community. A commonly mentioned idea was that the Mall's midsection would be demolished and replaced with parking or some kind of major retailer, leaving Kmart and Hill's untouched at either end. According to Johnstown architect Edwin Pawlowski, speaking to *The Tribune-Democrat* at the time, buildings like the Mall are constructed so that any part other than the main buildings can be removed.

Other local voices spoke in favor of non-demolition options. Tom Columbus Jr. of EADS Architects of Somerset suggested turning the Mall into a planned retirement community. In Tom's vision, everything needed by retirees, from exercise space to doctors' offices to small shops and a grocery store, could be included under one roof.

Whatever destiny awaited the Mall, it would be very different from the one imagined by Jim Streeter, Jim O'Roark, and the rest of the Unimich team back in 1974. Their particular version of the Richland Mall dream was almost certainly, and irreversibly, coming to an end on March 31st, 1998.

Tomorrow Never Knows

As the Richland Mall went down like a sinking ship, its tenants headed for the lifeboats – and, in some cases, toward a very hazy future. Though some were moving to the Galleria (including original tenant and longtime holdout Watchmaker's Jewelry), and others were closing for good, still others weren't sure what a Mall-free tomorrow would bring.

The future of the Encore, for example, was up in the air. Owner Larry Mummert was considering various options but hadn't found the right fit by October.

The former Jolly Roger Restaurant on Scalp Avenue had looked promising, and had just closed for business in August, but the owners weren't returning his calls.

Then there was the Keystone Chapter of the American Red Cross, which occupied 7,000 square feet of the Richland Mall. Chapter officials wanted to find a site in Richland, and they wanted more space – 8,000 to 12,000 square feet, enough to accommodate an expansion of the organization. A chapter task force conducted a site search, but resources were limited, and choices were few. For a while, Executive Director Catherine Madigan-Penrod worried that the chapter might end up homeless.

But even as terminal tenants chafed at the uncertainty, officials in downtown Johnstown tried hard to recruit them. There was plenty of space downtown, after all, including 26,000 square feet of retail space opening up in the Glosser Bros. building by early '98. Main Street Manager Richard Dill sent letters to individual tenants, encouraging them to give downtown a try.

George D. Zamias Developer, which had built the Galleria, had plenty of openings to offer, too. Though the Galleria was 90 percent full, Zamias had room in other local properties, including the Bel-Air Plaza and University Park Shopping Center in Richland and the Westwood Plaza in Westmont.

One way or another, it seemed, the castaway tenants would find new homes. Jim Streeter would make sure they all had time to make the transition and left on good terms. Life would go on.

But it wouldn't be the same. As of March 31st, 1998, everything that had made the Richland Mall special and meant so much to so many merchants, employees, and shoppers for so many years would be undone forever.

And the worst, after that, was yet to come.

Photos by Chuck Mamula

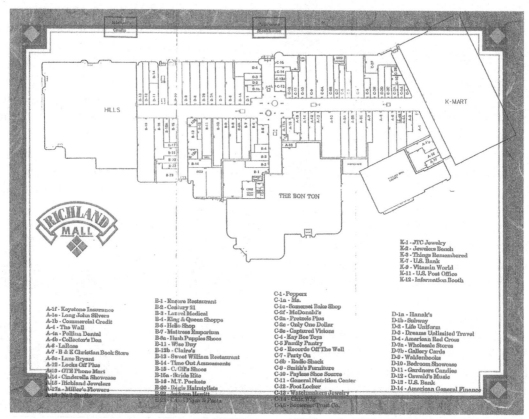

Richland Mall has been serving the Greater Johnstown market area for the past 21 years with a large variety of local and national retailers. Hill's, K-Mart, and The Bon Ton anchor the mall along with over 70 specialty shops. The mall store mix is very strong with over twenty-five percent long established local tenants.

Carousel
A turn of the century Carousel spins all day in the mall's Center Court area. Young and old alike are encouraged to ride and is handicapped accessible.

Information Center
Located at Center Court, our Information/Lottery Center offers free use of strollers and wheelchairs. Richland Mall Gift Certificates are also sold after 5pm and on weekends (they're sold daily in the Mall Management Office) and are good in all mall stores. Pennsylvania Lottery tickets can also be purchased as well as tickets for local and civic events. They're a wealth of information!
(814) 266-3155

Community Room/Booth
Both are available to non-profit groups for meetings, fund-raisers, etc. Call the mall management office for details and reservations at (814) 266-5876.

Richland Mall Store Listing and Phone Numbers

Hours Daily
Monday thru Saturday
10am - 9pm
Sunday 12-5pm

Route 219
Elton Exit
Johnstown, Pennsylvania

My memories of the Richland Mall are few due to my age, but as vivid as a then-seven-year-old's memories can be. One of those memories comes from after most of the Mall had closed. I often accompanied my mom to Kmart, one of the last anchors to close before the Richland Town Centre came into being. I remember that outside the entrance to Kmart, a makeshift door and wall had been set up to close off the rest of the Mall. Every chance I got, I made a point to stop and gaze through an opening in that wall at the once grand Mall on the other side. I can still see the empty storefronts and feel the sadness that I had at not being able to explore what looked like a grand place.

Photo by Jason Pozar

Randall Frye

I worked at Gardner's Candies in the Mall for about a year. I have memories of my daughter when she was competing for the Cambria County Outstanding Young Woman (Junior Miss) in '97 or '98, and they had to decorate rocking chairs in the Mall. That was a great mall, unlike the current one.

Darlene Lipuma

Photo by Chuck Mamula

I was there for the opening of the Richland Mall, transferring from the downtown Penn Traffic to work as the assistant manager of the men's department at the Penn Traffic Mall store. I later transferred to the display department and eventually moved to Miami.

Michael C. Wesner

229

I worked in the Richland Mall Sears store. I started in the catalogue department, then went to the switchboard, then Customer Convenience, and then Shipping. The job I liked best was RTV, which was where people would return their merchandise, after which we sent it to a big trucking company. I liked to aggravate the sales people in those days, too.

Maryann Estbanik

I will never forget the time my dad put out a fire at the Mall. There was a bad snowstorm, and my dad and I drove to the Mall to pick up my mother, who was working late at the bank beside Gardner's Candies. When we showed up, no one was there. As we walked to the front door entrance to wait for my mother to walk out, we noticed that one of the garbage cans was engulfed in flames. Someone must have thrown a cigarette into it, we guessed. There were flames about eight feet high shooting up the side of a brick wall. Luckily, my mother was walking toward the exit at that point and opened the entrance doors to let us in. My dad then ran and grabbed a fire extinguisher and ran back out and put out the fire. Fortunately, there wasn't much damage, though nothing much was left of the can, and there were ash marks about 10-15 feet up the wall. In my eyes (at age 7), my dad was a superhero! He still is to me. Who knows what would have happened if we hadn't shown up when we did?

Also, I remember that sometimes, when my mother worked late at the bank, she'd let me play in the Mall with my radio-controlled car from Radio Shack. I had the whole Mall to myself to drive it around, which I loved.

John Feathers

I didn't get to see much of the Mall until the late 80s-early 90s, though I remember going to see Michelangelo from the Teenage Mutant Ninja Turtles.

My grandparents loved shopping at the Richland Mall. I remember my grandfather getting his boots at or near Hills. Grandma loved shopping at Kmart. If we parked near Kmart's entrance (fingers crossed) we ate at McDonald's or Long John Silver's. It was heartbreaking when a wall was put up to separate Kmart from the closed portion of the Mall. But all the great photos help keep the memories alive.

Missy Toy

Photos by Chuck Mamula

chapter twelve

survival strategies

1998 - 2003

The Galleriazilla just kept getting bigger and better. By early '98, sales were up, and most of the tenant space was full. Meanwhile, out on the periphery, Wal-Mart, Staples, Sun TV, Applebee's Neighborhood Grill & Bar, and Red Lobster were open for business. Ryan's Family Steakhouse was under construction, and a big new multiplex movie theater was planned by Regal Cinemas of Knoxville, Tennessee. The future was so bright up there in Galleriaville, the shoppers all had to wear shades.

Photo by Philip Balko

A mile down the road, the Richland Mall closed its doors for the final time. Between Kmart and Hills, what had once been a bustling marketplace was now a boarded-up dead zone.

231

Imagine walking through there, where once you'd shopped and celebrated, and finding only silence and stillness. Your footsteps echo down the corridors, and the hairs bristle on the back of your neck. It doesn't seem right that this place is shuttered and empty. When you close your eyes, you can still almost imagine it the way it once was.

But those days are long gone. And soon, even the owners will change.

Conscious Uncoupling

The Richland Mall Associates pulled up stakes in 1999, giving up their control of the Richland Mall property. The changeover started soon after the closing of the main section in March 1998. It was then that the mortgage holder, TIAA, discounted the mortgage and sold it to Lehman Brothers Holdings, an international investment bank. In turn, Lehman Brothers offered to sell the mortgage to Jim Streeter, but he decided to pass on the deal. Instead, Jim structured a deal with Lehman that would get him and Unimich completely off the hook.

When the deal closed on July 9th, 1999, the Unimich partners were free of the mortgage and no longer had any kind of ownership stake in the Mall. They released the remaining Mall employees and walked away…kind of. Jim, though no longer in control of the Mall's fate, was still part of its future.

He went to work for Lehman Brothers as a consultant, managing the Richland Mall property until such time as another party bought and put it to use. That meant more trips to Johnstown for Jim, handling the issues that arose for Kmart and the other remaining tenants.

Right on Target

By July 2000, Richland Mall was still struggling along in its reduced state, with its two remaining retailers still operating at either end: Kmart and Ames (which took over for Hill's in 1998). The Richland Mall Cinemas were still in business, and so was Michael's (though Ponderosa had moved to the Galleria zone). Somerset Trust was finally pulling up stakes, though, and moving to the former Bob Evans restaurant building in front of Market Basket along Scalp Avenue.

But in July 2000, it looked like the Mall might finally be turning the corner. A new project was announced to convert the property into "a strip center of medium-sized stores that will include the national discount retailer Target."

Grand plan for Richland Mall

Wilton Partners envisions a major reworking of the Richland Mall that involves tearing down much of the current structure and building anew. Dark shade of gray shows the section of the current mall that will be removed for parking.

Elton Road.
Michael's
Former Ponderosa
Buchanan St.
Ames
Kmart
Hemlock St.
Parking
Theater
Proposed Target
Theater Dr.
Eisenhower Blvd.
☐ Existing buildings
■ Proposed buildings

© *The Tribune-Democrat*

According to *The Tribune-Democrat*, the Target-centered project would cost between $30 million and $40 million and would kick off in the fall of 2000. Work would be completed by fall 2001 or spring 2002.

Developed by Grubb & Ellis Co. of Pittsburgh, the new center would also include Barnes & Noble, Pet Smart, and Office Max stores. "We are repositioning the Richland Mall in the market place," said Michael Hendrickson, senior vice president of Grubb & Ellis. "It will be an open air, power strip shopping center."

Kmart, Ames, and Michael's would stay where they were, though they would be remodeled to match the new buildings that would go up on the site. As for the Mall's midsection, it would be bulldozed to make way for parking for 2,000 vehicles.

The Richland Mall Cinemas would be torn down as part of the demolition, but then rebuilt elsewhere on the property. Owner Ed Troll wanted to "continue the theater business on this site," after three generations of his family had done so for more than 50 years.

When construction was done, a freestanding 140,000-square-foot Target would face Theater Drive. A store that locals had clamored for for years would finally be part of Richland's retail landscape, bringing its trendy merchandise and style to a site that once been the epitome of trendy style back during the Richland Mall days.

Too Good to Be True

It was like a dream come true. Soon, a 600,000-square-foot shopping complex would rise from the ashes of the Richland Mall, replacing the crumbling structure with new or significantly renovated buildings – four or five "midsized boxes" of 20,000 to 40,000 square feet, plus a smattering of smaller retailers.

After years of declining business, the site would be jumping again. Richland residents would have good reason to be proud of it again.

Theoretically.

Though Grubb & Ellis were all-in, Target was playing its cards close to the vest. Contacted for comment in July 2000, Target spokeswoman Kristin Knach would only say, "We are interested in Johnstown, but at this time I can't confirm anything as final."

Was it a bad sign that Target was staying tight-lipped about the situation? Was it a bad sign that by July 2000, no plans had been submitted for approval to Richland Township for a project supposedly starting in the fall? Was it worrisome that for a project happening so quickly, Richland Township zoning officer Mark Walker could only say, "We just hear rumblings"?

Let's just say that a year later, there still wasn't a Target in Johnstown, and Grubb & Ellis had been replaced by Atlanta-based Hartfield Phillips as the ones trying to swing a deal for the old Richland Mall.

Second Time's the Charm?

"There's activity out there with developers working on it," said Ed Troll in July 2001. "There's stuff cooking."

That's about all anyone would say about the new deal that was apparently being brokered by Hartfield Phillips. It wasn't just that the plans were in the embryonic stages, either, with nothing set in stone. People were a little afraid to jinx whatever deal might happen, after the way the whole Target/Barnes & Noble/Office Max complex ended up stillborn in spite of promising early chatter.

"I do believe something is going to happen," said Richland Township Supervisor William Harris. "We remain optimistic."

According to Troll, an interested developer with holdings in the state was considering plans for retail use of the Richland Mall site. Hartfield Phillips was setting things in motion on behalf of that developer.

"We're looking at redevelopment possibilities but there is nothing concrete at this point we can discuss," said Conrad Nelson, a Hartfield Phillips assets planner. "Hopefully we'll have some positive movement on this in the near future."

It all sounded great, except for the complete absence of details. But maybe that would bring a better result than the Target hoedown, when a whole lot of talk had led to zero positive outcomes.

Or maybe not. A year later, nothing had changed at the Richland Mall site. The hoped-for new development had failed to come to pass.

So it was just as well they hadn't said much about it, after all.

Ambitious project

At least $25 million is expected to be invested in redoing Richland Mall to include a new strip mall, Kmart and Super Wal-Mart.

© *The Tribune-Democrat*

Say Goodbye, Richie

It wasn't until early 2003 that a new plan for the Richland Mall site finally got some traction. Almost exactly five years to the day after the Mall's closing in '98, Heritage Development Co. of Moreland Hills, Ohio found it had the magic touch.

It was the biggest news since Richie the Pook gave away a Volkswagen Thing. Best of all, every stakeholder got on board with the new plan; there didn't seem to be a single deal-killer on the horizon.

And things were going to move at warp speed. Heritage already had a permit for demolition of the Mall, which could get underway by April 1st. Construction would start soon after.

When it was all over, the classic but now neglected Mall would be torn down and carted away. Everything from the shuttered Ames Department Store to Kmart (soon to close, as its parent company was undergoing bankruptcy) would be obliterated. In its place would rise a new shopping complex, complete with new iterations of Michael's and Richland Cinemas, plus room for additional retailers.

And at the heart of it all would stand that temple of modern marketplace glory, that symbol of all that was grand and gigantic in American shopping culture – a Wal-Mart Supercenter.

Photo by Jason Pozar

The Tribune-Democrat, Johnstown, Pa.

Sunday, December , 199

Home for the Holidays

Shop our fine merchants for all your Holiday needs:

Department Stores
Hills   K-Mart   The Bon-Ton

Specialty Shops
Bedroom Showcase
B & K Christian Book Store
Captured Visions
Claire's Boutique
Collector's Den
Family Pantry
Gardner's Candy

GNC
Kay Bee Toys
Laurel Medical
Life Uniform
Mattress Emporium
Michael's Crafts
Only One Dollar

Party On
The Bridal Suite
Somerset Bake Shoppe
Vitamin World
Walden Books

Cards & Gifts
Hanak's I & II
Hello Shop
Gallery Cards & Gifts
Things Remembered

Footwear, etc.
C. Gil's Shoes
Footlocker
Hushpuppies
Stride Rite

Fashions
King & Queen Shop
Lane Bryant
La Rose
Wholesale Stores
Wise Buy

Services
American General Finance
American Red Cross
Century 21
Commercial Credit

Dr. Antinoro, Chiropractor
Pollina Dental
Dreams Travel
Excel Model Mgmt

GTE Phone Mart
Jackson Hewitt
Keystone Ins.
Somerset Trust

Jewelry
Jewelers Bench
JTC Jewelry
Richland Jewelers
Watchmaker

Comp., Elect., & Music
Oswald's Music Center
Radio Shack
Records off the Wall
The Wall

Beauty & Hair
Chic Wig
Locks Off Plus
Nail Studio
Regis

Seasonal
Personal Thoughts
Home for the Holidays

Treasures of the Earth
Over The Wall
Hickory Farms

Deepa Goal
Sievers

Restaurants
Capri's Pizza & Pasta
Encore
Ponderosa
Sweet Williams

Fast Food
Long John Silvers
McDonalds
Pretzels Plus
Subway

Movies & More
M.T. Pockets
Richland Mall Cinemas
South Mt. Kiddie Rides
The Carousel
Time Out

RICHLAND MALL

Here To Stay!
Just Off Route 219   Geistown/Elton Exit

VISIT SANTA:
11 a.m. - 8 p.m. Weekdays
Noon - 5 p.m. Sundays

Extended Shopping Hours:
Daily 10am-10pm
Sunday 12 noon-6pm

chapter thirteen

all the pook's horses and all the pook's men

2003

Jim Streeter could see the Richland Mall come down from his motel room. He was staying at the Sleep Inn across Theater Drive, and he would look out his window and watch as the Mall he'd helped build was reduced to rubble.

In those days, in the spring and early summer of 2003, Jim was working as a consultant for Lehman Brothers, managing what was left of the Mall. His responsibilities to the Mall were almost over now, though. Lehman Brothers had sold the place to Heritage Development Co., which was leveling the existing structures in favor of all-new buildings.

Photos by Jason Pozar

237

As the Mall went away, so did Jim's reasons for being there.

And so did a piece of his heart and soul.

"I was the only one, other than Bob McConnell, who was there from the beginning until the final day the Mall was open in '98.

"After that, I spent a year and a half unwinding and managing the project for Lehman Brothers. I was there every week going through the process of holding this piece of real estate that had died. It was like losing a member of my family.

"Then being there during the demolition, it was like the death of a loved one. It was devastating.

"At night, I would open the window in my room and look out at a perfect view of the Richland Mall site...but every night, there was a little less Mall there. Everything the partners and I had accomplished was being swept away.

"That Mall had had such a life force, and now it was in its death throes. It was truly the end of a life, of an era," remembers Jim. "It was gut-wrenching."

The Mayor of the Mall Reflects

As the wrecking balls flew and the bulldozers rumbled to make room for the incoming Richland Town Centre, there was plenty of pain to go around. Bob McConnell, who had worked as general manager of the Mall since its opening, was as deeply affected as Jim.

Bob, at least, was out of town, working his new job at the Clearview Mall in Butler, PA. He didn't have to witness the destruction first-hand – but knowing the Richland Mall was coming down was still a personal blow.

After all, he'd spent more time there, day in and day out for 23 years, than anyone. And now, the place that had been his home and community for all that time was leaving the face of the Earth. He couldn't go back again even if he wanted to.

"We'd all known it was just a matter of time," recalls Bob. "That size of a market could not support two malls.

"We'd seen the end coming for a while, but still. It was awful knowing that everything we'd worked so hard to make succeed was being obliterated. I was already long gone when they started tearing it down, but it was really heartbreaking," says Bob.

A Frozen Moment

Let's pause here for a moment and consider the last stage of the Mall. Let's pick a night – June 9th or July 15th, say – and freeze everything right there.

RICHLAND MALL COMING DOWN

Ken Brownson, above, an employee of Earthmovers Unlimited Inc., an excavating company in Kylertown, Clearfield County, recycles tin removed from the Richland Mall yesterday. At left is a remnant from the building. A Wal-Mart Supercenter will be built at the site.

PETE VIZZA/THE TRIBUNE-DEMOCRAT

© The Tribune-Democrat

Photo by Jason Pozar

Let's glide over the demolition site, with all those piles of rubble that used to be our favorite shopping center...those heaps of glazed multicolored brick, those mountains of fixtures and flooring. Everywhere we look, we see pieces of things we once loved – marquees from Time-Out and Karmelkorn, counters from Sweet William and the Kmart snack bar, shelves and racks and carpets and tiles from all through the place.

Gliding onward, we see drivers pulled off along the road, standing with hands on hips and staring...scowling...remembering. Some have tears in their eyes. Some just look lost and confused.

Across the street, we drift up to a window of the Sleep Inn and see a man standing there, also staring at the ruins. Maybe his head is cocked to one side. Maybe his jaw is clenched, and so are his fists. We recognize him from the photos – Jim Streeter, his necktie loosened, sleeves rolled up, illusions gone.

Photo by James and Frederica Rosenbaum

239

If he could have one wish come true, what would it be? That he'd done it all differently and saved the Richland Mall...or never built the Richland Mall in the first place?

Someone snaps their fingers then, and the moment unfreezes and is lost to history forever, just like the Mall.

There Was a Mall Here?

By July 25th, 2003, the demolition of the Richland Mall was complete. Workers just had to remove concrete and footers from the site, and that part of the new project would be done.

To those who gazed out at that leveled property, clear of structures for the first time since 1974, it was as if the Richland Mall had never existed.

Actual construction started later that year, and new buildings quickly rose, layer by layer. This time, instead of a central sprawl encircled by parking, the new center was arranged like a horseshoe, with the parking wrapped in the middle.

The site was a beehive of activity as the army of contractors erected one structure after another, then filled them with fixtures and furnishings. All around the plaza, signage went up to identify the new tenants – Circuit City, Petco, Bed Bath & Beyond, T.J. Maxx, Famous Footwear, Dress Barn, Dollar Tree. The new Richland Cinemas took shape on an outparcel,

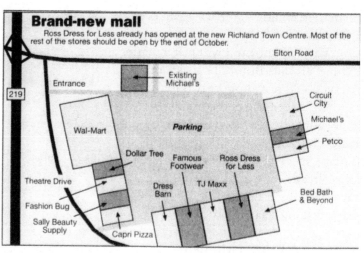

© *The Tribune-Democrat*

Photo by Philip Balko

complete with 10 screens and 2,000 seats (200 fewer than the previous theater, to allow for more legroom).

Looming over all of it was the single biggest tenant – Wal-Mart Supercenter. The combined general merchandise and grocery retailer would staff its latest location with some 200 employees, including those who moved over from the former Wal-Mart at the Galleria. All told, Richland Town Centre retailers were expected to employ more than 500 workers.

The first wave of these employees rushed through the stores in Fall 2004, getting them ready for their big debuts. The first opening, a soft one, took place at Ross Dress for Less in September 2004. Other store openings were staggered over the following weeks, welcoming shoppers as soon as they could after construction on their buildings was finished.

Those shoppers liked what they saw and came in droves. Suddenly, the site of the former Richland Mall was the place to shop again. The great wheel of retail had turned.

Was it just because the Town Centre was new? That it focused on the kind of big box stores that were popular in retail at the time? Or was it something else, harder to define, that brought back the shoppers? Because surely, if the Richland Mall people had known the secret, they would have put it to use.

The Galleria people would have done the same, instead of steadily losing shoppers and tenants over the next 13 years. And on any given Saturday, the Richland Town Centre's parking lot might not be as jam-packed, and the Galleria's might be more full.

Richland Mall Lives

Looking again at the theories of quantum physics, if multiple alternate realities do exist, there must surely be a parallel world where the Richland Mall still exists.

In that world, shoppers still flock to the Mall instead of the Richland Town Centre, which was never built. Visitors still stroll through those familiar hallways, laden with packages, chatting with friends and friendly employees. The sounds of laughter, music, and cash registers still fill the place, accompanied by the familiar smells of caramel popcorn and Sweet William ice cream.

Photos by Philip Balko

In that world, Jim Streeter never had to stand at the window of his motel and watch dust settle over the Mall's ruins. Bob McConnell never had to stop being the general manager and spending time with the tenant community he loved so well.

In that world, there are still disco parties in the Encore and videogame face-offs in Time-Out. The petting zoo, mini-circus, fishing pond, wrestling bear, and Harlem Globetrotter still show up regularly, entertaining thousands in the common areas. Sometimes, shoppers still dream up a new stunt to get into the Guinness Book of World Records.

In that world, maybe a new face shows up once in a while – new but familiar, the face of someone who belongs there. Maybe the face of someone who steps out of a shadowy doorway or corner when no one else is looking...someone who lights up with *waaaay* too much joy as they look around the place, as if they know it *so* well but haven't been back in forever and maybe never thought they'd be back again. Maybe it's someone who might have slipped through from a very different parallel world, one without this happy ending for the Richland Mall and its supporters. Maybe it's someone who can't believe his or her luck in getting here.

Someone like you. Or someone like me.

And we just start walking as children laugh and the carousel turns behind us in center court like a great and magical wheel. And neither one of us says a single word about going home.

Photos by Chuck Mamula

MEMORY SHOP

I started working at Sears in 1971. I was still in high school, and I actually started at the Scalp Avenue store before it moved to the Richland Mall. I worked in receiving merchandise, then tagging and pricing it. I did the same thing at the Mall. Then, they created a replenishment team, and I was the Replenishment Team Leader. We would come in early, stock the shelves, and do signage.

Jeannine Yannutz

Junior Achievement held trade fairs at the Richland Mall. I loved those weeks. Each company had a booth to sell products, and we participants were always treated so well at the Mall.

Kathy Glattke

My first job was at Hickory Farms in the Richland Mall. I worked after school and on Saturdays. I can still remember handing out samples: "Would you like to try our cheese ball? It's made with blue cheese and white cheddar rolled in old English walnuts." I can't believe I still remember that line!

Mary Mock

Photo by Chuck Mamula

My favorite memory is my kids getting treated to Karmelkorn or Capri pizza. It was the treat of the month.

Debby Yoder

The Encore had great food and pennies in the tabletops. I was one of the waitresses. It was a fun place, and the owner was great to work for.

At Christmastime, it was great to walk through the Mall, listening to the holiday music and seeing the lights and decorations in each store's windows.

Arvilla Harvey

243

The Richland Mall was a destination for me. It was about three miles from my home, and I started riding my bicycle there after work. It took me almost an hour, as it was all uphill. As days passed, it got to be less than thirty minutes. I wish I was in that shape now.

Dan J. Stutzman

I worked in the deli and snack bar at Kmart from 1972-1992. I really liked working at the Mall, because it was close to home, and the people were nice.

Lois Konchan

I worked in the ladies' department at Kmart for about three years. The people were great, and I had a lot of fun in those days. I'll never forget the good times we had.

Josephine Deshner

I got into walking at the Richland Mall in the mornings as the place was winding down. The distance was about three miles for four laps. Toward the end, a lot of the stores were closed, and there weren't many people around. I felt bad, because I had a lot of good memories of that place. It had been booming at one time.

I walked that Mall right up until it closed. It was sad, because I'd worked there for Sears for almost 20 years. Being there at the beginning, I'd seen the Mall at its height, when all the stores were open every night, and the place was packed with shoppers.

Bernie Roesch

Photos by Chuck Mamula

chapter fourteen

where are they now ?

People disappear all the time. They might have a profound impact on our lives, or not much impact at all, and they disappear all the same. They move on.

Photo by Chuck Mamula

In the case of the story you just read, the impact of the people who starred in it was definitely profound. Together, they made the Richland Mall a reality, bringing us happiness and a sense of belonging we might never have experienced in quite the same way otherwise.

Though they went their separate ways and disappeared when the story ended, they're still out there. We know what happened to them, and where they are now.

And we can thank them from the bottoms of our hearts for the gift of the wonderful Mall they gave us for those 23 magical years in Richland Township.

Whither Unimich?

When we think of the Richland Mall, no one looms larger than the legendary five partners of Unimich who built and owned it. Those five men have had very different destinies since the end of the Richland Mall era.

After the sale and demolition of the Mall, Managing Partner and Mall Co-Founder Jim Streeter continued to devote himself to the real estate development business. Based in Grand Rapids, Michigan, he negotiated deals and managed existing properties for a while, then retired to devote himself to other pursuits.

Jim O'Roark, the Mall's co-founder along with Streeter, is the only Unimich partner who lives in the region of West-Central Pennsylvania today. After years of entrepreneurial ventures and Pook projects, he lives a quiet life in the mountains near Boswell...if "quiet" means constantly hustling new business deals in search of another smash.

Photo by Philip Balko

Courtesy Ray Kisor

Unimich partner and Richland Mall Leasing Manager Ray Kisor returned to Michigan to work in commercial real estate. Back home in Grand Rapids, he remarried, and went on to own and operate a 400-acre cattle farm. These days, he has downsized to a lake house and retired from the working world, but he still remembers the Richland Mall days fondly.

As for the other Unimich partners, Steve Clause died some years ago, and Ron Sabin is retired and travels extensively. Before leaving the daily grind, he worked for many years as a partner at an engineering firm in Grand Rapids, making his mark on one project after another. He occasionally stays in touch with Jim Streeter, who also spends time with Ray Kisor and is still, as before, the central figure bonding the Unimich team together.

Bob, Karen, Sal, and Connie

Aside from Unimich, other members of the cast of our story have come a long way since their days as part of the Richland Mall team.

Bob McConnell, the "mayor" of the Richland Mall for 23 years, landed on his feet after the Mall closed in 1998. His mall management career took him from Richland to the Clearview Mall in Butler, then to Century III near Pittsburgh. After three years at Century III, he got out of the business, moving with his wife to Indianapolis, Indiana.

Photo by Philip Balko

"I paid my dues and was in the mall industry for 30 years, and it was great," says Bob. "But Century III was very stressful, with all kinds of challenges. By the time I was done there, I knew the industry was starting to wind down, and I was glad to get out. I kind of saw the beginning and the end of it in my career."

Photo by Philip Balko

Original Mall Promotion Director Karen Bevilaqua followed her own unique path that eventually led to the opposite end of the country. In 1976, she quit her job in promotions to open a Yogurt Hut in the Mall with her uncle, then moved to California and found work with a publishing company. She still works for the same company today and spends most of her time on the west coast, though she comes back to Johnstown from time to time to help with family matters.

Then there's Sal Garcia, the Stix and Stoned recording artist and voice of Richie the Pook. After the early days of the Mall, he went on to perform and record with various bands. These days, he lives in Sarasota, Florida, where he still finds steady work as a musician, mostly as a vocalist/pianist solo act.

Connie Hayes, who ran the Mall's information booth for 20 years, lives in Florida, too. She moved there after retiring from the Mall in 1995. A cancer survivor, she lives in the town of Indian Shores, which is located between Clearwater and St. Petersburg.

Courtesy Sal Garcia

Employee Roster

During our tour of the Mall in this book, we met some of the merchants and employees who worked in our favorite stores and restaurants. In the years since the Mall closed and was demolished, these folks have gone on to their own new adventures.

Dennis Petimezas moved Watchmaker's Jewelry from the Richland Mall to the Galleria to the store's current location across Scalp Avenue from Wendy's restaurant. In his spare time, he continues to travel the world in search of quality gemstones.

Ed Troll continues to own and operate the Richland Cinemas at Richland Town Centre, not far from where his previous theaters – the Richland Mall Cinemas and the Duke and Duchess – were located.

Shirley DiRosa is another Richland Mall merchant still in business on the same ground once occupied by the Mall. She owns Capri Pizza and Restaurant in the Richland Town Centre, plus another Capri store on Main Street in downtown Johnstown and a third Capri on Goucher Street in Westmont.

Courtesy Ed Troll

Photo by Philip Balko

When the Richland Mall died, so did the Encore restaurant. Owner Larry Mummert liquidated his assets, paid his debts, and never reopened. After his Encore days, he went on to sell CO_2 to bars, then sold cars for Laurel. He retired in 2013 and had quadruple bypass surgery four years later.

After Time-Out folded, Doug Brydon went to work in the packaging industry. In 2001, he was hired by Garnell Packaging in Johnstown, where he still works at the time of this writing.

Dorothea Stephens left Sweet William restaurant in 1992 and moved to State College, where she got another waitress job and took nursing classes in her spare time. Eventually, she found work as a nurse's aide and "float nurse" at Mount Nittany Hospital. She currently works as a receptionist for the AARP in downtown Johnstown.

Jim White of Spencer Gifts worked 12 years at Griffith Custer Steel, then served as Director of Community Development for the City of Johnstown, finally retiring in 2012.

Wendy Jeschonek became a teacher after leaving Shop 'n Save. She spent most of her 25-year career teaching English in the Richland School District in Johnstown and only recently retired from her position there.

What about the three Ponderosa Steakhouse managers? Larry Stahl worked at Ponderosas in Altoona and Indiana, then left the company to get into teaching. After working as a substitute teacher for a while, he became a TSS – therapeutic support staff giving students individualized support when needed. Terry Miller now works for Vet Advisor with the Veteran's Choice Program, scheduling appointments for veterans who can't be seen by their local VA. He is also in his 19th year as a bus driver for McIlwain

School Bus Lines. As for Barry Thomas, he has been a financial advisor for the past two decades. Currently, he's a partner in the Kabler-Thomas Financial Group, a Johnstown-based firm that is part of LPL Financial.

After 19 years at Kmart, Brian Mahon went to work at Home Depot and eventually retired. These days, he spends his time on car repair, home improvement, and his grandkids.

Bernie Roesch put in 43 years at Sears, working at all three Johnstown locations, before retiring in 2015.

Bob Enos continues to keep busy as Senior Vice President and Senior Commercial Lender at Somerset Bank and Trust.

The Breakfast Bunch

Speaking of Bob's pals Gil, Joe F., Joe C., and Frank, they've carved out their own interesting destinies in the Johnstown area.

Gil Demos, owner of C. Gil Shoes, has survived open-heart surgery and severe injuries from a biking accident, and he continues to be one of the biggest boosters of the Richland Mall.

Joe Fortunato continues to own and operate American Insurance Marketing and The Health Insurance Place.

Joe Cohen worked in real estate for ten years after closing the last La Rose store. He finally retired after suffering a stroke in 2012, though he's almost fully recovered and hard at work tending his house and grounds in Westmont these days.

Frank Koscis of Thom McAn and Grand Slam USA is also completely retired, but he makes time to see his buddies Gil, Joe Fortunato, and Joe Cohen every week. The four of them still get together for breakfast at local eateries on Saturdays, as you'll see in the very next chapter of this book.

Photos by Philip Balko

I spent eighteen years working in the Richland Mall. I started as an Assistant Manager at the Piercing Pagoda, where I worked for three years. Then I went to Shoe World as a Key Sales Leader and an Assistant Manager until 1996.

When I think about memories of my time working at the Richland Mall, they fill my heart with joy and laughter. I remember all the friendships I made there. I think my favorite memories were of the special Christmas parties. I remember getting dressed up in sparkles and making something to eat to share with everyone. At 10:30 p.m., we would pause and head down to the Duke and Duchess movie theater, which was inside the Mall, and we picked up our free tickets to any movie of our choice. We also had free snacks, popcorn, and drinks. Then, we exchanged gifts with our coworkers and went home.

I remember Gus, the massive doll in center court, who along with Santa Claus, listened to the children's holiday wishes. There were decorations like trumpets filled with flowers, plus ABC books, and toy soldiers. Of course, there was also an annual appearance by Richie the Pook, who was the Mall mascot. To this day, I don't know what on earth a "Pook" is, and I don't think that anyone else did, either.

Photos by Chuck Mamula

I remember the trick-or-treat parade, where all the children dressed up in costumes and marched up and down the Mall, stopping at each store to collect candy.

Don't forget the lovely carousel that came from Switzerland as a special gift to the Mall. What a lovely, soothing sight it was, and how the children loved to ride it!

I also remember all the long-gone restaurants that I loved. There was Sweet William, the Encore (with money embedded in the tabletops), Franks 'n Stuff (which served hot dogs of all kinds), KarmelKorn (where you could get popcorn, hot chocolate, coffee, drinks, and sweets), and Mary's Poppers with homemade fried chicken.

My favorite place to work was Shoe World. It was a fun setting. There were color-coordinated shoes with accessories such as pushers, shoes clips, stockings, shoe care products, and polish. I was the best sales employee, and so I won pushers, marked-down shoes, and sometimes money!

I made long-lasting friendships at Shoe World. I think that the feeling of family and friendship was the most special thing about working there.

A gentleman who lived across the street from my in-laws did all the cement work and designed the wave pattern in the Mall ceilings that was very unique for its time.

The day we found out that the Mall would be closing was heartbreaking to all of us. The final time that my coworker Jayne and I pulled down and locked the metal gate, we stood there and looked around at the ghost town that had once been a bustling, happy place full of shoppers. Farewell Richland Mall. We will miss you.

Linda Stufft

Photo by Philip Balko

chapter fifteen

memories
for breakfast

For four guys, it's like the Richland Mall never closed...at least on Saturdays.

Back in the old days, when Gil Demos, Joe Fortunato, Frank Koscis, and Joe Cohen worked in the Mall, they used to meet for breakfast every morning at Sweet William restaurant. It was these laugh-a-minute breakfast meetings that put them in the right frame of mind for a busy day in the world of retail.

"We would go over to Sweet William in the morning and just have a ball, laughing and carrying on," recalls Frank Koscis, who was then managing the Thom McAn shoe store. "The guys and I would have a great meal and catch up on the latest news, and then we'd be back in our stores by 10 to open to the public."

Photo by Philip Balko

According to Gil Demos, breakfast wasn't the only time the gang congregated at Sweet William. "We also had lunch there every day. We never missed breakfast or lunch at Sweet William.

"They had a salad called the Swiss Salad Supreme, which was like the most sought-after salad in the world. Everybody had to have one.

"They put this special dressing on, like a sweet-and-sour dressing, and you tried to duplicate it at home and you couldn't. They just had this salad down pat. They put some cheese on it, and it was perfect. Everybody ate the Swiss Salad Supreme. It was famous, like Isley's chipped ham. It was just really famous there."

Tradition Continued

Even as some of the guys found work elsewhere, and the Mall eventually ran out of steam and went under, they kept up the tradition. If they no longer worked close enough together to meet every day, and Sweet William no longer existed, they could at least find time on Saturday mornings for a lively breakfast at another dining establishment.

Down through the years, they kept meeting for Saturday breakfasts at local restaurants, sometimes joined by other pals from the Richland Mall days like the Encore's Larry Mummert or Jim White of Spencer Gifts.

The tradition continues to this day, as the gang meets for Saturday breakfast at Denny's or Panera Bread or Corner Coffee Shop.

"We talk about old war stories and what's going on in everyone's lives," says Joe Fortunato.

"We solve all the world's problems," says Gil Demos. "We have a really terrific time."

They also continue to help each other through the rough spots that are inevitably part of life. As they've aged, their troubles have focused more on health issues, like Gil's open-heart surgery and Joe Cohen's stroke. By being there for each other and talking things over, they've gotten through struggles that might otherwise have been much harder to survive.

And so they've resolved to keep the tradition alive and support each other as they have since the days of the Mall. You can find them every Saturday, talking around the breakfast table in one of their favorite haunts, discussing the ups and downs of life.

Also laughing their butts off as they talk about some old Halloween party or a run-in with a security guard or some crazy stunt one of them pulled with a farm animal at the dairy exposition in the Mall one time.

I had the honor of working as Gus and Melanie at the Mall during the Christmas holiday season. There was a little door on Gus's seat that I would crawl through to get to the mechanics that operated the puppets.

I sat on a swing that let me make Gus lean forward or backward. There were foot pedals and hand levers that controlled the other movements of Gus and Melanie.

And of course there was a microphone that I used to respond to shoppers' questions and wishes in real time as Gus or Melanie.

It was always fun for me to see someone I knew and call them out by name, as though it were Gus or Melanie talking directly to them. I think a few grown-ups once again believed in the possibility that Santa did indeed know if they were good or bad.

Pamela Krupa-Jeschonek

I filled out many entry slips during a contest at the Richland Mall to win a trip to Disney World. I went to many stores to enter as many times as I could and spent quite a while filling out my slips.

On a Friday night, I went with my daughter to the Mall. I had to write a check to pay for her purchase. The cashier said to me, "Are you the lady who won the trip to Disney?" She showed me the announcement that had been sent to each store, and sure enough, my name was on it…but I had to wait until Monday to verify that I had won because the Mall office was closed over the weekend!

That's how I won a fight to Florida, a week in Orlando at Walt Disney World, and a hotel with breakfast and other amenities!

Gail Hoover

Photo by Philip Balko

255

One of my first jobs after graduating from UPJ was as an assistant manager at Spencer Gifts. I loved "Mall life." There were Mall walkers who exercised indoors before the stores opened. I would pick up my favorite new albums or cassettes at National Record Mart.
Vanessa Spack Walker

My grandmother and I went to the Encore to see Thaao Penghlis, who played Tony DiMera on *Days of Our Lives*. I'll never forget it.
Al Reno

I remember spending a ton of time with my mother at work running the carousel in the Mall. She also worked in the lottery booth for a while.
Justin Lozar

My mom and I had lunch in a sit-down restaurant near Penn Traffic. We started to get a little silly, and then we got a *lot* silly. We were laughing about just about *everything*. I think the people at the next table wished we'd just leave. We had so much fun!
Gina Shelton

Photo by Chuck Mamula

When they put the carousel in, that was a nice feature. As a kid, I would go to the Mall with my grandmother and great grandmother on Saturday afternoons to shop and watch people. I loved to watch people.
Elizabeth Zilch Barto

I worked at Our Furniture, then Hoss's across from the Mall. Then, I worked at La Rose for 19 years, where I became manager. I loved working for Joe Cohen at La Rose.

Glenna & Mike Bodolosky

What I liked best about the Mall was all the people, the customers you got to know personally. At the Richland Mall, everyone was friendly and got along well. I still see a lot of those people today.
Glenna Bodolosky

Courtesy Joe Cohen

256

chapter sixteen

a reunion to remember

september 24, 2016

Richland Mall employees helped themselves to a delicious buffet, laughed about crazy goings-on, and danced to live rock 'n' roll and disco hits.

It was almost like a night at the Encore back in '79 instead of Ace's Lounge in 2016. That was kind of the point – to relive the Richland Mall's glory days, complete with music, food, drink, and a crowd who'd shared the unique experience of working in the Mall.

When the doors opened at Ace's at 6:00 p.m. on Saturday, September 24th, 2016, organizer Gil Demos greeted a long stream of Mall colleagues ("malleagues?") with smiles, hugs, and hearty handshakes. Some of them, he'd seen steadily or at least occasionally over the years since the Mall's closing; others, he hadn't seen in ages.

As they handed over their tickets and got their name-tags at the registration table, Gil was happier than ever that he'd decided to set up this reunion. Some of the best times of his life had happened at the Richland Mall; now, for one night at least, he would get to bring them back with a bunch of his favorite friends.

"I miss everybody," Gill said before the event. "I want to see some of the people, even the caretakers of the Mall, janitors, everyone. We all loved the Mall."

What They Missed Most

As guests entered and got their name-tags, they sat at tables according to where they worked in the Mall. One table was all Franks & Stuff employees, another was all Ormond employees, another was Kinderfoto alumni, and so on. Both Kmart and Somerset Trust had two tables each.

But they didn't stay confined to those groups as the party heated up. Before long, guests were mingling freely, regardless of where they'd worked in the Mall. They shared memories of the old days, retelling stories of the funny or wonderful things that had happened back when they'd all been part of the same Mall community.

They all had one thing in common: they loved the late, great Richland Mall.

"I do miss the Mall," said Chris Lugar, a former employee of Watchmaker's and Somerset Trust. "It was easy to get around, and you knew where everything was. There was a lot to do offered in a small area, instead of having two floors and nothing there."

"I loved the Mall," said Brian Peracchino, who worked four years in the Mall's information booth. "I loved working in the center of the Mall. You could see everything from there. I loved working in the information booth, where you got to know everyone, and I loved my boss, Connie Hayes. I truly miss the Richland Mall and have never even been to the Galleria."

Rose King also worked in the information booth, plus several shops in the Mall and Galleria.

"Those of us who worked at the Richland Mall were very close," she remembers. "All of us – managers, security, maintenance – we worked together. We would help each other out, and we would stand outside our stores and talk to each other. It was the friendliest atmosphere, and you just don't have that today. It was one big family, and I miss it very much."

Craig Keilman, who worked at Lester's and Chess King, was also a fan of the Mall. "I like working there because it was like a family. Everyone would go from store to store and get to know each other."

"They called me 'Miss Kmart,'" said Cindy Tomaselli, who worked at Kmart for 12 years. "What I liked most about the Mall was all the food places. It was also nice having Penn Traffic in the Mall. It was an old store I grew up with.

"I remember the Richland Mall fondly. I made a lot of good friends there, and we all hung out together," said Cindy.

The Longtimers

When most everyone had arrived, Gil made some opening remarks as emcee, officially kicking off the celebration and welcoming the guests – one in particular. Gil and the crowd gave a special ovation to Bob McConnell, the Mall's general manager for 23 years, who had come all the way from Chicago to attend the event.

For Bob, who had loved the Mall as much as anyone, coming to the party had never been in doubt. It was only the second time he'd been back in town in 20 years, but he hadn't been able to say no to Gil's invitation. Recapturing some of the magic of the Mall had been more than worth traveling all the way from Chicago.

"Those of us who worked at the Mall were like family," Bob said that night. "Everybody got along and was there for each other. We were all friends. I made my best friends here, in fact."

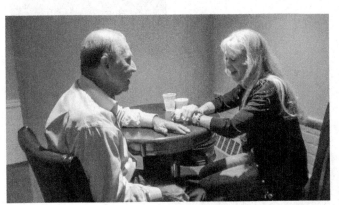

Photos by Philip Balko

Another guest who'd witnessed the history of the Mall from start to finish had also been unable to refuse Gil's invitation. Shirley DiRosa of Capri Pizza remembered the same friendly, family atmosphere that Bob talked about, with merchants chatting like neighbors and supporting each other.

"We were like next-door neighbors in the Mall," remembered Shirley. "It was like, 'come on over and have a cup of coffee.' We would talk about what was happening and what was going to happen – what items we would put on sale and what events were coming up.

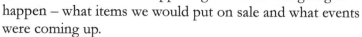

"We kept each other up to date and enjoyed each other's company. There were so many good times," said Shirley.

Richard Stern had a long career at the Mall, too. Starting in the 1970s, he managed the Mall branch of Somerset Trust, where he was responsible for all non-lending functions of the bank.

"Somerset Trust was important to the Mall because most of the tenants did their banking with us," explained Richard. "We had to satisfy the deposit and cash needs for the businesses to keep running there.

"The Mall and Somerset Trust always had a close and special relationship, which continues today. The bank contributed to the sponsorship of this reunion, in fact," said Richard.

A True Mall Musician

After dinner, live music started up, courtesy of the Tomcats, a band with a true Richland Mall pedigree. Ed Cominsky, who played lead guitar and harmonica, worked in security at the Mall from 1980 to 1993. He also played in Kindred Spirit, a popular band in the Johnstown area in the 1970s...though he gets recognized just as much for his time at the Mall.

"When I'm out playing, people who worked at the Mall or were customers there still tell me they recognize me," said Ed. "That's no surprise, because people at the Mall were very friendly. I got to know them on a personal basis."

More Reunions to Come?

Ed's band motivated plenty of guests to get on the dance floor, though others spent time off to the side, catching up with friends. Some of them hadn't seen each other in many years, after all; it had been a decade, for example, since the Kinderfoto group had gotten together.

However long it had been, the years melted away in the big room at Ace's, as friendships were reestablished and good times remembered. It was a testament to the magic created by Jim O'Roark, Jim Streeter, and the whole cast of pioneering dreamers, designers, builders, and merchants back in the early 70s. Even after everything that happened, even so long after the Mall went away, its spirit lived on in the hearts of the people who were once part of its unique reality.

Photos by Philip Balko

Even tearing the Mall down and replacing it with something else could not burn away the love and longing that the members of the Richland Mall community still felt for it.

But did they have enough fun that night at Ace's to continue to keep the legacy alive?

"I'm having a great time and seeing people I haven't seen for a while," said Brian Peracchino.

"It's great to visit with people who were a part of your life, and you've fallen out of touch with them," said Chris Lugar.

"It's always a good thing for folks to come together and remember the good times they had," said Richard Stern.

Though their lives after the Mall's demise had taken them in different directions, the people at that party agreed on two things. First, they all

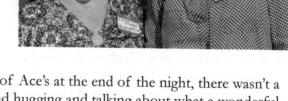

had a great time. When they finally streamed out of Ace's at the end of the night, there wasn't a sourpuss among them. Everyone was laughing and hugging and talking about what a wonderful time they'd had.

Many of them were also in agreement about one other thing: the Richland Mall might not return, but the reunions should.

Photos by Philip Balko

I worked at Kmart in the building materials department in 1974-75. One of my favorite times at the Mall was seeing the Vogues when they came to perform in Center Court. And the car shows were awesome, presenting all the latest new cars. There were classic car shows as well. Sometimes, it was just nice to stroll through the Mall, window shopping and getting some exercise.
Frank Burkhard

I remember shopping at Mommy and Me. I loved buying Leap Frog Knits for my son and the cutest pink sailor dress with white trim for my daughter. I also bought a pair of blue/green plaid knickers, a V-neck yellow sweater vest, and a matching plaid golf cap for my youngest son. Two giant toy soldiers greeted us at the entrance. These soldiers can still be seen in Richview Manor at Christmas time, adorning the front entrance to the former owners' home!
Joyce Phillips Baywood

My best memories are of my dad, Clair Rager, appearing as Santa Claus at the Richland Mall, which he did for many years. I would always be in Johnstown for Thanksgiving, so I had the opportunity to watch him work. One year, as we stood in line, a woman made a comment about Santa. My young son turned to her, and with a volume loud enough for the whole line to hear, said, "That's my Pap Pap."
Bruce Rager

I remember when one of the Teenage Mutant Ninja Turtles came to sign autographs and greet the kids. The line was so long, we must have waited an hour for the autograph.
Nancy Dickert

I remember when my daughter was small, as soon as we walked in the door of the Mall, she would run to the merry-go-round to see if she was tall enough to ride on her own yet. I also bought a beloved pet at the pet store. My "Lady" lived to be almost 13 years old.
Tracey Coughenour Wolk

In 1989, around Christmas, we decided to take our new Pekingese puppy, Rocky (who came from That Pet Place) to the Richland Mall to get his picture taken with Santa. I was in the picture, too. (I was almost 10 at the time.) My older brother, Bill, had Rocky tucked inside his Westmont letterman's jacket with just his little head sticking out between two snaps. I think a security guard was trying to give him a hard time for bringing the dog in, but my mom was able to convince the guard to leave my brother alone. (The guard was probably a former student of hers from Bishop McCort). When we got to Santa, I sat on one side of Santa's lap, while he held Rocky on the other side. The following year, we brought Rocky back with my grandma's dog, Tobie (also a Pekingese). The people at the Santa photo kiosk told us that we'd started the pet photos with Santa thing at the Mall because we'd brought Rocky the previous year.

Jodi Warren Uhron

I worked at Regis in the Richland Mall. On one of my breaks, while walking to Karmelkorn, I met Richard Simmons. He reminded me that caramel popcorn was unhealthy.

Lisa Vivis Giffin

For years after the Richland Mall closed, I dreamed of that place. I dreamed about walking through the Mall, and my stores still being there, and me working in the Mall. This went on for maybe five, six, or seven years. I kept dreaming that I was still working at the Richland Mall. That's how much of an impression it left on me.

Gil Demos

Photo by Chuck Mamula

chapter seventeen

where the mall never closed

Brick and mortar retail is dying. That's what they say.

Some people say good riddance. Why waste your time driving across town, then parking, then walking across the parking lot, walking across a mall or big-box store, when the thing that you want or need might not even be

Photo by Chuck Mamula

in stock? Why waste your time searching for a cashier or standing in line or fumbling with coupons that don't even work for what you're buying half the time?

Why not just find what you're looking for online? Why not tell your phone or voice-activated home assistant to order it for you? Why not get a rock-bottom price and free two-day shipping without leaving the comfort of your couch?

These days, all that and more is at your fingertips...and the options are constantly evolving and multiplying. As brick-and-mortar shopping centers close and crumble, and major retail companies like Sears and J.C. Penny shut down stores, scientists and engineers keep cranking out new ways to make buying easier.

265

But can you order friendship – *real* friendship – over your phone? What about a sense of community?

Can you find true human contact and the personal touch? Satisfying face-to-face relationships that last a lifetime?

In 20 or 30 years, will you go to reunion parties for people who met while shopping online? Will you have tons of stories you can laugh about with those people? Will you share favorite songs and movies and dance moves and jokes and memories?

And what about surprises? How many of those will you come across when shopping online? How many unexpected events will come along by random chance to change your destiny or the way you live your life?

If you remember the Richland Mall, you already know the answers to all these questions. You already know how special brick-and-mortar shopping can be. And you know how much we have to lose if it all goes away.

Though it's true, if a place is special enough, we can hold it in our hearts forever. We can dream about it, write books about it, post tributes online about it. Long after it's closed and demolished, we can keep the best parts of it alive and use them to continue to enrich and inform our lives.

But maybe that doesn't mean we should be so quick to give things up in our never-ending quest for what's new and exciting. Maybe we should slow down a little and make the most of what we have. Maybe that's the true lesson we can learn from a dead-and-gone mall born in the 70s.

Photos by Chuck Mamula

Insert Smiley Face Here

Earlier in the pages of this book, the theories of quantum physics let us imagine realities parallel to our own in which the Richland Mall never died. Does that mean those worlds are all the better for it? And would you, if given the chance, pass over to one such world and spend the rest of your life there?

If you're holding this book, your answer is pretty obvious. And in that answer lies the answer to a bigger question.

Should brick-and-mortar retail be saved before it's too late? Or should we get out of the way of progress, let online shopping dominate as we dream of fairy tale parallel worlds where the Pook still tiptoes through the trees in center court?

If, given the chance, we would live in a world where the Richland Mall still thrives, maybe we should do what we can to bring that Mall back to life in the shopping choices we make and the way we do business.

Maybe we should make a conscious effort to put friendliness and community front and center. From the beginning, those qualities were featured prominently in the Richland Mall's promotions and advertising. Looking back, it's easy to see them as a feel-good gimmick in the "Have a nice day" 1970s…but maybe the folks who cooked up those campaigns were on to something.

Because look around at the retail experiences in your world. Do you feel good about them? Do you feel like they are gratifying in ways other than the exchange of money for goods and services?

And do you think they would be *more* or *less* enjoyable with a stronger component of friendliness or community?

Let me ask that question again: Would your shopping experiences be more or less enjoyable with a stronger component of friendliness or entertainment or community?

Talk about a no-brainer.

Richland Mall 2017

Visit one of those alternate realities, and the answer is right there in your face.

Walk in the door of the Richland Mall 2017, and there's a mini-circus happening near center court. Music plays as an aerialist flips between trapezes, clowns frolic with cream pies and balloons, and dogs in costumes do tricks.

You pause and take it all in, laughing and clapping with the crowd. Then, you move on toward the Kmart end, where a band plays on a stage near National Record Mart. Again, you stop and watch, enjoying the show.

Photos by Chuck Mamula

People you know swing by and chat you up, dishing out the latest gossip. Some of them are employees from stores in the Mall, who've become good friends of yours over the years. One tells you there's a big sale coming up, and they're putting aside an extra coupon just for you. Another mentions an outfit you liked that finally came in in your size.

Leaving the stage, you head for Kmart. Briefly, you recall another world where there was once a wall between Kmart and the rest of the Mall...and then you forget. Your memories of a tragic end for the Richland Mall fade away, becoming like dreams or echoes of other possible realities that mean nothing to you.

So what if there are alternate worlds where the Richland Mall no longer exists, and shopping is strictly a no-frills, businesslike affair...where the goal is just to get what you came for and get out, with minimal interaction. Where people have stopped asking, "Where's the fun in *that?*"

You're just happy to exist in a reality where you can still eat at Sweet William, play games at

Courtesy Jim O'Roark

Time-Out, or dance under the glitter ball at the Red Lady Disco in the Encore. You're just glad that you live in a world where the Richland Mall is still a big part of the community and your daily life, a tradition to be shared with generations to come.

Just then, as if he senses your happy thoughts, Richie the Pook catches your eye, waving from down the hallway toward McDonald's. Grinning, you wave back at him.

At which point, you laugh, because you forgot why the heck you came to the Mall today in the first place. And the funny part is, you just don't care.

Photo by Chuck Mamula

bonus section

small talk
newsletters

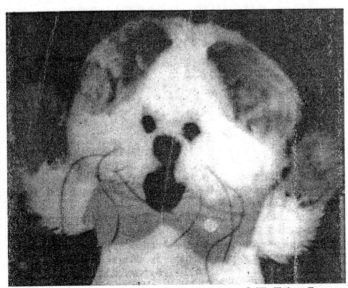

richland sMall talk

August/September, 1973 | VOLUME I | ISSUE I

THANK YOU

On page 12 of the May/June, 1973 issue of the Saturday Evening Post, The Post, in co-sponsorship with the National Municipal League, announced the 1972 winners of the ALL AMERICAN CITY awards. As most of you know, Johnstown, Pa. is one of the 11 award winners. So, pardon us while we take a short ego trip, after all, The Post has now publicly confirmed our opinion of Johnstown. We'll delve into this issue in later editions, but for the time being, let us say once again, "Thank you, Saturday Evening Post, for recognizing the community spirit and hard work of the citizens of Johnstown, Pennsylvania, THE ALL AMERICAN CITY."

YOU'VE COME A LONG
WAY BABY!

Eighteen short months ago, a dream was born. This dream existed in the minds of two men, and soon expanded to the mind of three others. Unlike many dreams in the minds of men, this dream has become a reality.

On May 3, 1973, ground was broken for the Richland Mall in Johnstown, Pa. Construction is well under way, and the partners of Richland Mall Associates are confident that the September 1974 opening date will be met.

Yes, we've come a long way, and the next 13 months will be even more exciting. This newsletter is to keep you, the tenant, abreast of the news and progress of Richland Mall. We plan to announce each tenant as leases are signed, keep you up to date on construction and let you know of any new developments or changes in the mall. In other words, this is YOUR letter. If you have any questions or suggestions, we want to know about them, so please direct all mail to:

Richland sMall talk
P. O. Box 8101
Grand Rapids, MI 49508

The paper will originate from the home office until the opening of the mall, when the responsibility will then be assumed by your Merchants Association. This transfer will keep your newsletter close to home and in touch with YOU, the tenant. But, until then . . . .

oh where,

oh where,

DID OUR LEASES GO?

"I signed a letter of intent several months ago, but . . . ." We've heard some of our tenants say those very words. All we can do is say, "We're sorry." According to Ray Kisor, the leases are now in the attorney's hands, and are being prepared for mailing. We wish we could mail them to you today, but cutting red tape is a long, slow process. We hope to have the leases in the mail within the next two weeks, and ask that you continue to be patient. We are working at top speed, but a person can only accomplish so much in a day. Please be assured that we will continue to do everything in our power to have the final leases to you in very short order.

UP. UP, &
AWAY!

On May 3, 1973, the first shovel of dirt was turned on the site. Since then, many, many things have happened. According to Ron Sabin, our construction engineer, the area has changed from a drive-in theater site to a Mall site, with construction crews already beginning to pour the concrete foundations. All work is "on schedule", for our September 1974 Grand Opening date. More Construction news next month.

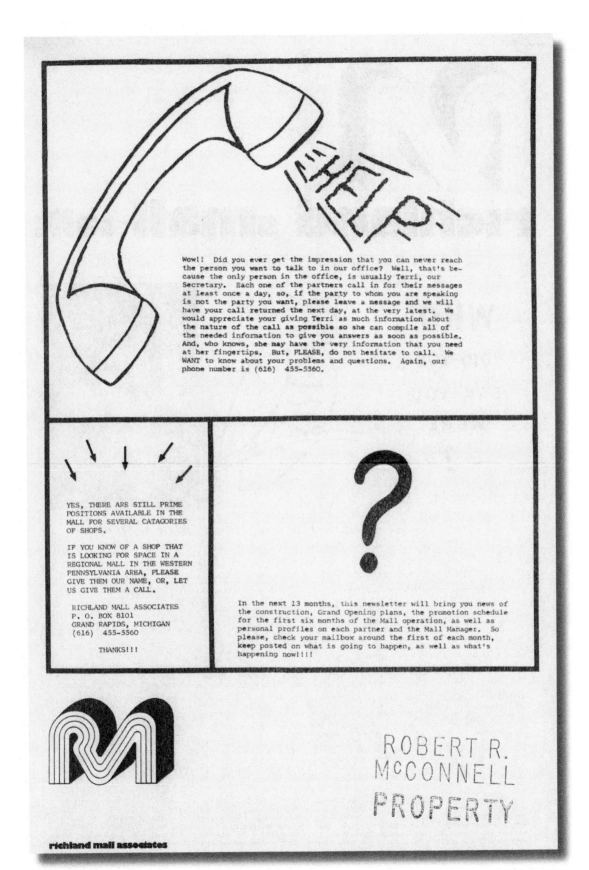

Wow!! Did you ever get the impression that you can never reach
the person you want to talk to in our office? Well, that's because the only person in the office, is usually Terri, our
Secretary. Each one of the partners call in for their messages
at least once a day, so, if the party to whom you are speaking
is not the party you want, please leave a message and we will
have your call returned the next day, at the very latest. We
would appreciate your giving Terri as much information about
the nature of the call as possible so she can compile all of
the needed information to give you answers as soon as possible.
And, who knows, she may have the very information that you need
at her fingertips. But, PLEASE, do not hesitate to call. We
WANT to know about your problems and questions. Again, our
phone number is (616) 455-5560.

YES, THERE ARE STILL PRIME
POSITIONS AVAILABLE IN THE
MALL FOR SEVERAL CATAGORIES
OF SHOPS.

IF YOU KNOW OF A SHOP THAT
IS LOOKING FOR SPACE IN A
REGIONAL MALL IN THE WESTERN
PENNSYLVANIA AREA, PLEASE
GIVE THEM OUR NAME, OR, LET
US GIVE THEM A CALL.

RICHLAND MALL ASSOCIATES
P. O. BOX 8101
GRAND RAPIDS, MICHIGAN
(616) 455-5560

THANKS!!!

In the next 13 months, this newsletter will bring you news of
the construction, Grand Opening plans, the promotion schedule
for the first six months of the Mall operation, as well as
personal profiles on each partner and the Mall Manager. So
please, check your mailbox around the first of each month,
keep posted on what is going to happen, as well as what's
happening now!!!!

richland mall associates

ROBERT R.
McCONNELL

PROPERTY

271

Courtesy Bob McConnell

richland small talk

October 1973   VOLUME I   ISSUE 2

WHO
DID YOU
SAY YOU
WERE
?

Jim Streeter . . .

During our first few months of business, the above question seemed to be all we ever heard!! That response has changed (thank goodness!), and we can now look back and laugh at our growing pains. We thought you might enjoy doing the same, so, here are a few facts and figures:

-We started our Company on a shoestring, a dream, lots of energy, and a whole lot of faith in our ability.

-We've paid over $2,900 in turnpike tolls.

-We've used well over 100 reams of paper.

-We've made 3,736 blue prints in our office alone.

-Our phone bill has topped $16,500.

-Our poor copy machine has spilled out over 40,000 copies.

-Uncle Sam has collected over $1,000 in postage from us.

-We've driven over 520,000 miles, gone through 12 cars, "totaling" two in four accidents.

-We've hand applied 17,064 feet of graphic tape to the maps in our Market Studies, (that's nearly 3¼ miles), and we're not done yet!

-Our office looked like a blizzard in July when we assembled over 15,000 pages into 200 basic leases of 75 pages each.

-Since our medical policy went into effect June 1, 1973, we've claimed 150 stitches from a collision with a sliding glass door, one crushed foot, one appendectomy, one sprained ankle, one ear drum restoration, a lanced abcess and three facial stitches. Before June 1, we were healthy!!

And now, we'd like to thank Linda, Joyce, Evelyn, Jan and Cheryl, the wonderful wives of our guys for helping to apply that graphic tape, assemble those market studies, put up with our hectic schedules, spend ever-so-many weeks (and weekends!) alone, take the responsibility of raising our children, and keeping those home fires burning. Because of the help and support of these great gals, we've had the freedom and peace of mind to be able to make Richland Mall a reality, and stop that nearly forgotten question of, "WHO did you say you were?"

We'd like you to meet Jim Streeter, one of the two men that started our Company. Those of you who have met Jim will remember him as that super looking guy that walks into your office and causes your Secretary to make 8 typographical errors in that letter that had to go out in the 2 P. M. mail. Now we'd like everyone to know Jim the way we do, a great guy to work and play with.

Jim is 33, and a native of Grand Rapids. He and his beautiful wife Joyce have two darling children, Susan and Mike. His winter hobbies are work, work, and work some more in order to have time in the summer to enjoy Golf (he's the best in our Company), and Tennis. He is taking flying lessons this year, so we'll someday have a pilot among us.

Unfortunately for us, you see that cheerful face of Jim's more than we do. His hectic schedule keeps him on the road most of the time. Jim serves in two capacities with us. He's in charge of Land Acquisition, and was recently appointed to the position of Lease Coordinator for Richland Mall Associates. This position was designed to free Ray Kisor's time and enable us to be more efficient in final lease negotiations with you, our Tenants. We know you will enjoy working with Jim as much as we do.

Leases, Leases

EVERYWHERE ! !

Mailing a lease, it sounds so easy!! If all we had to do was put it in the envelope, plop on a stamp and drop the whole thing in the mail box, each and every one of you would have your lease in your hands right now.

Unfortunately, the process is not as simple as one would like to believe, (if only it were!!) Each and every one of you have special needs... therefore.... each and every lease is "made to order" by our attorney, according to the intent letter you signed.

Needless to say, this is very time consuming. So far, over 20 leases have been mailed, and many others are waiting for the proper approval from our office before they are transferred to yours. If you haven't received your lease yet, thanks for waiting. We are all working on them as fast as possible, and you should have them in the next few weeks.

richland mall associates

Richland Mall, that's us!! Now that our name and Logo are fast becoming associated with our Company we decided that we must give credit where credit's due, and let you know how, who, and why the design of our name was chosen.

The art and type style were designed by Dan Bridy, one of the owners of Rainbow Grinder, a three year old design and illustration studio in Pittsburgh, Pennsylvania. Dan and his two partners, Jim Deigan and Bill Schmidt, have a combined 35 years in this business, and their approach to these areas are very contemporary and "today".

The symbol in our Logo combines the initials R & M into one, which graphically relates to the contour and design of the Mall structure. The bands going through the symbol are muted earth tones on the full color versions of the Logo.

We're pleased with our Logo and identification program, and thank Dan, and the Rainbow Grinder for creating such a fine piece of work for us.

terRi's NotE-book

If we used the 1,200,000 bricks in Richland Mall to build a wall 30 ft. high, that wall would be 1 mile, 434' long.

The materials used in Richland Mall would be equivilent to building a subdivision of 315, four bedroom homes.

Over 2,400,000 pounds of steel will be used in the construction of the Mall.

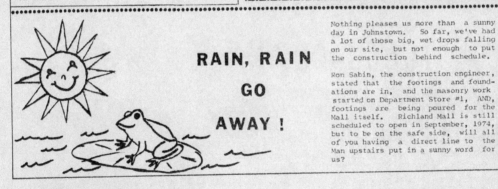

RAIN, RAIN GO AWAY !

Nothing pleases us more than a sunny day in Johnstown. So far, we've had a lot of those big, wet drops falling on our site, but not enough to put the construction behind schedule.

Ron Sabin, the construction engineer, stated that the footings and foundations are in, and the masonry work started on Department Store #1, AND, footings are being poured for the Mall itself. Richland Mall is still scheduled to open in September, 1974, but to be on the safe side, will all of you having a direct line to the Man upstairs put in a sunny word for us?

ROBERT R.
McCONNELL
PROPERTY

richland mall associates
p.o. box 8101,
grand rapids, michigan 49508

Courtesy Bob McConnell

richland sMall talk

NOVEMBER 1973   VOLUME 1   ISSUE 3

TOUCH-DOWN !

Last month, we began personal profiles for each member of our "Mini" team. As it will take several months to complete the lineup, you'll find the following program helpful in directing your passes to the correct player:

JIM O'ROARK - Quarterback - Jim carries the ball for major tenant leasing and calls the plays for the entire team.

JIM STREETER - Fullback - Jim is our "legal mind" for land acquisition and grabs the ball on lease communications.

STEVE CLAUSE - Guard - Steve protects the checkbook and "eagle eyes" the sites for market analysis.

RAY KISOR - Halfback - Ray picks up yardage for internal mall leasing which keeps him running all the time.

RON SABIN - Tackle - Ron tackles the problems of construction, blocks interference between the Contractors, Architects and Engineers.

BOB McCONNELL - End - Bob is in strict training for Mall Management, learning to catch tenant passes.

TERRI WEST - Center - Terri centers communication, hikes the sMall Talk, and blocks as much interference as possible.

LINDA, JOYCE, JAN, CHERYL, EVELYN, KATE and FRANK - The better halves of the team and the greatest cheering section any team could ask for.

That's our team!! We may be "Mini" in size, but we're "Maxi" in team spirit and ability. Keep on reading the personal profiles and learn all about the "real" people behind the plays!!

Jim O'Roark

This month, we'd like you to meet Jim O'Roark, one of the two men who started our Company. Those of you who have met Jim will not be likely to forget that fantastic mind and the energy that seems to infect everyone around him.

Jim, heading toward 30, is a native of Stoystown, Pa., a little town of 400 or so in the vicinity of the Mall. Jim and his wife Linda, (who is as pretty as Jim is intelligent) have two of the "cutest" children you'll ever meet, Brook and Jamie. His wide range of interests include Golf, Tennis, mixed double Bowling, and antique collecting. They also collect frogs in all sizes, shapes and forms (except living)!!

While the rest of us are "doing our thing", Jim is the coordinator and "Master Mind" of the Company. He's the guy on top of everything, making sure each of us keeps pace with the rest, and that our work is turned out fast and perfect. He knows when to push, when to bend, and when to have fun!! Quite a job for an average man, but anyone that knows Jim knows he's far above average. His unique mind, and his ability to enjoy life to its fullest truly make Jim "one of a kind", and one which all of us are proud to be associated with.

GIVE THANKS?

Thanksgiving, the beginning of the Holiday season! The beginning of the mad rush in our stores, heavy traffic on the roads, long shopping hours, and the beginning of the end of another year!

When we were kids, Thanksgiving meant a trip to Grandma's for one of the yummiest meals of the year!! No school, and loads of time to play with our friends and be pampered by Gram and Gramps!! Of course we were thankful that there was plenty of food, a nice warm house and all that stuff! Mom and Dad said we had to be, but that wasn't as important as all the fun things!!

In our teenage years, Grandma's house just didn't seem to hold that same magic anymore. We'd much rather be home with our friends, shopping for new party clothes for the up-coming holiday season and worrying about dates for the Christmas Formal. Yeah, the meal was good! Sure, we were thankful for being able to live in this country. There are just so many other things that...well...you know!!!

Then we were married, with a young family of our own! Here comes the hassle---WHICH set of parents do we visit? Certainly we're thankful for everything we have, but WOW! We don't want to hurt any feelings!! And with Christmas so-o-o close, how will we possibly manage to buy the kids what they want with all these other bills? The heating season's here---more money going out!! Regardless of tradition--almost hate to see the season come!! Only....so homesick in the fall!!!

With the twilight years approaching, our viewpoint changes once again! Will the kids bring the grand-children here---or will the in-laws see them instead? Look at the shape of the country!! Will the taxes ever stop going up? Are we headed for another war? What's the younger generation coming to? Yes, we're thankful, it just seems that there's an awful lot not to be thankful about!!

Thanksgiving today!! Isn't it a bit old fashioned? After all, the world...the country...our lives...so totally different now from the original concept of this day so many generations ago!! Why...NOW we can live...love...dress...work...act...in any manner we choose without being put down by our peers!!

Come to think of it, this old-fashioned holiday of Thanksgiving can still be summed up in a single word!! The very same word that's been used for generations!! Only now, in our modern world where we have so much more than our forefathers could ever conceive, where we take for granted the liberties that they fought.. and died for, where we are surrounded by luxuries unheard of in their day...now, the concept of that word is enlarged to encompass more than our forefathers wildest dream!! Yes, that word means more today than it has ever meant in the past!! What word? FREEDOM!!

WALLS!

Ah, yes, 'twas much simpler in ye olden days to 'ave a barn raisen' than 'tis t'day to 'rect ye Mall!!

But we're off and running, and this month have we got news for you! Ron Sabin, our construction engineer, is keeping our contractors busy! The foundations are in for nearly all of the Mall and WALLS are going up for Department Store 1. You bet we're happy!! Instead of a vacant piece of land with a big hole and lots of concrete, we've got WALLS!! Keep up the good work Ron!!

terRi's NotE-booK

We could pave a residential street for one full mile with the material we'll use on the 30 acre parking lot!

The buildings erected on the site will consume a full 15 acres!

The articles in this newsletter are written only by me. If I sometimes sound a little too enthusiastic, it's because I love my job and have 5 of the greatest guys in the world to work for!!

So you're a health nut! Just jog around the Mall 1½ times to equal 1 mile!

ROBERT R. McCONNELL PROPERTY

richland mall associates
p.o. box 8804,
grand rapids, michigan 49508

Courtesy Bob McConnell

richland small talk

December 1973   VOLUME 1   Issue 4

100% OPEN

That's our goal, "100%" open for Grand Opening next September!!

So-o-o, we're asking that you keep your eyes peeled for the Tenant Coordination Folder and Block - Out drawings that are in the process of being prepared at this very time!!

And---we'd like to ask you to run, not walk, to your favorite Architect's office as soon as that package arrives in your office!!

Why? 'Cause we want to avoid as many last minute problems as we can!! Let's face it, if everyone used the allowed amount of time for each set of drawings, approvals, revisions, etc., and no one gets the edge by beginning a bit early, we won't have any construction on Tenant spaces started before June of 1974!! Can you imagine 80-odd shops trying to get Contractors, building permits, etc., and be open in 3 short months? Even without the problems that the fuel crisis may have in store for us, that would be like having a 3 month long marathon race.

So, we're asking you to jump the gun a bit. Put in a few extra hours in the coming month, and save everyone a whole bunch of hours, problems, and perhaps a migraine or two next summer.

AN HOUR TODAY MEANS OPENING ON TIME

We're Getting BIGGER !

Richland Mall isn't the only thing under construction right now, even if it does seem like we are laying each and every cement block via long distance!

We are enlarging the home office to nearly twice it's existing size!! It's not that we need more room, after all, just 'cause it takes Ron 20 minutes to locate a drawing that is buried under how many others, and just 'cause we have only four rooms and six people, and we were going to have to lay out our next months issue of sMall talk while it hangs on the walls, well, we could get by for a few more months before we enlarge! But, we'd much rather enlarge now instead of waiting till no one can walk into the office because of the tons of paper that block the door!! (That would be a great opportunity to get everything caught up without interruption tho, wouldn't it?)

So, please, overlook that extra ring it takes to answer the phone and the sounds of saws and hammers that may accompany our greeting!! It takes a bit more time to walk around ladders, and one just can't build without noise!! Be patient with us for a month, and you'll reap the benefits of increased efficiency in the very near future!!

Steve Clause

That's not Santa, that's our Steve! Steve's the guy that very few people meet but everyone loves, 'cause like Santa, he hands out the money! The majority of Steve's time is spent in the home office correcting spelling errors and keeping books!

Steve, 32, hails from Cincinnati, Ohio. Steve and his fantastic wife Jan, who is constantly working on arts and crafts, have two darling children, Connie and Ronnie. Steve loves to play golf and tennis, and also coaches a little league football team.

Steve is one of the most valuable assets in our company. His duties are many, but basically, he's the guy that cuts through the frosting and sees the cake. He takes care of the books, picks out sites, and does market analysis for our developments. While Steve is indispensable in these areas, if we had to pick the one, most important thing about him, it would have to be his ability to remain calm during any crisis. While the rest of us are climbing walls, pulling our hair out, and in general, losing our minds, Steve remains cool, calm and collected. He's straight forward and honest, the guy we all count on for everything from a helping hand to a shoulder to cry on if we need one. That's our Steve. With him, our Company runs smoothly, without him? God help us!!

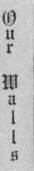

Richland Mall is popping right up!! The above pictures show the walls of Department Store #1 as you would see them from Buchanon Street looking towards Theater Drive and Eisenhower Blvd. Of course, these walls are now complete, as is the front wall for the Mall!! The footings and foundations are well underway for Department Store #2, the supermarket and the theater, and are completed for the entire Mall and Department Store #3. Our steel is scheduled for delivery about the time that you read this article, and everything is full steam ahead (provided, of course, that the steam is not generated by gas!!)

When this report was given to us by Ron Sabin, our Construction Engineer, Ron also noted that work on the site is ahead of schedule, and that with the recent forecast of an exceptionally mild winter, we will have no problems what-so-ever in meeting our Grand Opening schedule!!

Keep those walls heading skyward Ron!! You're doing a GREAT job!!

The Night The Wall Talked!

'Twas the night before Christmas, and all through the Mall
Not a creature was stirring, 'cause I've only one wall!

   The employees are home, enjoying the night
   And me, I'm stranded, alone in my plight!

The machinery is idle, the hammers are still
And everything's silent in the Christmas eve chill.

   No decorations, no crowds, no lights for this year,
   Just one lonely wall, and not very much cheer.

But my wall WILL grow, I know 'cause I've seen
The plans and the specs all shinny and clean!

   Of walls, and courts, and corridors and such,
   Yet right now I'm alone, and I don't look like much!

But next year I'll show them, I know what I'll be
The most popular place in Johnstown, you'll see!

Thru Christmas and Easter and the Fourth of July
I'll get bigger, and bigger, and bigger, shall I!

   And then around Labor Day of next year
   I'll open to toasts of huge mugs of beer!

Open in time for the Christmas season
To enjoy the crowds, the songs, and the fun!

   Decorations, and lights, and a fat Santa too
   And Tenants, and shoppers, I can't wait, can you?

The hustle, the bustle, the fun and the joy
And the cheer that I'll bring to each girl and each boy

   Will be worth all the tears that I shed on this night
   'Cause next year I'll be open and fly high as a kite!

Yes, next year I'll show them, I know what I'll be,
The most popular place in Johnstown, you'll see!!

ROBERT R.
McCONNELL
PROPERTY

richland mall associates
p.o. box 8104,
grand rapids, michigan 49508

Courtesy Bob McConnell

richland small talk

January 1974   Volume 1   Issue 5

HEADLINE EDITION !

When will YOU make headlines?

The Leases Are Coming In!

Where's your lease? Peeking out from the bottom of that stack of work you've been meaning to get to for the past, HOW-long? Or does your Attorney have it, peeking out from the bottom of that stack of work HE's been meaning to get to for the past, HOW-long?

Well, now that the Christmas rush and vacation season is over and we all have our heads back on in the right position, please run, don't walk, to your Attorney's office and ask him (use force if necessary!!) to set things in motion for execution of that lease! Time is growing short and we must have the leases signed before work can begin on your space! (And at the rate the mall is going up, that will be in the VERY near future!!)

So, unless you want your customers greeted by stacks of panelling, studs, nails and lumber when entering your shop during Grand Opening, please, take a moment today, track down that lease and make sure it's headed toward execution in the very near future!! That few minutes today may be all it takes to assure your future customers of an excellent first impression of your new shop, and that means future $$$$$ in your pocket for the life of your lease!!!

Ron Sabin

Long, lanky and loveable, that's our Ron!! He's the man with the "Weight of the Mall" on his shoulders and he needs every inch of that 6' 6" frame to hold up the "problems" that go along with the building of a Mall!!

Ron's not only the tallest of our group, but, believe it or not, he is the oldest too!! Ron, 41, and his lovely wife, Evelyn, have 3 children, Bruce, Jody and Doug!! All three consistently make the honor roll, which, needless to say pleases both parents very much!! Ron's favorite sports are tennis, golf, hunting, fishing and both winter and water skiing. A taste of his dry grape wine will confirm that Ron is one of the original "Little Olde Wine-makers!"

Ron, our Civil Engineer, is fast becoming the most popular person in our Company!! He's responsible for ALL phases of construction and every problem from permits to roof supports will be crossing his desk in the next few months, if it isn't there already!! We rarely see Ron in our office, he's just too busy running from meeting to meeting to solve all the problems that go with erecting a regional Mall!! Rest? Well, next September, after the Mall is up....keep up the good work Ron, our Mall looks better every day thanks to you!!

Courtesy Bob McConnell

Meet Your Neighbor!

So, you're going to lease space in Richland Mall and some of those names on the leasing plan are foreign to you!! Well, relax, get yourself a cup of coffee and sit down for a well deserved break in your day! Beginning this month, we'll be bringing this article to you as a regular feature to acquaint you with your new neighbors!!

Hello Shop - This distinctive gift and card shop, started in 1962 in Johnstown, now has 16 locations in Pennsylvania, Ohio and W. Virginia. The 2,100 square foot prototype shop in Richland Mall will be the 17th in their chain and will have recessed lighting with a traditional decor, and will be able to fill any special order request. One of the most unique features of each Hello Shop is that every store manager visits major gift markets to select merchandise of particular interest to their own market area, creating a specialized shop to serve the needs of their customers! We're happy to have this unique shop on our central court!!

Walden Book - With over 350 stores and 3,000 employees, Walden Book is certainly considered a "national" tenant, even though this dynamic company is new to the Johnstown area!! Founded in 1933 with the home offices in Stamford, Conn., the name of this company was derived from the pond immortalized by the great Henry David Thoreau!! Walden Book will feature thousands of books to suit every taste and interest, from the smallest child to the grandest senior citizen!! Textbooks, cookbooks, novels and best sellers are but a few categories to be offered in the 5,850 square foot shop in Richland Mall. Welcome to Johnstown, Walden! Your shop will help make our Mall a one-stop shopping center!

Where'd You Go?

What happened to you, 1973? All of a sudden, you're not a baby any more!! In fact, you only exist in our memories!!

According to Ron Sabin, our Construction Engineer, 1973 isn't the ONLY baby that's grown up!! Our 1974 baby may be going thru winter "growing pains", but is still expected to mature for its debut in September.

At this time, all trades are working on the underground utilities for K mart and the Mall!! All of the footings and foundations are completed with the exceptions of Sears and Shop 'n Save!!

But the best news of all is that the Steel is set for K mart and is already started in the Mall! Keep up the great work Ron!! September is but a few, short months away!!

Over 200,000 cubic yards of earth have been moved on the Richland Mall site!!

From the mouth of my four-year old when he saw the first quarter moon one evening: "Look Mom!! There's a Lucky Charm in the sky!

terRi's NotE-booK

Thanks Steve!! Without your help this issue of "sMall talk" would still be sitting on my desk!!

The shortest distance between two points is generally under construction!!

There is a time to speak and to keep silent . . . may heaven help us to know the difference!!

Why are we so obsessed with the fear of what others think of us, when, really, we seldom cross their minds?

richland small talk

february 1974   Volume 1   Issue 6

This Merry Month Of February!

George chopped cherry trees, Lincoln split rails, and the Cupid shot arrows, BUT the biggest happening in February (at least in our opinion!), is that the steel is set for Blocks C and D, as well as the K mart store!! Not only that, but according to Ron Sabin, our Construction Engineer, footings and foundations are complete for the entire project!! Granted, truck strikes have slowed our deliveries, but we've "re-vamped" our construction schedule to make up the time we've lost and we're still on target for a September Grand Opening!!

Ray Kisor

This month we'd like you to see the many sides of Ray Kisor. Ray's face is very familar to our Mall Tenents as he's the guy that leases space for Richland Mall! If you haven't seen Ray lately, you're in for a suprise! He's taken off 30-odd pounds and looks fantastic!!

Ray is 29 and from Lancaster, Ohio. He and his darling wife, Cheryl, have no children yet, (if only he could get home more often!), but they do have a "nearly human" Miniature Schnauzer, Trina. Ray, an outstanding athlete in school, now confines his sports to golf, tennis and skiing. He collects antiques and enjoys working on them in his workshop. Sailing is another of Ray's favorites—he crewed for races on "The Intruder" last summer. He also enjoys building things for their home when he isn't watching football on television.

Ray spends more time away from home than anyone else in the Company. Perhaps that explains why he holds a record for auto accidents! Unfortunately, Ray's car is not like Cinderella's coach!! It won't turn into a VW on the stroke of midnight or if someone hits him in a parking lot! Even tho our Insurance Company may get a bit uptight, we think he's the greatest! His level head, winning personality, and perfection combined with his "I can - I will" attitude, and his ability to converse on nearly any subject make Ray one of the most valuable assets our Company has, and a person we're all proud to be associates with!!

Try Again ?

How would you like a second chance at being a Valentine! Well, for those of you that may have missed the big day, (and for those of you that remembered the day but forgot us!!), we're going to give you an opportunity to make up for it!! How? Just send us your preliminary drawings TODAY!! Deliveries are getting tighter every day and everyone wants to open on time with a FINISHED store, so please do your part to help us open with a finished Mall, one we can all be proud of and that will attract customers from the moment we open the doors to the public!! Send us your drawings TODAY!! You'll not only be helping yourself, you'll get a great big Valentine from us!!

Courtesy Bob McConnell

ROBERT R. McCONNELL PROPERTY

Meet Your Neighbor!

No matter what your listening pleasure, from top pop to classical or foreign, on tapes, cassettes or records, you'll find it in **National Record Mart**, the largest chain of record "department stores" in the U. S. And, if you can't find it in stock, they'll be glad to order it for you! Variety, speed in receiving special orders and ease in finding what you want, help account for the success of all 37 stores!! The "Complete phonographic needs of every customer" is their goal, so it's easy to understand why we're so pleased they've joined us, you see, we want only the best for our future customers!!

Tiny bits of glitter and gold will fascinate area residents at **Piercing Pagoda**, a uniquely styled kiosk. It's service and structure have named this chain, and this, the 22nd shop, will offer over 1,200 pairs of 14K solid gold earings and free piercing service. A bit squeamish about having holes put in your ears? Relax! 60 years of experience have gone into the design, manufacturing and distribution of a disposable device that offers fast, painless and safe piercing! So get ready to wear your heart on your ears, Piercing Pagoda is coming to town!!

Calling all men!! If you love to dress in fashion but your pocketbook says "No", then march yourself down to **Lester's** where you'll find all the latest name brand clothing at popular prices!! Lester's is opening it's fourth store with us, and tho the decor will be rustic, the facilities and styles are completely "Today"!! "Changing objectives with the changing times", and the flexibility of each store manager to make their own decisions are two keys to their success. Welcome to Johnstown, Lester's, your shop is a big plus to us!!

Tradition began in 1919 when the leading cook in the U. S. licensed her name to a small candy store. Today, with 350 shops in the chain, **Fanny Farmer Candy Shops** still use the exact recipes that made them famous! Many candies are still made by hand, and all use creamery butter, fresh whole milk and the finest imported chocolate. Also available in all stores is the Fanny Farmer cookbook, now in it's 11th edition, and first published in 1896. Richland Mall will contain one of only about a dozen kiosks in the chain and will feature their new design. Welcome to Richland, Fanny Farmer, our Mall wouldn't be the same without you!!

50 years of experience has produced 100 stores in the **Brooks Fashion** chain! This progressive Jr. fashion shop features an in-depth selection of top name brand Jr. apparel in every item from bikini's to formals, and blue-jeans to dresses!! As their first venture into the Johnstown area, this shop will feature contemporary decor and a woman manager!! (After all, who best knows women's tastes!!) Welcome to Richland Mall, Brooks, Johnstown area Jr's will welcome your unique merchandising techniques!!

The only problem you'll have when you walk into the **Hickory Farms** shop, (one of over 250 in their chain) is deciding which of the many cheeses and sausages to buy! But aren't we lucky!!! That smiling girl behind the counter will be only too happy to slice you a bite to help you make up your mind! Area residents will have their first experience tasting the delights from this "old fashioned country store" in Richland Mall, and one taste will keep them coming back!!

Five years ago, the Isaly Dairy changed the name of their fast food operation to **Sweet William**, in honor of the founder of the Company and the flower used in their advertising. Today, they boast 16 shops with 10 more on the drawing board!! The Richland Mall shop will be slightly larger than average, using the basic prototype decor. Between 100 and 115 employees will be needed to properly run this restaurant, so, if you want a quick, quality meal, topped off with an ice cream treat, stop in, then trot next door to the **Sweet William Deli** and check out their line of outstanding gourmet items to take home to your family!! The Deli will be unique in that there is no store like it in the chain. The Isaly Company manufactures all the dairy products, as well as many of the other items, and take pride in the fact that, "A lot of care goes into our products." We are proud to announce the involvement of the Isaly Co. in our project!!

The largest chain of family shoe stores, **Kinney Shoes**, is coming to Richland Mall!! Kinney, with 950 stores operating in the U.S., has built their reputation on top value for the entire family at popular prices, and they own 14 factories to make sure this reputation is held!! Kinney's success is based on their philosophy that buying shoes for the family is a major investment, and they strive to give individual service and style. The only way up in the Kinney family is to start at the bottom, a fact proved by their President who started 45 years ago as a part-time salesman!! We're proud to add Kinney to OUR growing family in Richland Mall!!

terRi's NotE-booK

Pity the poor family who has no teenager. The parents never know what they're doing wrong!!

Old age is that time of life when you know all the answers but no one asks you the questions.

A pedestrian is a man who has 2 cars, a wife and a son!!

Failure is a word that should not be in your vocabulary!!

What is life? To me, it's sunshine, lollipops, rainbows and roses with a touch of fog for confusion and mixed with large quantities of love!!

To encourage Rick, my six year-old to take more interest in school, 5¢ was offered for each paper bearing a star. Robby, age 4, came home from nursery school with 2 stars and received 10¢. Upon closer examination, I noticed the stars were a bit crude, and ask how he got them. He promptly replied that he made them himself!!

Meet Your Neighbor!

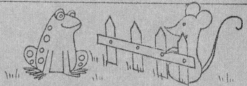

A pleasant retail experience awaits the woman at **Matchmaker Ltd.** in their second store opening in the greater Johnstown area. They feel that it's the woman who knows what she wants who counts. Their philosophy is "You know life...you know what you want. You wear what is best for you...not what "fashion" dictates. You are sure, confident...aware of yourself. You are a woman." Matchmaker's first store was opened just three years ago by owner, Bob Erallier, and in a few short months Bob's brother Dave will join him to assure that the new store in Richland Mall will be as successful as the present one. We are proud to announce Matchmaker as the first local Johnstown tenant to become a part of our Richland Mall family...and what a nice addition it is.

Every smoker's wish will be fulfilled when he or she walks into **Tobacco Village.** This store will be the most beautiful and complete shop in Frank Jennican's small but growing chain of four. The shop will be stocked with pipes ranging in price from a few dollars to a few thousand dollars, along with dozens of blends of domestic and foreign tobacco. A wide variety of cigarettes and cigars will also be found stored in a special humidified vault to insure their freshness. Many pipe and tobacco related items, along with a fine selection of hard-to-find newspapers and magazines, will also be offered to round the shop out. We welcome this excellent specialty shop to Richland Mall.

Right next door to the smoker's heaven is another dream come true, especially for those interested in art. The **Framing Hut,** as the name implies, is a custom frame shop owned by Dick Halbritter, master craftsman and artist, who also owns a shop in Altoona, Pennsylvania. Dick and his staff offer as complete a line of frames as can be found in any major city along with the skill and knowledge to assemble pictures that will be treasures for a lifetime. Besides custom framing, the shop will have a complete line of art and artist supplies which will satisfy both the amateur and professional artist's needs. Another section of this 825 square foot store will be a unique art gallery with a fine selection of prints and original art work. Richland Mall welcomes this fine shop to our growing family. We know you will help to make our mall "framous."

It's some kind of drink. No it's not. It's some kind of fast food place. Well, you're both right because **Orange Julius** is really SOME KIND of operation. In fact, it is a smart looking 800 square foot fast food restaurant named after the famous Orange Julius drink. This "devilious good drink" is made from a secret formula developed almost 46 years ago using freshly-squeezed oranges. In their chain of over 300 stores, they have at least one Orange Julius in every state and many in foreign countries. So if you have never tasted an Orange Julius, be prepared to join the many people all over the world who have enjoyed this drink. While you are enjoying your drink, you'll want to try some of their other fast food items including delicious hot sandwiches. Welcome aboard, Orange Julius, with your "devilious good drink" (and food)!!

Pizza Chef is not just pizza. Pizza Chef is spaghetti, ravioli, rigatoni, lasagna, and many other delicious Italian dishes, not to mention their scrumptious sandwiches and salads. That's right! A full course Italian restaurant. Although pizza is their most popular item, salads are not far behind and many people claim that Pizza Chef makes the best antipasto salad in the whole wide world. According to Louis Tannous, President of the five-store chain, this restaurant will seat 200 people in an elegant atmosphere. So get ready for some exciting Italian cooking in very pleasant surroundings. We are proud to welcome this Morgantown, West Virginia based restaurant to Richland Mall.

Did you ever see Easter rabbits, Christmas Trees, Valentines, Snowmen and Jack-O'-Lanterns--all made out of popcorn? That is some of what you will find in the **Karmelkorn** shop. They not only do clever things with popcorn but feature many high-quality confections with their original Karmelkorn being the specialty. One taste of Karmelkorn and you'll realize how they grew into a 135 store chain since 1929. You will also enjoy watching most of their products being made on a daily basis right in front of your eyes. This is done not only to entertain you, but also to insure maximum freshness. Be sure to try some of their home-made candy and you'll see why Karmelkorn is another plus in our lineup of tenants at Richland Mall.

If you are one of the millions of people who have become conscious of long life and good health, then you'll welcome as we do the addition of the **General Nutrition Center** to our mall. This shop will open in 1600 square feet of space just jam-packed with hundreds of vitamins, health foods, and physician prescribed diet foods. General Nutrition is headquartered in the city of Pittsburgh. They began operating 40 years ago, and today over 250 General Nutrition Centers can be found throughout 40 states. In fact, General Nutrition is the largest chain of this type in the country, and I'm sure they will be the answer to all your vitamin and health food needs. We look forward to the opening of your unique store in the Richland Mall.

Everyone who plans to shop at Richland Mall will be happy to hear that **Our Furniture** is one of the larger internal mall tenants, occupying 10,030 square feet plus a full mezzanine area. With all this space, you can expect to see a decorator store displaying 110-room settings with full colonial Kling galleries in Early American along with Ethan Allen furniture and a full line of Lee carpets. John Jones, the owner of Our Furniture, started his business in Altoona, Pa. in 1946. He has since expanded this high-quality furniture store into three malls with Richland Mall being the third. Mr. Jones plans to move to beautiful Indian Lake, near Johnstown, and along with one of his four sons will open this new store in September. We are proud to have Our Furniture in "our mall" to help make Richland Mall a truly one-stop shopping center.

ROBERT R. McCONNELL PROPERTY

richland small talk

April, 1974   Volume 1   Issue 8

What Drawings?

Although this is an April newsletter, it is no April fool's joke that on May 6, Blocks A and C will be ready for Tenant construction to begin. Blocks B and D will be turned over to Tenants starting May 20. In order to begin your construction, drawings must first be submitted and approved by our architects, Steenwyk and Thrall. The majority of our Tenants have already submitted preliminary drawings and are well on their way. But a few still need to get on the ball (or should I say on the egg this month) and send store front drawings and merchandising plans to us. If you have any problems, please do not hesitate to call our Tenant Coordinator, Bob McConnell at the site (814) 266-8748 or at his home (814) 255-1195. Who will be the first Tenant to begin construction? Will it be you? Find out next month in our May issue of "Richland sMall Talk."

Construction Notes

There was more activity at the site this month than at an Easter egg hunt. According to Ron Sabin, our construction engineer, Peter Rabbit wasn't the only busy one this month. The roof is in place on one-half of the entire mall which means, as we said before, that by May 6, all Tenants with space in Blocks A and C can hop in and begin their work. Concrete is poured in the K mart store and in the common area from K mart to the central court of the mall. All of the steel is on the site with approximately 98% of it erected. THE OUTSIDE WALLS ARE 75% COMPLETE ON THE MALL. The Sears Auto Center is under roof and steel for the Sears retail store area is all in place. Work has begun on widening Theatre Drive which will help to accommodate the increased traffic flow this fall. You'll have to agree that if the Easter Bunny did hide any eggs at the site, they have all been uncovered by now.

"Lets Go Expo"

The Richland Mall Associates put on their new Easter outfits and participated in the Johnstown area's Industrial And Related Services Exposition at the Cambria County War Memorial on April 25, 26 and 27, 1974. The exposition included over 90 displays representing many of the area's leading businesses. The Richland Mall booth was filled with many colored architectural renderings of the mall and a scale model of the central court. Admission was free to the public and the thousands of visitors were greeted by various members of our company. Interest in the mall was great and everyone was busy answering the hundreds of questions that people were waiting to ask. "When will the center open? How do I get a job?"--they went on forever!! The general reaction was one of enthusiastic anticipation with "It is about time we got something nice in this area--I can't wait until it opens," being the most repeated comment throughout the three day period. Even Peter Rabbit would have dropped his eggs due to exhaustion as the exposition ended, but it was very successful and we were happy to have the opportunity to share the Richland Mall with approximately 20,000 future customers.

ROBERT R. McCONNELL PROPERTY

Meet Your Neighbor

Streaking onto the fashion scene at Richland Mall is the **Bon Ton** , the quality fashion center for everyone BUT "Streakers." Here, men, women and young people will find fashionable answers to all their clothing needs. This month Bon Ton is celebrating the 72nd anniversary of stylish service to its home community, Altoona, PA. Bon Ton stores are located in downtown Altoona and the Logan Valley Mall, also in Altoona. The Richland Mall store will feature women's fashions, accessories and lingerie, Men's sportswear, and two departments devoted to the young at heart--the Male Bag for the Guys and the Coal Bin for the Dolls--all with a brand-name-brand-new approach to fashion. 11,400 square feet of space will house this handsome new addition to the Richland Mall.

You'll find no problem taking **Time Out** to visit this fantastic family amusement center. The Time Out shop will be built on a space tunnel concept with a tubular effect running the length of the 1,874 sq. ft. store. Round mirrors will fill the back walls along with flashing lights to carry out the theme. Inside the fully carpeted shop you will find a large variety of the newest coin-operated electronic games. Time Out goes to great lengths to insure that they are providing the newest and most popular games available, which is one reason why they have grown over the past three years into ten locations. The Time Out shop will be managed by a uniformed store attendant who will give change, check machines and insure that there is no loitering. Time Out was recently featured in the National Mall Monitor, and as you can see is a first class operation. That is why we're excited to announce their involvement in Richland Mall. Get ready to take time out in TIME OUT!!

Ormond's makes a girl's shopping experience an exciting adventure! It starts with the unique exterior and interior design concept developed by world renowned Italian designer, Nick Tricarico, and continues with a tremendous merchandise selection. The Ormond Shops specialize in contemporary and Jr. women's fashions. They are headquartered in North Bergen, New Jersey, just minutes from the fashion capital of the world--New York City. This enables their leading fashion buying staff to visit the many clothing manufacturers daily, which guarantees a steady flow of exciting and up to date merchandise to their stores. The Richland Mall Ormond Shc will be number 60 in their chain of stores located throughout ten states and the District of Columbia. We welcome Ormond's 8,400 square foot shop as a super addition to our Tenant mix.

Just like apple pie and hot dogs, **Thom McAn** shoes have become an American tradition over the past 52 years. Almost everyone has worn these fine shoes at one time in his or her life, either as a growing child or as an adult. One reason why Thom McAn has been so successful is because once you wear their shoes you stick with them. Thom McAn was the first shoe store chain to make and sell their shoes in their own stores. Elimination of the middle man enabled them to provide better quality at better prices. This idea was the basis for a chain which now has over 1,050 family shoe stores with the best selling shoes in America. Richland Mall is one more "step" ahead with the addition of Thom McAn's second store in the Johnstown area and their 55th store in Pennsylvania. We welcome this 3,250 sq. ft. store to our mall.

Do you ever yearn for the "Good Ole Days"? Well then, you'll have to visit **Cottage Crafts Boutique** which will be located on the central court of the Mall. Some of the American-handcrafted specialty items that you will find in this shop include metal jewelry, wood and coal figurines, lamps, clocks, candles, tapestry and a feature line of leather goods. Beautiful stone, heavy timber and rough cut lumber will add to the decor of this re-created 18th Century Craftman's Shop. We know you will be as excited as we are when you see this fine addition to the Richland Mall.

Did you ever have to buy something for the person who has everything? Do you remember looking and looking and looking? Well, next time you can stop--and I mean stop--at the **Spencer Gifts** shop in Richland Mall because they specialize in unusual domestic and imported gifts at popular prices. In the past ten years this very successful operation has expanded into over 180 stores throughout 32 states. Spencer Gifts is headquartered in Atlantic City, New Jersey and coordinates all its buying and distribution efforts from that city. So if you are the type of shopper who doesn't have unlimited resources but who likes to buy unusual gift items such as games, toys, puzzles, candles or gadgets, then you'll feel at home in the Spencer Gifts shop. We welcome you to Richland Mall because the Johnstown area is waiting to shop at your unique 2,500 sq. ft. store.

No modern shopping mall is complete without a children's paradise and we have ours--it's **Childrens World**. This exciting addition to the mall will be the eighth toy store for this growing 17 year old chain which is headquartered in Pittsburgh, Pennsylvania. Childrens World attributes their success to top notch men who keep a tight reign on their operations. The 5,950 sq. ft. store will be completely stocked with toys of all kinds including many wheel goods and craft items. Parents will also enjoy strolling through this maze of toys because they will discover that Childrens World has many ADULT games and puzzles, too. The "young at heart" ages 1 to 100 will find many wonderful surprises in Childrens World. Everyone at Richland Mall welcomes you to Johnstown. Your shop will add a great deal to our outstanding tenant mix.

CAR POOL

richland small talk

May, 1974   Volume 1   Issue 9

We're In The SPOTLIGHT

We are proud to announce that the spotlight focused on the Richland Mall in the May,1974 Executives Edition of Chain Store Age. The feature article entitled, "K mart to Retain One Entrance in First Mall," outlined the philosophy behind K mart's decision to enter its first regional mall in the United States. Special emphasis was placed upon the importance of K mart's decision to connect their free standing unit to the mall by turning it 90 degrees, which placed the standard K mart entrance directly on the main mall corridors. As a result of this move, every K mart customer must enter typical mall entrances to approach the only entrance to K mart. As Jim O'Roark, our president, stated in the article,

Frontal treatment of entry into store from the mall is done in bas relief fashion, the image of a free-standing store in an interior environment

"Would you like to have a retail shop at the front door of K mart, where every K mart customer must pass your store? It's a fantastic leasing situation." Chain Store Age also reiterated the two industry firsts that Richland Mall enjoys. Those industry firsts are:

1. First time that K mart and Sears, the nation's largest general merchandise chain, have ever been teamed together in either a strip shopping center or mall anywhere in the world.

2. First time K mart has entered a regional mall in America.

The May,6,1974 issue of Discount Store News also had a front page article on the two industry firsts that the K mart and Sears combination will create. The spotlight has turned in our direction and the exciting Tenant mix is going to make the Richland Mall a unique and successful feature attraction.

  # CONSTRUCTION PROGRESS

Excellent weather during the past two months has contributed to tremendous progress on both exterior and interior construction. We are right on target for our fall Grand Opening. K mart is nearing completion. Exterior masonry work is complete, the ceiling grid is in place, and auto center equipment is being installed. Penn Traffic has taken a great leap forward in the past few weeks--jumping from 70,000 square feet of thick mud to 70,000 square feet of hard concrete. Masonry is

80% in place; HVAC ductwork, plumbing and electric are nearly ready for ceiling in one-half of the area; and a large mezzanine in the receiving area is nearly complete. The Sears TBA store is virtually complete and work in their main store is progressing well even though the roof membrane is not in place. At least 95% of their concrete floor is in place,with all trades working vigorously. Rough floors are poured in the Mall corridor areas, awaiting terazzo. Our plas-

tering contractor has begun work at one end of the Mall and our terazzo contractor is starting at the opposite end. We'll keep you posted on their progress. Practically the entire Mall is under roof and all Tenant spaces-- Blocks A, B, C & D--are ready for Tenant construction. Many Tenants have been in to review their locations and to take the final steps towards a construction start. HAVE WE SEEN YOU??

Courtesy Bob McConnell

ROBERT R. McCONNELL PROPERTY

Meet Your Neighbor

Hanover Shoes announces the opening of its second store in the Johnstown area in Richland Mall. The new store will occupy 1200 square feet. This men's specialty shoe store will feature a rich Early American decor accomplished with walnut paneling, red wall-to-wall carpeting, black and brass store fixtures and extensive use of gold wrought iron coach lamps. Dramatic presentation of its shoes is accomplished by a unique revolving display window and extensive display bars. The entire line of fine shoes can be viewed quickly and easily by the prospective customers. Hanover is one of the oldest maker-to-wearer retailers in the country today. Hanover opened its first retail store for men in 1900 and has since expanded into nearly 200 stores throughout the U. S. Hanover believes that good personal service and professional selling are important to a quality shoe operation and devotes much effort to teaching store managers and salesmen a program of FULL SERVICE SELLING together with furnishing them a steady flow of product information. Welcome to Richland Mall, Hanover Shoes!! We know our customers will get a "boot" out of you.

With Father's Day just around the corner, we know the thinking caps are on for that special gift for Dad. When **Scot Ties** opens their shop, your troubles will be over because they've got the greatest selection of ties and bow ties imaginable. You'll be able to choose from over 4,000 American made ties at low, low prices. They will also carry men's popular gift items---everything from hosiery to lighters to belts. The Scot Tie operation consists of 27 stores concentrated on the east coast and Richland Mall is proud to house this handsome addition to their chain.

Why not enjoy an evening out starting with dinner at **The Encore**. Relax in their cocktail lounge and bar, and then delight in an epicurean dining experience with a varied menu consisting of specialties in Italian food (yummy!) plus seafood and aged western beef. You'll be surrounded by a provincial decor with displays of original artwork done in oils. Continue the evening with entertainment and dancing into the wee hours of the morning. You'll be happy to know that you can join The Encore every day for both lunch and dinner. What more could anyone ask for!!

If you have a little trouble seeing the sign that says **Family Vision Care Center**, be sure to enter this shop and when you leave an hour later, you won't have a problem seeing anything. That's right--in just one hour Dr. Arnold Hecht, registered optometrist, will examine your eyes and prepare your glasses or contacts while you wait! This almost unbelievable accomplishment is possible because all of the work is done right on the premises. Dr. Hecht will have a large selection of frames to choose from for regular or sunglasses and a contact lens room for both hard and soft lenses. A full money back guarantee is also part of their complete service. This fine optical company will be the first of its kind in the area and we know you are as anxious as we are to welcome them to Richland Mall. Keep your eyes open wide this fall for all your optical needs at The Family Vision Care Center.

You'll find yards and yards of fabric in Richland Mall because **Jo-Ann Fabrics** is one of our new tenants. Over 250 stores comprise the Jo-Ann chain--the largest fabric operation in the United States. Jo-Ann attributes its past 30 years of success to indepth control over operations and to excellent management. Although its primary concentration is on fabric, Jo-Ann also carries a fine variety of related notions and sewing items. So for the woman in the family, we have the answer to all your fabric needs. We're happy to have this Beechwood, Ohio based firm associated with Richland Mall.

Just about everyone will agree that among the favorites in his or her wardrobe is a pair of blue jeans. Well, **The Depot** feels the same way so they will merchandise just that--jeans, jeans and more jeans, plus matching sportswear and accessories for men, women and children. The Richland Mall will house the first of what we hope will be many Depots. Best of luck to this contemporary levi shop. We wish you many, many more.

Wouldn't you like to shop in a quaint old-fashioned seaport type shop? Well, Richland Mall is bringing the shore to you via the **Portside Shoppe**. Gifts, decorative pieces and unusual jewelry from all over the world are just a few of the items that will be found in the quaint atmosphere of the Portside Shoppe. You'll find imports from as far as Spain, Pakistan, and India--all moderately priced. From our neighboring community of Jennerstown, Pa., we welcome the Portside Shoppe.

Calling all girls 13 to 21 (and everyone else who can get away with it)! If you like the young contemporary fashion scene, then you'll really dig **Stanyan Street**. Their emphasis is on what's NOW in sportswear, coats and jewelry for the young junior and pre-teen. Stanyan Street, Inc., is a young company (only two years old) featuring merchandise at popular prices. So if you're looking for a fun place to shop in a "street" type atmosphere and rock musical background, it's Stanyan Street. FAR OUT!!

288

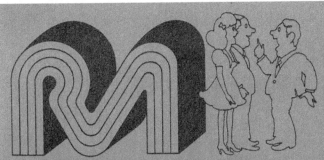

richland small talk

June, 1974   Volume 1   Issue 10

Construction Notes

Fair weather has continued to allow good progress on exterior site construction work. The concrete curb and gutter work is nearly completed, and blacktop paving has begun. Construction of roadway improvements has progressed well beyond the half-point.

Most work is completed in the K mart store, and workmen have moved over to the Mall and Penn Traffic store. Drywall and grid ceiling are being installed in the Penn Traffic. Progress is very good in the Sears store, with the concrete floor completed, most walls completed, and drywall started. Ceiling work will commence very soon.

Our Mall is shaping up, with the planters in place, terazzo moving along rapidly, and the plaster ceiling taking shape!

Most tenants are either bidding construction work or actually working in their space. CAN WE SEE YOU SOON ?

Bird's Eye View

It's about time to let you SEE how construction is progressing. If you check the aerial photo below, you can see that the entire mall is now under roof, and if you look closely, you can see the HVAC roof-top units are all in place on the K mart (More roof-top units have been put in place since this picture was taken.) You don't have to look too hard to see that the separate Sears TBA building is nearing completion, the concrete curbing and gutters are poured, and the blacktop work has begun. Turn the page and you'll see more pictures of construction progress. If you haven't started construction on your shop,-
G E T
M O V I N ' - !

G r a n d
O p e n i n g
i s   j u s t
a r o u n d
t h e
c o r n e r !

Bob Fowler

We would like you to meet our man behind the scenes. Bob Fowler. He will be instrumental in keeping our mall in tip-top shape! Bob will handle Tenant construction coordination until the mall opens this fall. At that time he will assume total responsibility for mall maintenance supervision which includes maintaining all air-conditioning, plumbing and electrical equipment.

Bob has come to us with a background of maintenance supervision dating back to 1961. His work experience includes maintaining an office building and a hospital in Washington, D.C. and a 650,000 square foot mall in Greensburg, Pennsylvania.

Bob's a real outdoorsman: he enjoys boating, fishing and hunting, but as he says, "Unfortunately, I always come home empty handed." Join us in welcoming the newest member and a vital part of our team------
Bob Fowler.

Courtesy Bob McConnell

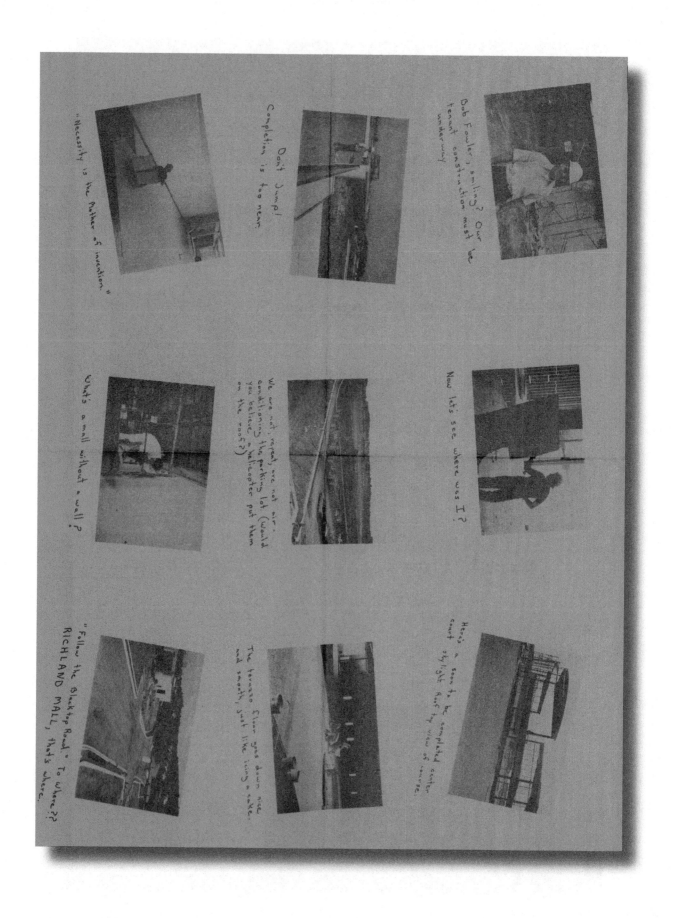

ROBERT R. McCONNELL
PROPERTY

Meet Your Neighbor

For Things Remembered is a colorful and unique gift shop that will carry a full line of personalized gift items, including pewter mugs, charm bracelets and serving trays. To make that personal gift item even more meaningful, you can have your selection expertly engraved while you shop. For Things Remembered will also duplicate keys (an extra set comes in handy for those of us who lock our keys in the house or car). Cole National, the parent company, operates 150 of these shops and kiosks throughout the country, and their Richland Mall kiosk will be located in the central corridor! The perfect place to shop--For Things Remembered!

No one-stop shopping center would be complete without a drug store and Richland Mall is proud to report that **Thrift Drug** will fill that need. Thrift will occupy 10,725 square feet of space and feature complete drug, cosmetic, greeting card, candy and tobacco departments. A new addition to this operation will be a machine that automatically counts the prescribed number of pills, allowing Thrift Drug to give their customers fast and accurate service. Thrift was founded in 1935 in Pittsburgh, Pennsylvania, and they operate 235 drug stores in 14 states. Thrift's management and directors are all registered pharmacists which may explain why 25% of their business is prescription drugs. We're happy to welcome Thrift Drug's 236th store!

95 years of experience have made **Richman Brothers** a household word. This men's clothing store features an indepth selection of sportswear, suits, slacks and furnishings all for that special guy. Shop in a warm and comfortable decor which is specially designed so that you can easily find what you're looking for. We welcome this strong American institute to Richland Mall.

If you're wondering what to do with all your money, then we've got the solution for you. The **Somerset Trust Company** will be opening a 3,080 sq. ft. full service branch bank in the mall with a separate, two lane drive-in facility located in the parking lot for your convenience. The Somerset Trust Company has been a favorite of ours for a long time (they provided our operating capital and they handle our banking needs) and we know you will enjoy the friendly service and progressive attitude they exhibit in handling all your banking needs. Our hats go off to Somerset Trust Company! We're rolling out the red carpet for you!!

Tune in to the sounds of **Lafayette Radio & Electronics** !! This dynamic young chain handles top name audio equipment such as Pioneer, Sansui, JBL, Altec and Kenwood. A highlight of their Richland Mall operation will be an audio clinic which will be conducted periodically throughout the year to test your stereophonic and high fidelity equipment. Their personnel are all highly qualified specialists who can lend expertise and guidance to both the novice and the connoisseur of audio equipment. During their 10 years of operation, this Lafayette Radio chain has established locations in Greensburg, Indiana and Johnstown, and we welcome the 1,350 square feet of musical vibrations that Lafayette will bring to the mall.

Step into the fashion scene this fall with **Teeks Fine Shoes**. This excellent shoe store will feature 2,700 square feet of men's, women's and children's nationally known, quality shoes displayed in an early American decor with contemporary accents. The Teeks chain started in 1949 and has expanded to fifteen stores located in Pennsylvania, West Virginia and Ohio. The Richland Mall will house Teek's sixth mall operation. We give Teeks Fine Shoes a hearty hello.

Who can offer you over 100 different varieties of delicious candies that will make your mouth just water? The **Candyman** can. The Candyman can because this shop will be filled with the best imported and domestic sweets in the world. Most of the candies will be individually wrapped and will be sold by the piece or by the pound. The entire shop will be built on an old-fashioned candy store theme with many original and unusual antiques used throughout the interior of the shop. The employees will be dressed in styles of clothing that store keepers wore years ago. Although this is the first venture of this kind for the originator of the Candyman, we are sure it will be successful and add to the completeness of our total tenant mix. We are happy to announce the opening of this "sweet" operation in Richland Mall.

Courtesy Bob McConnell

richland small talk

August, 1974   Volume 1   Issue 11

SPECIAL EDITION

INTRODUCING

RICHIE THE POOK

This is "Richie the Pook," the newest member of our team. Isn't he cute?! Richie's part in Richland Mall is more than that of any other partner because Richie is what Richland Mall stands for--"Just For You"! His position with the company is an exciting one. He will be the highlight of an extensive mall pre-opening promotional plan. We couldn't have chosen a more lovable fellow! Another area that will involve Richie is public relations. He'll be in every newspaper and on every major television and radio station in the area. We're creating a star!! "Richie the Pook" is new to the Johnstown area. Originally from Pittsburgh, Richie is now residing on the mall site and he has said he plans to make it his permanent home. Richie has no family. At the present time he said he's not serious about anyone, but who knows what lies ahead. Richie's a young fellow, only two weeks old, but boy what a big baby--all seven feet of him. That's seven feet of cuddly white fur with accents of grey at the paws and floppy ears, little beady eyes, and a big red nose and tongue!! We give him a warm lovable welcome. From all of us at Richland Mall to all of you, we present--"Richie the Pook"!

Ribet Productions 1974

the THING

What a super way to travel! Richie sure knew what he was doing when he asked Steve, our comptroller, for a company car! Not only did he ask for a car but he was particular about the model. One thing we know for sure is that Richie has a mind of his own, and he knew what he wanted!--a brand new Volkswagen "Thing." Well, Steve began to scratch his head, got out his adding machine and started juggling figures. With the help of those great people at Suppes Motors, the Johnstown Volkswagen dealer, Steve was able to make

Richie's wish come true!! We're all equally happy for Richie. We didn't want to tell him, but we knew the "Thing" was THE car for him! This story isn't over. Richie decided that after his assignment was complete, he would humbly turn his car over to someone else. And that's exactly what he's going to do. Richie will give the Volkswagen "Thing" to a lucky winner as the Grand Prize Saturday evening of Grand Opening week. He is really something special!!!

RICHIE IN HIS "POOK CAR".... THE "THING".
HE'S SO PROUD!

Richie's Construction Notes

Richie is happy to report that construction has again moved rapidly during the past month, with a "finished" look becoming apparent. Store fixturing has begun in the K-mart Department Store and according to Richie, it is creating a swarm of activity. Penn Traffic is beginning to look like a store on the inside, with plastered walls and ceiling work proceeding rapidly. At the other end of the mall, Richie observed that Sears is making excellent progress with the outside

masonry complete, the auto center nearly finished, concrete curbs in place, and plaster walls started on the inside. Richie is so proud! Our mall has a floor and ceiling under construction. Work is well under way in both trades and is showing significant change every day. Our center court "pool" is fabricated and is awaiting finishing touches. In all areas, we are closing in on our big Grand Opening.

Courtesy Bob McConnell

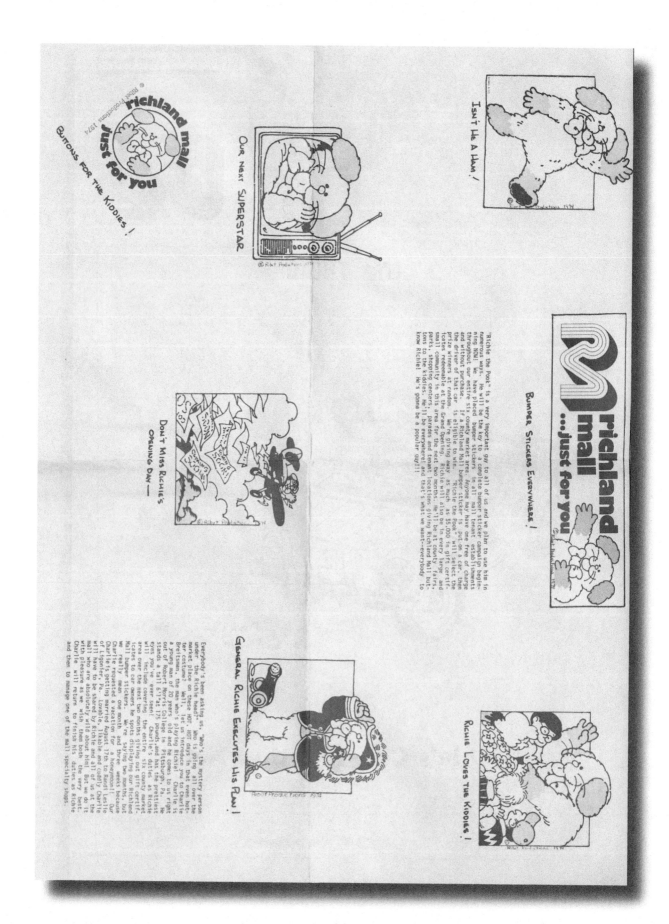

richland small talk

September, 1974   Volume 1   Issue 12

RICHIE EVERYWHERE

...and he sure has been everywhere! Since August 15, the day Richie the Pook was introduced to the public, he hasn't had one free minute! But that's the way in is in the trying life of a star and Richie is no exception. Everyone's been asking for him. Richie has made many personal appearances in the area including his debut in the Western Pennsylvania Firemen's Association Parade in Somerset on August 15 and in the Richland Township Volunteer Firemen's Parade in Johnstown on August 16. He's been seen at baseball games, fairs, merchants' locations, on television, in the newspaper and in many large and small communities in the area. Indeed, Richie the Pook has been charming young and old with his lovable, warm personality, but he's so irresistible we knew he'd be loved.

Karen Bevilaqua

The spotlight this month goes to the gal who's usually behind the scenes when you see a newspaper ad or a television or radio spot. She is Karen Bevilaqua, Promotion Director. Karen is a new member of the team having started with Richland Mall Associates in May, and she's been busy ever since! Her duties include planning and executing all promotional events, advertising, and public relations. Right now she is in full swing with mall pre-opening activities and is looking ahead toward an exciting Christmas season. Karen has been our direct link to the people of the six county area. She has given frequent talks to clubs and civic organizations and she feels right at home because she was born and raised right here in Johnstown. Karen attended the University of Pittsburgh where she received a Bachelor of Arts in English and speech. Her promotional experience began at Penn Traffic Company (yea!) where she worked as Special Events Director for two years. She recently graduated from the International Council of Shopping Centers Promotional School at Michigan State University and is bubbling over with new ideas. Karen and her husband Rick live in the Richland area of Johnstown. They both enjoy many of the same hobbies including music and skiing. They have one daughter, Richene, who's 1½ years old and the cutest thing you've ever seen!! Welcome aboard, Karen!!!

Meet Your Neighbor

If you like fairs but don't enjoy spending your money on rides, trinkets and arcades, then you'll really fancy the "fair" at Richland Mall--**Dollar Fair**. A subsidiary of Action Industries, Dollar Fair will be the first store in this chain that will carry only Action's proprietary manufactured and imported merchandise, consisting primarily of hardware and housewares products. A very inviting atmosphere will be created with warm colors and carpeting throughout the 3,531 square foot Dollar Fair interior. A dark wood front and wood grain fixtures will complete the decor. Action Industries originated more than 50 years ago and has expanded into 47 stores located in Pennsylvania, Ohio and West Virginia. Of these stores, 22 are company-owned and 25 are franchises. We are proud to have the FIRST Dollar Fair in our mall and we wish them the best of success in their new venture.

The most royal of theatres will enhance the Richland Mall when County Amusement Company unveils **The Duke & Duchess Twin Theatres**. The Duke & Duchess will make use of one large lobby to serve both theatres. The lobby will be elaborately decorated in shades of brown and white, with paintings and art work adding that certain touch of elegance to the walls. There will be seating capacity for over 750 people in the theatres--over 500 seats in one and 250 seats in the other. Great steps have been taken to sound-proof the theatres so that even the boom of cannon won't penetrate the sound barrier between the two. The Duke & Duchess will have a truly unique feature: directly above the concession stand a 4' x 6' screen will flash previews of their currently featured movies. To enable everyone to enjoy movies year-round, one of the theatres will feature family movies 52 weeks of the year and Kiddie Matinees will be shown daily. County Amusement Company owns and operates five other theatres and drive-ins around the Johnstown area, and at one time they had a drive-in where Richland Mall NOW STANDS. That's right--County Amusement is our Ground Landlord and we're as excited as they are to add the Duke & Duchess to our super tenant mix.

Courtesy Bob McConnell

ALTMEYER'S
Thick 'n Thirsty Terry Hand or
Kitchen Towels, 5 for *$5.00*.
Limit 10.

C. GIL'S SHOES
Let's Get Acquainted...
$5 OFF Any Purchase of $50 or More.

CAPRI PIZZA
30% OFF All Dinners.
25% OFF All Subs.
$1.00 OFF Whole Pizza, or
One Free Topping.

CINDERELLA SHOWCASE
40% OFF
Mother's Dresses.

CROWN JEWELERS
Buy One Scarab Bracelet *50% OFF*,
Get Second One Free.

DREAMS UNLIMITED TRAVEL
$50 Savings Per Cabin on 7-Night Cruise.

ENCORE FAMILY RESTAURANT
$2 OFF Any Dinner. *$1 OFF* Any Platter,
Buffet or Special. One coupon per person.
Not valid for banquets.

FAMILY PANTRY
Buy 1 lb. M & M Peanut Butter,
Get 1 lb. of M & M Plain or Peanut *Free*

FOXMOOR
20% OFF
Entire Purchase.

FRANKS 'N STUFF
Buy One Hot Dog, Get One *Free*.

GALLERY CARD & GIFT
20% OFF Large Paper Mache
Clothtique Santas.

GREAT IDEAS
20% OFF
All Christmas Ornaments.

GTE PHONE MART
Free 4-Book Webster's Student Set
When Signing Up For any GTE
Custom Calling Feature.

THE HELLO SHOP
20% OFF All Halloween Merchandise –
Counter Cards excluded. Free Creepy
Classics Video with $10 Purchase.

HESS'S
25% OFF Lowest Ticketed Price.
One Item Only with this coupon.
(Excludes Fragrances,
Cosmetics & Electronics).

HUSHPUPPIES SHOES
$5 OFF $50 purchase or More.
$10 OFF $100 Or More.
Regular-priced merchandise only.

K-MART
2 Liter Regent Beverages *29¢* (reg. 50¢).
Limit 4 with *$10* purchase.

KARMELKORN SHOPPE
Free Large Box of Cheesekorn with
Purchase of Large Box of Karmelkorn.

KAY JEWELERS
Free Jewelry Refurbishing.
Limit 1 item.

KWON'S JEWELERS
Buy One Scarab Bracelet *50% OFF*,
Get Second One Free.

LaROSE
20% OFF Lowest Ticketed
Price on Sweaters.
"The perfect holiday gift".

LIFE UNIFORM SHOP
20% OFF One Item.
Regular-Priced Merchandise Only

LONG JOHN SILVERS
$1.99 Value Meals (reg. $2.79)
2-pc. Chicken w/Fries
Fish & Chicken w/ Fries

McDONALD'S
Side Salad *79¢* with any purchase
(reg. $1.39)

MILLERS FLOWERS
20% OFF All Fresh Flowers –
Arrangements and Loose flowers.
Cash & Carry (no deliveries).

NATURAL COMPLIMENTS
Sterling Silver earrings
regular $12.99, now *$6.99*

OSWALDS MUSIC CENTER
Up To *20% OFF* on Pianos,
Keyboards, Guitars, Amps,
Drums and PA Equipment.

PEARLE VISION CENTER
50% OFF Specially Tagged
Designer Frames Only.
No other discounts or coupons apply.

SHOE WORLD
Buy One item, get *One half-OFF*
the regular price or choose from the
many items at great sale prices.

THAT PET PLACE III
20% OFF Any Item In Dog
Department. Puppies excluded

WATCHMAKER'S JEWELRY
All Watch Batteries Professionally Installed
Only *$1.99*. Limit 5 Per Customer.
Tax is Additional.

ZACK'S FROZEN YOGURT
16 oz. Soft Drink from Pepsi in
Tiffany Glass – only *99¢*.

Photo by Chuck Mamula

acknowledgements

"Just for you," was the slogan of the Richland Mall in the beginning, and it applies to this book, too. There is so much love out there for the Mall, this book just *had* to happen sooner or later. Though "Couldn't have done it without you" also fits.

This book wouldn't exist without all the eyewitnesses, collectors, and preservationists who contributed their stories, photos, clippings, artifacts, and insight to the project. Imagine a book about the Richland Mall without firsthand accounts of the Mall's history, photos of the Mall's exterior and interior, or accurate facts recorded in the same timeframe as pivotal events. Thanks to this book's contributors, you don't have to.

Let's raise a glass to all of them, from the people who donated photos to the individuals who were personally interviewed, from those who attended the Richland Mall reunions to the Facebook followers who provided recollections for the "Memory Shop" chapters.

Let's also raise a special toast to those who went above and beyond in making this book complete, including: Chuck Mamula, retired *Tribune-Democrat* staff photographer, who supplied exquisite images of the Mall from his photo archives; Jason Pozar, whose incredible vintage videos opened a window on the Mall's last days; and Jim Streeter, Jim O'Roark, Ray Kisor, Bob McConnell, Dennis Petimezas, Larry Mummert, Gil Demos, Joe Cohen, Larry Stahl, Terry Miller, and everyone else who loaned their personal collections of photos and memorabilia for use in the book.

Now that we've raised our glasses for the book's many guiding lights, let's give three cheers for the book's all-star production team, whose outstanding efforts made it shine so brightly: Philip Balko, photographer and photo editor beyond compare; Ben Baldwin, mega-talented cover artist and graphic designer; Kendra McConnell, transcriptionist, copy editor, proofreader, and all-around publishing assistant extraordinaire; and the Pie Press interns – Amanda Eckenrod, Alayna Tomaselli, Danielle Myers, Kyler Smith, and Ashley Back – who also transcribed interviews and performed research and other tasks in support of this project.

When it comes to all-stars, my wife, Wendy is at the top of the batting order, as always. Her support, love, and sacrifices during the creation of this book are too many to count. She did the work of many people, scanning tons of photos, helping with planning and staging special events, and serving as the first reader of the manuscript. Her name might not be on the cover, but without her, there would be no book.

While we're handing out the toasts, we can't forget all the shoppers, employees, and executives who made the Richland Mall and all its stores, restaurants, and attractions such a success for so many years. Together, you (yes, *you*) created something special with a lasting impact that will endure as long as we keep the story alive.

Finally, let's offer a standing ovation to the men who started it all – the founders, Jim O'Roark and Jim Streeter. Their vision, determination, courage, and brilliance changed the state of retail in Johnstown and brought the most wonderful dream of a true community Mall to life for all of us for 23 years. No one else, we can truly say, would have done it the same way, and we are all the richer for it.

Keep standing. Keep clapping. Those guys deserve it.

July 18, 2017, Johnstown, Pennsylvania

Courtesy Jim O'Roark

about the creators

robert

Author Robert Jeschonek grew up in Johnstown, Pennsylvania and has made it his mission to keep the rich history and culture of the region alive in his writing. His books and stories include *Penn Traffic Forever, Long Live Glosser's, Christmas at Glosser's, A Glosser's Christmas Love Story, Easter at Glosser's, Halloween at Glosser's, Fear of Rain,* and *Death by Polka,* all set in and around Johnstown and Cambria County. He's written a lot of other cool stuff, too, including *Star Trek* and *Doctor Who* fiction and *Batman* comics. His young adult fantasy novel, *My Favorite Band Does Not Exist,* was named a top ten first novel for youth by *Booklist* magazine. His work has been published around the world in over a hundred books, e-books, and audio books. You can find out more about them at www.piepresspublishing.com and www.robertjeschonek.com or by looking up his name on Facebook, Twitter, or Google. As you'll see, he's kind of crazy...in a *good* way.

phil

Philip Balko is an internationally published and award-winning portrait and wedding photographer. When not engaged in providing personalized custom-designed photographic art for his individual and commercial clients, Phil can be found wandering local hills, valleys, and towns, recording the daily life and natural beauty of the Allegheny Highlands. Phil's commissioned work can be found at www.philipbalko.com and his landscapes and lightscapes can be viewed at www.laurelight.com.

ben

Cover artist and graphic designer Ben Baldwin is a self-taught freelance artist from the UK who works with a combination of traditional media, photography, and digital art programs. He has been shortlisted for the British Fantasy Award for Best Artist for the last seven years and has also been shortlisted for the British Science Fiction Association Award for Best Artist. In 2013, he won "Best Artist of the Year" in the annual This Is Horror Awards. You can find out more about Ben and his work at www.benbaldwin.co.uk and https://www.facebook.com/pages/Ben-Baldwin/343132594365

300

bibliography

Reabuck, Sandra K. "Richland, Developer Reach Agreement on Shopping Mall." *Johnstown Tribune-Democrat*, February 6, 1973.

"Residents Have Mixed Feelings Over Mall." *Johnstown Tribune-Democrat*, April 4, 1973.

Jones, Bill. "Groundbreaking Is Held for Mall." *Johnstown Tribune-Democrat*, May 4, 1973.

richland small talk, issue 1, August/September 1973.

richland small talk, issue 2, October 1973.

richland small talk, issue 3, November 1973.

richland small talk, issue 4, December 1973.

"New Mall to Provide Employment for 700." *Johnstown Tribune-Democrat*, January 25, 1974.

Jones, Bill. "Richland Mall to Have Greenery Outside, Inside." *Johnstown Tribune-Democrat*, January 30, 1974.

richland small talk, issue 5, January 1974.

richland small talk, issue 6, February 1974.

Jones, Bill. "Richland Mall Signs 20 More Stores." *Johnstown Tribune-Democrat*, March 20, 1974.

richland small talk. volume I, issue 7, March 1974.

"McConnell to Manage Mall." *Johnstown Tribune-Democrat*, April 24, 1974.

richland small talk, issue 8, April 1974.

"K Mart To Retain One Entrance In First Mall Store." *Chain Store Age*, May 1974.

richland small talk, issue 9, May 1974.

richland small talk, issue 10, June 1974.

Jones, Bill. "Hard Work, Luck Behind New Mall, Developer Says." *Johnstown Tribune- Democrat*, July 17, 1974.

Jones, Bill. "Pre-Yule Opening Assured for Mall." *Johnstown Tribune-Democrat*, August 14, 1974.

richland small talk, issue 11, August 1974.

richland small talk, issue 12, September 1974.

"A Pook Is Born." *Johnstown Tribune-Democrat*, November 1, 1974.

"Clause Believes in Johnstown's Future." *Johnstown Tribune-Democrat*, November 1, 1974.

"Dedication Turned a Dream Into a Mall." *Johnstown Tribune-Democrat*, November 1, 1974.

"Good Effects Of Mall Seen." *Johnstown Tribune-Democrat*, November 1, 1974.

"Joe Ypma Put It All Together." *Johnstown Tribune-Democrat*, November 1, 1974.

"Karen Bevilaqua Promotes Joy." *Johnstown Tribune-Democrat*, November 1, 1974.

"Kathie Patty Finds Mall Life Exciting." *Johnstown Tribune-Democrat*, November 1, 1974.

"Kisor Lone Leasing Agent." *Johnstown Tribune-Democrat*, November 1, 1974.

"Mall Brings Outdoors Indoors." *Johnstown Tribune-Democrat*, November 1, 1974.

"Mall Compared With Birth of Child." *Johnstown Tribune-Democrat*, November 1, 1974.

"Mall Is City Unto Itself." *Johnstown Tribune-Democrat*, November 1, 1974.

"McConnell Reaches Top as Mall Manager." *Johnstown Tribune-Democrat*, November 1, 1974.

"Miles of Ducts." *Johnstown Tribune-Democrat*, November 1, 1974.

"O'Roark -- A Man And His Dream." *Johnstown Tribune-Democrat*, November 1, 1974.

"Plastering a Work of Art." *Johnstown Tribune-Democrat*, November 1, 1974.

"Richie Plays Peek-a-Pook in Area." *Johnstown Tribune-Democrat*, November 1, 1974.

"Richland Mall -- the Practical Dream." *Johnstown Tribune-Democrat*, November 1, 1974.

"Sabin Lauds Mall Team." *Johnstown Tribune-Democrat*, November 1, 1974.

"Shove From Rear Made Shopper First." *Johnstown Tribune-Democrat*, November 1, 1974.

"The 'Thing' Is Special Car." *Johnstown Tribune-Democrat*, November 1, 1974.

"Trio Provides Words, Music, Pictures." *Johnstown Tribune-Democrat*, November 1, 1974.

"Unimich Agreed to Provisions." *Johnstown Tribune-Democrat*, November 1, 1974.

"Weeks Before Opening Hectic." *Johnstown Tribune-Democrat*, November 1, 1974.

"Richland Mall Is Opened." *Johnstown Tribune-Democrat*, November 6, 1974.

"Mall Sales Better Than Anticipated - O'Roark." *Johnstown Tribune-Democrat*, January 13, 1975.

"Mall to Be Scene of State Lottery Drawing Wednesday." *Johnstown Tribune-Democrat*, March 29, 1976.

"Millionaire Chimp to Be At Richland Mall." *Johnstown-Tribune Democrat*, August 12, 1976.

"Monkey Business a Lot of Fun." *Johnstown Tribune-Democrat*, September 22, 1976.

"Circus to Highlight Mall's Anniversary." *Johnstown Tribune-Democrat*, November 1, 1976.

"Globetrotter Show Success." *Johnstown Tribune-Democrat*, August 18, 1977.

Jones, Bill. "Partners Pleased At Mall's Status." *The Tribune-Democrat*, April 30, 1978.

McCready, Jeff. "Mall tenants' sales gaining." *The Tribune-Democrat*, May 17, 1981.

Reabuck, Sandra K. "Mall boosts area economy." *The Tribune-Democrat*, February 27, 1987.

McCready, Jeff. "Mall work may start by middle of next year." *The Tribune-Democrat*, December 15, 1988.

Hiles, Brenda. "Mall owners worried about Galleria impact." *The Tribune-Democrat*, April 3, 1990.

Potts, Ted. "Mall plans update work." *The Tribune-Democrat*, July 29, 1992.

Reabuck, Sandra K. "Malls seek lower taxes." *The Tribune-Democrat*, March 2, 1993.

Reabuck, Sandra K. "Richland Mall fighting date with auction block." *The Tribune-Democrat*, July 25, 1996.

Reabuck, Sandra K. "Mall comes up with $94,141 tax payment." *The Tribune-Democrat*, July 27, 1996.

Reabuck, Sandra K. "Mall saved from tax auction." *The Tribune-Democrat*, September 5, 1997.

Blair, Bill. "Tips flooding in as police probe window shootings." *The Tribune-Democrat*, October 14, 1997.

McCready, Jeff. "Mall closing on March 1." *The Tribune-Democrat*, October 14, 1997.

Hudkins, Linda. "Mall stores face future." *The Tribune-Democrat*, October 19, 1997.

"Richland Mall's history runs through good and bad times." *The Tribune-Democrat*, October 19, 1997.

McCready, Jeff. "Mass exodus: Santa's visit won't bring good tidings for Richland Mall." *The Tribune-Democrat*, November 9, 1997.

Reabuck, Sandra K.. "Tax compromise for Richland Mall." *The Tribune-Democrat*, January 24, 1998.

McCready, Jeff. "Retail sector suffers from give and take." *The Tribune-Democrat*, February 17, 1998.

McCready, Jeff. "Mall revamp in the works." *The Tribune-Democrat*, July 16, 2000.

McCready, Jeff and Pete Bosak. "Richland Mall plan in works." *The Tribune-Democrat*, July 7, 2001.

Griffith, Randy. "Retail giants may face off." *The Tribune-Democrat*, February 16, 2003.

Griffith, Randy. "Closing may aid developer's plan." *The Tribune-Democrat*, March 7, 2003.

McCready, Jeff. "Competitive, economic factors cited." *The Tribune-Democrat*, March 7, 2003.

McCready, Jeff, "Region losing fourth big retailer in three years." *The Tribune-Democrat*, March 7, 2003.

Hurst, David. "Out with the old..." *Altoona Mirror*, March 25, 2003.

McCready, Jeff. "Retailer recruited." *The Tribune-Democrat*, May 2, 2003.

McCready, Jeff. "Survival Flick." *The Johnstown Tribune-Democrat*, , July 25, 2003.

McCready, Jeff. "Centre of activity." *The Johnstown Tribune-Democrat*, October 3, 2004.

Griffith, Randy. "East Hills offers 'good exposure' to retailers." *The Johnstown Tribune-Democrat*, April 10, 2005.

Hirschberg, Peter. "Time-Out Tunnel History." http://www.peterhirschberg.com/mirrors/timeout/history.html (accessed August 17, 2017).

O'Roark, Jim. Interview by Robert Jeschonek. Digital recording. January 18, 2016.

Pisczek, Bernie. Phone interview by Robert Jeschonek. Digital recording. February 1, 2016.

Dufseth, Linda. Phone interview by Robert Jeschonek. Digital recording. February 4, 2016.

McConnell, Bob. Phone interview by Robert Jeschonek. Digital recording. February 11, 2016.

Streeter, Jim. Phone interview by Robert Jeschonek. Digital recording. March 21, 2016.

Demos, Gil. Interview by Robert Jeschonek. Digital recording. March 14, 2016.

Kisor, Ray. Phone interview by Robert Jeschonek. Digital recording. March 16, 2016.

Bevilaqua, Karen (Belle). Interview by Robert Jeschonek. Digital recording. March 23, 2016.

Garcia, Sal. Phone interview by Robert Jeschonek. Digital recording. April 14, 2016.

DiRosa, Shirley. Phone interview by Robert Jeschonek. Digital recording. April 21, 2016.

Mahon, Brian. Interview by Robert Jeschonek. Digital recording. May 30, 2016.

Petimezas, J. Dennis. Interview by Robert Jeschonek. Digital recording. June 29, 2016.

Stahl, Larry. Phone interview by Robert Jeschonek. Digital recording. May 2, 2017.

Hayes, Connie. Phone interview by Robert Jeschonek. Digital recording. May 3, 2017.

Enos, Bob. Phone interview by Robert Jeschonek. Digital recording. May 4, 2017.

Stephens, Dorothea. Phone interview by Robert Jeschonek. Digital recording. May 6, 2017.

Thomas, Barry. Phone interview by Robert Jeschonek. Digital recording. May 8, 2017.

Roesch, Bernie. Phone interview by Robert Jeschonek. Digital recording. May 13, 2017.

Miller, Terry. Phone interview by Robert Jeschonek. Digital recording. May 16, 2017.

Fortunato, Joe. Phone interview by Robert Jeschonek. Digital recording. May 18, 2017.

Mummert, Larry. Phone interview by Robert Jeschonek. Digital recording. May 31, 2017.

Mastovich, Paul. Phone interview by Robert Jeschonek. Digital recording. June 14, 2017.

White, Jim. Phone interview by Robert Jeschonek. Digital recording. June 15, 2017.

Barto, Elizabeth Zilch. Phone interview by Robert Jeschonek. Digital recording. June 17, 2017.

Brydon, Doug. Phone interview by Robert Jeschonek. Digital recording. June 21, 2017.

Cohen, Joe. Phone interview by Robert Jeschonek. Digital recording. July 2, 2017.

Largent, Karen. Phone interview by Robert Jeschonek. Digital recording. July 6, 2017.

Koscis, Frank. Interview by Robert Jeschonek. Digital recording. July 8, 2017.

Jeschonek, Wendy. Interview by Robert Jeschonek. Digital recording. July 11, 2017.

image note

Some photos are credited "Courtesy of" without a photographer credit because the photographer of such images was unknown at the time of publication. We hope to provide additional details regarding these images in future editions of this book.

Can you smell the roasting peanuts?

The Glosser Bros. Department Store has reopened, just for you, just in the pages of this one-of-a-kind book. For the first time, the whole true story of Glosser's has been told, on the 25th anniversary of the fabled department store's closing. Step through the famous doors on the corner of Franklin and Locust Streets and grab a brown-and-white-striped shopping bag. You're about to embark on a journey from the humble beginnings of Glosser Bros. to its glory days as a local institution and multi-million dollar company...and the thrilling battle to save it on the eve of its grand finale. Read the stories of the executives, the employees, and the loyal shoppers who made Glosser Bros. a legend and kept it alive in the hearts and minds of Glosser Nation. Hundreds of photos, never before gathered together in one place, will take you back in time to the places and people that made Glosser's great. Experience the things you loved best about the classic department store, from the roasted nuts to the Shaffer twins to the Halloween windows and the amazing sales. Discover secrets and surprises that have never been revealed to the general public until now. Relive the story of a lifetime in a magical tour straight out of your memories and dreams, a grand reopening of a store that never really closed in your heart and will open its doors every time we shout...

Long Live Glosser's

Also Available from Pie Press

**The Real-Life Story of Another Great
Johnstown Department Store**

Penn Traffic
VIP

SAMUEL H. HECKMAN
PRESIDENT AND GENERAL MANAGER
YEARS OF SERVICE 57
1901-1958

BOLD
BRIGHTS

PENN TRAFFIC COMPANY
QUALITY
JOHNSTOWN'S GREATEST STORE
MERCHANDISE

Meet you on the mezzanine...

The Penn Traffic Department Store is back in business in the pages of this one-of-a-kind book. Now's your chance to revisit this Johnstown, Pennsylvania landmark or experience its magic for the very first time. The whole true story of the legendary store, its employees, and the shoppers who loved it is right here, complete with all your favorite treats and traditions. Help yourself to Penn Way candies...have a burger and fries in the Penn Traffic restaurant...relax on the mezzanine...and wait on the sidewalk on a cold winter's night for the grand unveiling of the most spectacular Christmas window in town. You'll never forget this trip through history, from the store's pre-Civil War beginnings to its dramatic finale 123 years later, with three devastating floods, an epic fire, and a high-stakes robbery in between. Hundreds of photos, never before gathered in one place, will whisk you back in time to the people and events that made Penn Traffic great...and carry you forward for a special tour of the Penn Traffic building as it stands today, complete with traces and treasures from the store's glory days. You'll feel like you've returned to the store of your dreams, especially when you cook up the authentic goodies in the Penn Traffic recipe section, handed down from the store's own bakery and candy kitchen all-stars. If you've ever longed to go back to the magical department store where you always felt at home, or you just long for a simpler, sweeter place where the air smells like baking bread and the customer is always right, step inside. Welcome to the grand reopening of the store that comes to life every time we shout the magic words...

Penn Traffic Forever

Other Johnstown and Pennsylvania Books
By Robert Jeschonek

(A Johnstown Flood Story)　　　(A Johnstown Mystery)　　　(A Cambria County Adventure)

Order from Amazon, Barnes and Noble, Books-A-Million,
or any bookstore or online bookseller.

Ask your book dealer to search by title at Ingram or Baker and Taylor.

Also available from Pie Press at www.piepresspublishing.com
or call (814) 525-4783

pie press publishing

CPSIA information can be obtained
at www.ICGtesting.com
Printed in the USA
BVOW07*0931051117

499001BV00001B/2/P

9 780998 109770